PA 19
1A95
J6C
(Wal)

RESEARCHING THE POWERFUL IN EDUCATION

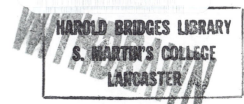
1

185 7281349

SOCIAL RESEARCH TODAY

Series editor
Martin Bulmer

Researching the powerful in education

Edited by

Geoffrey Walford
Aston University

UCL
PRESS

First published in 1994 by UCL Press
UCL Press Limited
University College London
Gower Street
London WC1E 6BT

The name of University College London (UCL) is a registered
trade mark used by UCL Press with the consent of the owner.

British Library Cataloguing-in-Publication Data
A CIP catalogue record for this book is available from the British Library.

Library of Congress Cataloging-in-Publication Data are available

ISBNs: 1-85728-133-0 HB
       1-85728-134-9 PB

Typeset in Palatino.
Printed and bound by
Biddles Ltd., Guildford and King's Lynn, England.

Contents

CONTENTS

Notes on contributors

Stephen J. Ball is Professor of Education at the Centre for Educational Studies, King's College London, UK. His books include *Beachside Comprehensive* (Cambridge University Press, 1981) and *The micropolitics of the school* (Routledge, 1987). His research on the powerful in education has been published in *Politics and policy-making in education* (Routledge, 1990) and *Reforming education and changing schools* (with Richard Bowe and Anne Gold; Routledge, 1992). He is currently researching market forces in education and palliative care provision for families with children with cancer.

Peter W. Cookson, Jr is Assistant Dean in the School of Education, Adelphi University, Long Island, New York, USA. He received his PhD in the sociology of education from New York University. His areas of interest include social inequality, international education and educational reform. He is the co-author of *Preparing for power: America's elite boarding schools* (with Caroline Hodges Persell; Basic Books, 1985) and *Exploring education* (with Susan F. Semel and Alan R. Sadovnik; Allyn & Bacon, 1993) and editor of *The choice controversy* (Corwin Press, 1992). Recently, he has conducted a national study of school choice in the United States, the results of which appear in *School choice: The struggle for the soul of American education* (Yale University Press, 1994).

Rosemary Deem is Professor and Head of Educational Research at Lancaster University, UK, and was previously Senior Lecturer in Education at the Open University. An experienced school governor, she was also a county councillor in Buckinghamshire from 1981 to 1989. She has researched and published extensively in the fields of gender and education, as well as the sociology of leisure, and co-directed the ESRC-funded project "Reforming school governing bodies: a sociological investigation" with Dr Kevin Brehony. She currently chairs the British Sociological Association's Publications Committee and is a member of the Council of the British Educational Research Association.

Tony Edwards is Professor of Education and Dean of the Faculty of Education at the University of Newcastle-upon-Tyne, UK. His recent books include *Investigating classroom talk* (with David Westgate; Falmer, 1987), *The state and private education: An evaluation of the Assisted Places Scheme* (with John Fitz and Geoff Whitty; Falmer, 1989) and *Specialization and choice in urban education. The City Technology College experiment* (with Geoff Whitty and Sharon Gewirtz; Routledge, 1993).

John Fitz is lecturer in Education Management and Policy at the School of Education, University of Wales Cardiff, UK. His previous work includes an investigation of the assisted places scheme *The state and private education: An evaluation of the Assisted Places Scheme* (with Tony Edwards and Geoff Whitty; Falmer, 1989). He is co-director (with David Halpin) of two ESRC-supported studies of grant-maintained schools policy and is co-author with David Halpin and Sally Power of *Grant Maintained Schools. Education in the market place* (Kogan Page, 1993).

Sharon Gewirtz joined the Open University in 1988 as a Research Assistant on the "Elites in Education Policy-making" project. She has since been engaged in researching contemporary education policy and is co-author (with Geoff Whitty and Tony Edwards) of *Specialisation and choice in urban education: The City Technology College experiment* (Routledge, 1993). Currently based at King's College London, she is working with colleagues on an ESRC-funded study of market forces in secondary education.

David Halpin is lecturer in Education Policy and School Management at the Department of Education, University of Warwick, Coventry, UK. He has published numerous articles on the National Curriculum, comprehensive schooling and grant-maintained schools, and is co-director of two ESRC-supported projects investigating grant-maintained schools policy. He is also convenor of the Education Reform Act Research Network, UK, and co-author (with John Fitz and Sally Power) of *Grant maintained schools. Education in the market place* (Kogan Page, 1993).

Phillip W. Jones directs the graduate programmes in International & Development Education and Human Resources Development at the Faculty of Education, The University of Sydney, Australia. Professor Jones has researched international organizations in education for many years, and is a frequent adviser on educational policy and development assistance. He is a former Deputy Director of the International Development Program of Australian Universities and Colleges, and author of *World Bank financing of education: Lending, learning and development* (Routledge, 1992).

Maurice Kogan is Professor of Government and Social Administration, and the Director of the Centre for the Evaluation of Public Policy and Practice, at Brunel University, London. He is the author of many books and articles on educational policy and government and on other areas of public sector policy including higher education, health, social services and science policy. His more recent books include *The encyclopedia of government and politics* (edited with Mary Hawkesworth; Routledge, 1992), *In support of education: The functioning of local government* (with Philippa Cordingley; Jessica Kingsley, 1993) and *Graduate education in Britain* (with Tony Becher and Mary Henkel; Jessica Kingsley, 1994).

J. Daniel McHugh is Director of the Maryvale Institute, Birmingham, a Catholic centre for further and higher education, specializing in distance learning theology and religious education. He is also Director of Religious Education for the Archdiocese of Birmingham. He is currently conducting research for a PhD on the political processes that led to the Act of Worship and Religious Education amendments to the 1988 Education Reform Act for England and Wales.

Roslyn Arlin Mickelson, a former high school teacher, received her PhD from the University of California, Los Angeles, in 1984. Currently she is Associate Professor of Sociology and Adjunct Associate Professor of Women's Studies at the University of North Carolina at Charlotte, USA, where she teaches graduate and undergraduate courses in research methods, sociology of education, and the sociology of women. Her publications investigate the relationships among educational processes and outcomes and race, class and gender. In addition to a critical examination of school reform in the United States, her research interests include explorations of the ways differences in the opportunity structure influence the secondary school performance of adolescents from diverse race, ethnic and class backgrounds.

Jenny Ozga holds the Chair of Education Policy at the University of Keele, Staffordshire, UK. Her books include *Teachers, professionalism and class* (with Martin Lawn; Falmer, 1981), *Policy-making in education: The breakdown of consensus* (co-edited with Ian McNay; Pergamon, 1985), *Curriculum policy* (co-edited with Rob More; Open University Press, 1990) and *Women in education management* (ed.; Open University Press, 1992). She chaired the Open University's course "Policy-making in Education" and is currently researching the impact of market forces on primary schools.

Susan F. Semel is Assistant Professor of Education at the School of Education, Adelphi University, Long Island, New York, USA. She received her AB in European History at Wheaton College (Norton, Mass.) and her MAT, EdM and EdD in history and philosophy of education at Teachers College, Columbia University. She is author of *The Dalton School: The transformation of a progressive school* (Peter Lang, 1992) and *Exploring education* (with Peter W. Cookson, Jr and Alan R. Sadovnik; Allyn & Bacon, 1993) and co-editor of the *International handbook of education reform* (with Peter W. Cookson and Alan R. Sadovnik; Greenwood Press, 1992). She is currently writing the histories of the City and Country School and the now defunct Downtown Community School.

Geoffrey Walford is Senior Lecturer in Sociology and Education Policy at Aston Business School, Aston University, Birmingham, UK. He is author of *Life in public schools* (Methuen, 1986), *Restructuring universities: Politics and power in the management of change* (Croom Helm, 1987), *Privatization and privilege in education* (Routledge, 1990), *City Technology College* (with Henry Miller; Open University Press, 1991) and *Choice and equity in education* (Cassell, 1994). He is currently researching the campaign for state funding of evangelical Christian schools.

Geoff Whitty is Karl Mannheim Professor of Sociology of Education at the

Institute of Education University of London, UK. Some of his research on the powerful was published as *The state and private education: An evaluation of the Assisted Places Scheme* (with Tony Edwards and John Fitz; Falmer, 1989) and as *Specialization and choice in urban education. The City Technology College experiment* (with Tony Edwards and Sharon Gewirtz; Routledge, 1993).

Introduction

CHAPTER ONE

A new focus on the powerful

Geoffrey Walford

Introduction

Most educational research has been conducted on children. Sociologists and psychologists have observed children in classrooms and playgrounds, they have interviewed them, given them questionnaires to complete, set them tests, conducted experiments on them and generally treated them as a convenient source of information for the next academic article or book. Although the situation is changing, most children in schools have little choice about whether to become involved in research projects. Once an adult has given permission for the research to take place, children have little power to refuse to participate.

A second large group on which much educational research has focused has been teachers, and teachers in training. Although teachers have more power than children to refuse to co-operate with educational researchers, their position within various social and organizational hierarchies means that to refuse to co-operate might reflect badly on them. In schools, power resides with headteachers and principals, and it is difficult for individual teachers to object if the headteacher or principal wishes research to go ahead.

In this focus on children and teachers, educational research has echoed that of sociology, psychology and political science more generally in "researching down" rather than "researching up" – looking at those with less power than the researchers themselves rather than those with more power.

But not all educational research has been of this type. Over recent years, in both the USA and UK, there has been a growth in the number of studies that have attempted to "research up" and examine those with power in educational situations. At the school level, there have been several studies of headteachers or principals and of school governors. "Leadership" in schools is now an important research topic. A further growth area has been research on education policy at both the local and national level. This development of policy studies in education is clearly linked to the recent rapid pace of change within education, but it also relates to the increasing lack of consensus about education. Although there was never complete consensus about the nature and purpose of education, recent political polarizations about the content of schooling and how schools are best organized have led many academics, particularly those on the political left, to investigate the ways of working of those with power.

It is thus not coincidental that the growth of educational policy studies occurred in both the USA and UK at a time when the political right was in ascendancy. Most academics research the powerful not simply because they find them interesting, but because they wish to understand the nature of their power and how they achieve their aims. In many academics' minds, one objective for the research is that they, or others with similar ideals, may be in a better position to influence future policy because of their increased understanding of the powerful. This emphasis is one of several reasons why researching the powerful is problematic. Indeed, as the chapters here show, research on the powerful has several features that differentiate it from most other research.

Although there is a growing number of studies that have looked at the powerful in education, there are few published accounts of the process of doing this research, and no edited collection with this particular focus. This book brings together a set of such accounts, and seeks to place itself in what has become a tradition of books that explore the practical, social, ethical and theoretical aspects of research. The contributors to this volume were asked to write reflexive accounts about the major research projects on the powerful in education with which they have been involved. The majority of the chapters examine particular segments of the process of a research project that led to a major book or series of articles. It is hoped that these chapters will mean that readers are better able to assess the validity, reliability and theoretical basis of these particular research projects. But it is also hoped that these discussions of particular research projects will help the reader to reflect critically on research methodology, and may provide a source of ideas and comfort to students and fellow researchers setting out on their own research projects involving the powerful.

Overview

For convenience, the chapters in this book have been gathered into four broad sections according to the central focus of each chapter, but there is considerable overlap between the sections. It is evident, for example, that all studies of the powerful involve an element of historical work, and that feminist ideas and perspectives have percolated into the methodologies of most researchers. However, sectional divisions are an aid to presentation.

The first group of chapters is concerned with research into central government policy in education and the activities of the various powerful participants. Geoff Whitty and Tony Edwards have now directed two major studies of educational policy that have involved interviewing British politicians and high-ranking civil servants. In their studies of the Assisted Places Scheme and the City Technology College initiative they have investigated the process by which two controversial policies passed from their initial broad outlines to practical schemes in action. Both of these policies were contentious from the outset, and have remained so. Both policies can be regarded as overtly politicized interventions into an educational system regarded by the government as too homogeneous. In each case the researchers studied the development of the schemes at the national, local and individual school levels, but they paid particular attention to the origins of the initiative, the interest groups that supported it, and the wider policy strategies it can be seen as serving. In each case they were also anxious to follow the initiative through "from policy to practice", and so avoid the top–down approach that starts with the perspective of policy-makers and largely remains there.

Research at the national level necessitated interviews with senior politicians and government officials. When a policy initiative is controversial and fiercely contested, researchers' normal problems of access to key informants are likely to be intensified. Whitty and Edwards show that those promoting or implementing the initiative may resist any scrutiny from researchers not already vouched for from their "side", while those opposing the initiative may refuse to co-operate because they feel that any research might help to legitimize the policy itself. Once access is achieved there are still formidable problems to be overcome. Politicians and senior government officials are well versed in controlling any information they provide, and present considerable difficulties in decoding the views expressed.

In addition to reporting on problems of access and of maintaining the role of objective enquirers, the writers consider the tension created by attempts to examine a controversial policy initiative in terms defined by its supporters and critics while also going beyond those definitions to a wider and more theoretically informed analysis.

The chapter by John Fitz and David Halpin discusses some of the methodological and practical issues that arose in the course of their research on grant-maintained schools. These schools, which mark a significant change in the way schools are funded and controlled, are the result of changes within the 1988 Education Reform Act for England and Wales. The general shape of this research has many similarities to the two studies by Whitty and Edwards in that Fitz and Halpin followed the development of policy on grant-maintained schools at the national, local and individual school levels and interviewed the powerful in education at those three levels. This chapter concentrates on the aspect of their research centred on the origins and development of central government policy and that involved interviews with high-ranking politicians and government officials. Fitz and Halpin describe and discuss their decision to use fairly closely structured interviews and their use of a two-person interviewer technique. They look at the limitations that are imposed on what may be obtained from such interviews as a result of the British Official Secrets Act, the civil service's own guidelines on accountability and the clash of class and cultural assumptions between the civil servants and the interviewers. They outline the nature of the interviews they conducted and show the extent to which these people were able to control the interview situation. They argue that, in the end, the factual information gathered through such interviews may be less important that the knowledge gained about the social and political context of policy-making at this high level.

The following chapter by J. Daniel McHugh is concerned with an ongoing research project that investigates the ways in which amendments were made to the 1987 Education Reform Bill such that the final

1988 Education Reform Act brought about significant changes to religious education in schools and school acts of worship. Prior to 1988, the only subject that the law insisted had to be taught in all English and Welsh schools was religious education. As the 1988 Act supplemented rather than replaced earlier Acts, the National Curriculum did not include religious education and it was assumed that religious education would simply continue as before. Many saw this as a recipe for the effective downgrading of the importance of religious education and began to campaign and lobby for changes. Others took the opportunity afforded by the Act to try to re-establish the centrality of Christianity within religious education and school acts of worship rather than the broad diversity of multi-faith teaching that had become common in many schools. In short, religious education and worship became an important site of controversy as the Bill progressed and, in both cases, the traditionalists met with considerable success.

J. Daniel McHugh's study of pressure group politics in education was based upon interviews with key actors in the Catholic Church and Church of England and with prominent Members of the House of Commons and House of Lords. In the chapter here, McHugh explains the ways in which he was able to gain access to these powerful people and obtain revealing interviews with them. He shows the way in which his local contacts led to national ones, and the way in which he was able to ascend the political hierarchy as he gradually made an increasing number of contacts. The chapter also examines the necessity of thorough preparation for semi-structured interviews with powerful political people who are well able to avoid answering questions if they wish to.

Maurice Kogan was one of the first academics in Britain to see the importance of researching the powerful in education and elsewhere. His work spans more than two decades and can be divided into four somewhat overlapping groups of studies. The first group of studies are collaborative books written with former ministers of education and directors or former directors of education within local education authorities. Here the powerful worked alongside Kogan to produce accounts of their roles in education policy-making and implementation. These books, especially that involving former ministers, had considerable popular as well as academic appeal. The second group of studies are more analytic investigations of the education policy-making process and draw upon a wide range of interviews with the powerful as well as documentary evidence. The third group consists of research commissioned by the powerful themselves, while the fourth includes two polemical works that were designed to report on and influence current events.

This wide variety of studies required a corresponding range of research methods and procedures. In this chapter, Kogan discusses questions of access to the powerful, the methods of interviewing used, the importance of the framing of questions, potential interview bias, and the ethics of publication. He argues that there are many similarities between the work of academics researching the powerful and that of good journalists. He points, however, to the significance that academics give to developing and testing theory and to the triangulation of evidence as two elements that distinguish the best academic research from journalism.

The chapter by Geoffrey Walford is concerned with some ethical and power issues that he encountered during an ongoing study of the Christian Schools Campaign in Britain. This small campaigning group represented about 65 private new Christian schools, and met with considerable success in achieving its objectives. Following the announcement of grant-maintained schools in 1987, which were popularly known as "opted-out" schools, many small schools wished to see the alternative possibility of "opting-in" such that small private schools would be able to obtain funding from the state. A campaign was started in 1988 and worked throughout the late 1980s and early 1990s to publicize its cause and to convince those in government of the legitimacy of its objectives. By strategically linking with members of the political New Right (with which the schools have no necessary "natural" affinity), the campaign was influential in achieving amendments to the 1992 Education (Schools) Act and the 1993 Education Act. As a result, from April 1994, faith-based schools have been able to apply to the Department for Education to become a new form of grant-maintained school.

In this chapter, Walford describes the development of his research project and examines some of the ethical issues involved in interviewing those with whom the researcher profoundly disagrees. Questions of self-disclosure and honesty are considered. He then discusses some of the special implications of researching the powerful, looking in particular at the possibility of self-censorship and the powerful's ability to exclude. Finally, he suggests that Becker's injunction to be clear about "whose side we are on" is not always straightforward.

The second group of chapters focuses on the interpretation of interviews. The chapter by Stephen J. Ball examines in detail some of his interviews with high-ranking politicians and civil servants. He gives extracts from his interviews with a highly influential county councillor, a former Secretary of State for Education and Science, a former minister for education and a senior civil servant at the Department of Education and Science and shows the different styles of interviewing that he adopted. He argues that, at least within the tenets of ethnographic interviewing, the interviewer must respond to and adapt to the style adopted by the interviewee, but shows through his examples that the powerful are well able to control the interview process such that certain topics are discussed and others dismissed. He recognizes that these policy-makers are also highly skilled interviewees and that they have both public and personal investments in being interviewed. These political interviews are themselves highly political, and Ball illustrates the "game-like" nature of some of these interviews. He argues that, in interviews with powerful policy-makers, researchers need to recognize and explore more fully the interview as an extension of the "play of power" rather than separate from it. But Ball does not see the interview as irretrievably flawed as a research instrument for studies of the powerful; rather, the interview should be seen as both richer and more difficult to interpret than is usually acknowledged.

The chapter by Peter W. Cookson Jr considers the methodological and ethical problems associated with his national study of advocates and critics of greater school choice. His sample included about 50 male and female educational decision-makers in the United States who have played a leading part in championing greater deregulation of school choices and others who have serious doubts about the efficacy, constitutionality and equity of such changes. They were drawn from government, academe and both public and private school systems, and were interviewed in person or by telephone using semi-structured interview techniques.

Cookson argues that school choice advocates and their opponents create "power discourses", which are ideological perspectives supported by political, economic and social power, and which set policy agendas and shape public perceptions. As a consequence, they influence not only what policies are implemented but also the way the public perceive these policies. Cookson describes the methods he used for identifying powerful policy-makers and for gaining access to them. He considers the particular problems of interviewing those who are well used to being interviewed, and discusses the ethical issues of reporting on the study's findings even where they conflict with personal beliefs. Cookson gives consideration to the problem of objectivity and argues the need for a thorough evaluation of one's own neutrality, and a recognition that researchers can be influenced by power discourses as much as are the public at large. As power discourses profoundly shape public perceptions and the formulation of educational policy, educational researchers need to develop sophisticated methodologies for investigating these power discourses. Without such methodologies, our understanding of the process of policy formation will be underdeveloped, naïve and sometimes inaccurate.

The next two chapters consider some feminist perspectives on researching the powerful. Roslyn Arlin Mickelson has conducted research on educational reform in Charlotte, North Carolina,which has involved interviews with both the locally and nationally powerful in education. Since 1971, the Charlotte school system had successfully used mandatory bussing to racially desegregate the county-wide district. In the 1980s and early 1990s, however, a new business elite attempted to reshape the system, and a controversial parental choice system based around a series of magnet schools was introduced. In her chapter here, Mickelson presents excerpts from interviews she conducted with some of the most influential figures in the USA concerned with school choice. She argues that it is often both necessary and desirable for interviewers to challenge those with power and to provide academic evidence that might question the basis on which policies are promoted. She considers some of the ethical dilemmas faced by feminist scholars in terms of lack of complete candour in interviewing, the need to confront racism, sexism and elitism, and the desire to combine the aims of scholarship with those of a political activist within the local community.

Rosemary Deem's research on school governing bodies is concerned with the locally powerful in education. It was not specifically designed to be feminist research, but much of the methodology and discussion here are heavily influenced by feminist perspectives. This four-year qualitative study of the processes and micro-politics of governing schools in England, following significant legislative changes during the 1980s, focused on 10 schools in two contrasting local education authorities. The researchers attended meetings, collected documents, administered two questionnaires to governors, and conducted semi-structured interviews with a large sample of governors.

This chapter concentrates on three main issues – the relative power of researcher and researched in gaining and maintaining access to research locations, the balance of power between researchers and researched during the research process and in defining the outcomes, and the issue of the extent to which research on the powerful can empower or disempower those being researched. Deem also gives explicit consideration to feminist critiques of research and argues that following some feminist suggestions would severely curtail research possibilities.

The three final chapters are concerned with research that has a strong historical dimension. Phillip W. Jones discusses his study of the World Bank, which has become a major influence on educational systems through its financial might, the conditions attached to its loans, the impact of the projects, and its attempts to exert direct influence on the educational policy-making processes of governments the world over. His research focused on the historical development of the Bank's policies on education, how these were put into loan form for particular projects, and how the Bank reshaped its policies as it looked back on completed projects. He was able to obtain remarkable access to the Bank to explore its documentary sources and to conduct interviews with many of those involved. In this chapter he describes his method of access to the Bank and to international civil servants, and reflects upon his methodology. He shows the importance of triangulation of data sources and, in particular, argues that documentary evidence must not simply be taken at face value. The story behind the production of any document has to be probed and analyzed if the researcher is to get behind the "official line" of such international organizations. Jones also discusses some of the ethical dilemmas and constraints imposed on researchers of such international organizations, but argues that the benefits of such work make it well worth while.

Sharon Gewirtz and Jenny Ozga's study was concerned to explore the world of post-1944 education policy-making in England, concentrating on the influence of high ranking officials and on the construction of the postwar system. They sought to challenge conventional, pluralistic accounts of the policy-making of the period and, instead, investigate the sources, scope and pattern of educational policy. Thus, in addition to archival research, they conducted extensive unstructured interviews with 15 former directors of education or senior Department of Education and Science officials. The objective of these interviews was to interrogate the assumptions held by a key group of postwar policy-makers, through an examination of their views on education and the impact of their views on the pattern of provision. The nature of the group itself, as an elite fraction of the state apparatus, was explored in an attempt to understand the source of education policy.

In this chapter they describe their research methods and discuss issues related to access and gatekeeping, the modified form of life-history interview used, the use of two interviewers, the necessity for thorough preparation and ethics. They also discuss some gender issues and raise some important questions about the supposed difficulty of interviewing the powerful compared with the "ease" of interviewing those less powerful than the researchers. Finally, they consider the process of analysis of their interviews and how this relates to their theoretical objectives.

The final substantive chapter by Susan F. Semel is concerned with a historical study of one particular school. The school in question is The Dalton School in fashionable Upper East Side Manhattan, which played a major part in the development of progressive education and which is now a highly prestigious school serving New York's elite. Semel's association with The Dalton School spans over a quarter of a decade – as a student, teacher, parent and researcher – but her account of the school is far from the self-congratulatory histories of private schools usually written by insiders. It is the result of painstaking study of documents and interviews with those involved and sets out to trace and analyze the transformation of an experimental progressive school into a high-status, competitive, college preparatory school. The book is not one that was wholly welcomed by the school itself, and is not the one that many of her interviewees would have wished her to write.

In her chapter here, Semel describes and discusses her research methods and her search for objectivity. She examines the strengths and weaknesses of her insider position, and the special difficulties of interviewing members of New York's academic and social elites.

The collection ends with a chapter by Geoffrey Walford that draws out some general conclusions from the preceding accounts. It is shown that, although the studies here use a variety of research methods and have a range of research foci, there are several common threads worthy of consideration.

PART I

Researching central government policy-makers

CHAPTER TWO

Researching Thatcherite education policy

Geoff Whitty & Tony Edwards

Introduction: levels of analysis

Researching education policy has become fashionable in recent years, especially amongst those taking refuge from the threatened redundancy of sociology. It was perhaps predictable, then, that such research is partly shaped by a traditional sociologist's interest in power and control. Some are intrigued by the myriad negotiations and struggles that go on between interest groups at national and local governmental levels and within institutions. Others seek beneath the surface of events to identify broad patterns underlying apparently disparate developments, and perhaps to develop some overarching theory to explain them.

Such different concerns can reflect different notions of who the "powerful" are in education and how their power is exercised. It can also involve different perceptions of rationality in policy-making. If the official view is taken, albeit with some qualifying scepticism, then policy is handed down in legislation and regulations by politicians and government officials to be implemented (more or less) at street level. This is to overplay the role of central government, and downplay what happens before and after legislation. It risks assuming a unity and clarity of purpose among the "makers" of policy that may well dissolve under scrutiny. And it is almost certain to exaggerate the extent to which the policy-makers can predict the consequences of their reforms by channelling the actions of those charged with implementing them. As judged by its real effects, policy is often made in the process of implementation. And that process may be only broadly and vaguely shaped by the

14

sketches from which it began. As Maurice Kogan (1978: 118) puts it, education policy is "the product of conflicting claims, painfully and painstakingly resolved", through many individual and collective decisions taken at various levels in the system. As has recently been argued, and persuasively documented in relation to current reforms, treating education policy as what is done to schools ignores the extent to which it is open to different readings, recontextualisations and re-creations (Bowe et al. 1992).

Power relations figure at all levels in the system, and power struggles may occur in and around the policy's design and construction that derive only loosely from its formal objectives. But to reduce education policy to the sum of innumerable individual decisions, even decisions seen as partly predetermined or considerably constrained, is to ignore what in some analytical traditions would be called the power relations between different parts of the system and in others how decision-makers are positioned by different discourses. Kogan, who tends to present policy-making in terms of the political interplay of interest groups, recognizes that those groups may be very unequally placed to advance their interests. Their relative power to do so may also change markedly over time (Ranson 1985: 106). It is therefore important to consider policy-making in relation to underlying trends emanating from changing structural relations between different parts of a system. Ozga (1990) claims, for instance, that only by studying the "bigger picture", rather than little pieces of policy-making that are part of it, can researchers avoid legitimating the very process of fragmentation and atomization being pursued by the present government. Treating power as entirely situated, or even entirely diffused, could exacerbate that tendency. We therefore regard the study of education policy as involving the study both of detail and of broad trends. Most crucially, it involves the attempt to demonstrate the complex relationships between them or, as McPherson & Raab (1988: xii) put it, relate "individual identity and the micro-politics of personal relationships to a wider analysis of power".

This chapter offers a largely experiential account of "researching the powerful" during two research projects funded by the British Social Science Research Council (SSRC) and its successor, the Economic and Social Research Council (ESRC). In the terms outlined in this introduction, both the Assisted Places Scheme and the City Technology College programme had conspicuous architects and promoters, and attracted strong support and strong opposition from quite clearly identifiable interest groups.

Each was seen at the time as heralding more radical and far-reaching reforms, and both are identified in the 1992 White Paper as significant first steps in the government's strategy of creating "a new framework for schools" through the enhancing of "choice and diversity" (Department for Education 1992).

Researching the Assisted Places Scheme

The Assisted Places Scheme (hereafter APS) was the first education initiative to be announced by the incoming Thatcher government in 1979. It provided government assistance with fees to enable children from families of modest means to attend academically selective independent schools (Edwards et al. 1989). In evaluating the Scheme's impact, we began from what its advocates and critics predicted would be its effects, and then compared their claims with what actually happened. Our most widely publicized finding was that the Scheme contained far fewer inner-city children than its rhetoric of justification had led people to believe. We also located the study in broader contexts by considering how it fitted in with other policies, historical and contemporary, and how it became reinterpreted by government ministers during its implementation to fit in with a new privatization agenda being pursued in the second Thatcher government. We were also interested in what that might reveal about broader social and cultural changes.

The Scheme's announcement in June 1979 represented a considerable success for the powerful private education lobby, and in particular for the pressure group within it that represented the highly academic former direct-grant grammar schools and their traditional commitment to providing scholarships for able children from "less well-off homes". That it also appeared to opponents as a sponsoring of "independent" schools from public funds raised in heightened form long-standing disputes about the relationship between public and private education. This meant that any attempt to research in this field was likely to be more than usually contentious. Its intensely political nature produced attempts to control the researchers' access to data and enquiries into the use to be made of any findings. In many ways, this issue became the subtext of our research programme and, at times, a main preoccupation. We certainly learned a great deal about the political and methodological

16

difficulties of undertaking research in such sensitive areas.

Our original application to the SSRC came at a time when the Council was short of funds and was itself the object of close political scrutiny. Having originally been identified by the then Educational Research Board (ERB) of the SSRC as a high priority for funding, our proposal was referred back to the ERB by the chair of the Council, Michael Posner, who had asked that any proposals of a politically sensitive nature be brought to his personal attention. Meanwhile, he had asked Jack Wrigley, the chair of the ERB, for his personal assurance that we were "professionally competent and by implication that [we] were not Marxists" (Wrigley 1989: 11). We understand that additional referees were also consulted informally with a specific request to comment on the likelihood of our using our findings for politically motivated purposes. Posner was clearly concerned that our project might not be the sort of research that the Council ought to be supporting while the whole future of SSRC was being reviewed by a government that suspected it of sponsoring left-wing propaganda. His concern was no doubt reinforced by a note from a Department of Education and Science (DES) official stating that the Department would follow the progress of the research proposal "with interest".

As far as we can ascertain, however, there was no attempt by government to obstruct funding directly. Instead, its influence operated through the Council's awareness of official surveillance in a situation where it might well have been politic to play safe. In the end, the academics on the Education Research Board were not inclined to do so, and instead chose to back the original judgement made in the course of the peer review process. Nevertheless, Jack Wrigley has since stated that "academic freedom hung by a thread" (Wrigley 1989: 11) and he saw the whole affair as an important defence of academic freedom against political pressure. The political sensitivity of this particular project nevertheless led the SSRC to insist on a steering group, unusual for a grant of such a modest size, to assist us in avoiding any "misinterpretation" or "premature disclosure" of our findings. Given that this group never actually met, and that its chair's moderating influence was limited to requesting that a single word ("Thatcherism") be changed in an early paper (Edwards et al. 1984), its significance may seem merely symbolic. It is possible, however, that our own awareness of potential surveillance may have encouraged self-policing or even self-censorship in a situation where a steady flow of external funding was becoming increasingly important to academic careers and institutional standing.

These difficulties contributed to a delay in starting the project, and so in beginning what were certain to be difficult negotiations about access. It is sometimes argued that it is easier to research "down" – that is, below the researchers' own social level – because those studied will feel less able to deny access and be less equipped with strategies for with-holding information. Certainly there have been few good studies of elite decision-making, researchers having found it hard to break into the net-works of influence well practised in maintaining secrecy. But we doubt if matters are as simple as that. For example, the top–down approach to policy-making may make it easier to identify key informants, which then simplifies the collection of evidence. But the apparently critical importance of such informants obviously increases the difficulties if access is withheld. There is also the risk that they exaggerate their own role while the "real" makers, reshapers or implementers of policy remain firmly behind the scenes. In short, the hierarchy of credibility may or may not fit well with the formal hierarchy of the system or insti-tutions being investigated. That possibility is greater where key inform-ants are accomplished definers of reality so as to highlight their own importance. As we report later, we had doubts about some self-reported roles in both our projects.

In relation to the APS, access at government level proved easier than we had expected once the investigation actually got underway. We were able to interview 10 ministers, political advisers and civil servants actively involved in the Scheme's administration, an HMI who had offered advice on the selection of suitable independent schools, as well as some of the leading independent school heads who had worked closely with these individuals in developing the Scheme. The small unit at the DES responsible for the notably light monitoring of the distribution and financing of assisted places gave us unrestricted sight of their school-by-school records, which allowed us to analyze the take-up of those places in more detail than was being done by the DES itself (Edwards et al. 1989: 81–95). A former senior civil servant in the Depart-ment volunteered his services as an honorary consultant to the project, providing us with valuable background knowledge and with access to both people and data that might otherwise have been difficult to obtain. Those contacts worked in both directions. Officials at the DES were kept informed of our activities and our consultant was certainly consulted informally when we requested some further funding from the ESRC.

The project also gave us some insight into conflicts, and cultural changes, at official level. Particularly obvious was the conflict between career civil servants of the old style, such as our project consultant, and the new breed of political advisers with whom politicians of both parties had surrounded themselves since the mid-1970s. Stuart Sexton, successively policy adviser to Norman St John Stevas (Conservative shadow minister for education at the time when the party committed itself to an APS of some kind) and then to Secretaries of State Mark Carlisle and Sir Keith Joseph, was in his own view the Scheme's architect. Certainly he was vigorously effective in mobilizing political support and in ensuring that there were sufficient independent schools interested in offering places to launch it quickly. In his enthusiasm for it, and for his own role in its creation, he gave us access to all his (unsorted) DES papers. These related both to the Scheme and to other policy matters, and included some that we clearly should not have seen. Our civil servant consultant found the laxity appalling, and sought to make us return the papers unread on the grounds that they had been improperly obtained. This may have led to our experiencing two sides of the Establishment. On the one hand, we were dined at the Athenaeum and advised on the decent thing, while on the other there was a break-in at the home of one of the research team that even mild paranoia could interpret as a Special Branch warning. In the end we made some use of the papers, taking the view that we were bound not by a civil service code but by an obligation not to ignore evidence put before us. His very different frame of reference led our consultant to terminate his association with our project.

Those papers, and some of our interviews, illustrated a sharp contrast in outlook at government level. Civil servants were still settling in to their relationship with policy advisers. They were both formally and actually apolitical to an extent undermined during the subsequent Thatcherite sifting of "us" from "them". There was thus a potential tension between their trained judiciousness and caution, and the ideological enthusiasm that policy advisers were likely to display. In this case, Stuart Sexton was an enthusiast, with a commitment to retaining or restoring as many grammar schools as possible and a determination (not clear to us at the time) to replace "state" provision with what he later advocated as an open market subject only to the free interplay of supply and demand (Sexton 1987, 1992). For both reasons, he wished many more assisted places to be provided than was politically feasible at a time of large cuts in public expenditure, and many more than could possibly have been seen as academically credible contributors to so overtly meritocratic a scheme. Both points were made forcefully by civil servants at the DES. Also apparent in the official and semi-official papers was the hard work that civil servants had to do to turn a scheme that Sexton believed was ready-made for implementation into detailed arrangements, and the relief in the private sector when they took over from a "broad-brush" political enthusiast the task of making the scheme work.

Researching the locally powerful presented its own and often acute difficulties. A controversial policy innovation of this kind engenders such loyalty and hostility that its institutional gatekeepers are inclined to doubt whether any research can be impartial. Research into independent schools by sociologists also provoked memories of Royston Lambert's work, which had been seen as damaging to the image of boarding schools (Lambert & Millham 1968, Lambert et al. 1968, Lambert et al. 1975, Walford 1987). In some independent schools, however, the grounds for resisting or limiting their co-operation were not so much suspicion of possible hostility as what they perceived as the impossibility of any systematic comparison of schools or types of schools in the educational opportunities they offer. The controversy surrounding attempts to compare the effectiveness of selective and non-selective schools might be thought to support this scepticism. Nevertheless, it seemed to us a position difficult to justify in principle when the essential defence of this publicly funded Scheme has been that it offers opportunities to able pupils in schools with established academic reputations not available in the comprehensive schools they would otherwise have attended. Much more readily understandable was the unwillingness of some heads to allow any enquiry in their school that might make assisted place pupils an object of special attention and so hamper their equal treatment.

For all these reasons, negotiating access to schools proved to be very time consuming. Working from King's College London, which had strong links with the independent sector, gave us some initial advantages in that direction. The College's sister school at Wimbledon initially offered any help we needed. But objections from the head of another school led the Headmasters' Conference APS Committee to advise its members to withhold any information that was not already in the public domain, and some schools that had initially offered assistance (including King's College School) became wary. Fortunately for us, there were others who valued their institutional independence too much to take advice from outside, the head of one leading school being especially helpful both in his own right and through reassuring fellow heads in the area that our research deserved co-operation. To get more general sponsorship or at least acquiescence, however, we had to attend a difficult meeting with the Independent Schools Joint Council (ISJC) and a civilized lunch in the study of the chairman of the Headmasters' Conference Assisted Places Committee. It was clear that the agenda on both occasions went well beyond specific questions about the research, which were many, and provided an opportunity to evaluate our pedigree. At the first of those meetings, the questions from one Committee member highlighted a reluctance evident in many justifications of the Scheme from inside the private sector to see it evaluated in any other way than by the benefits to the individual holders of assisted places. Consideration of possible effects on maintained schools, whether those locally affected or more generally, was regarded from that perspective as being quite irrelevant.

In some ways, it was maintained schools and opponents of the Scheme who posed the more formidable barriers to the investigation. Apart from an initial right of veto to entry at 16-plus, the Scheme was protected from any LEA involvement. Most Labour-controlled authorities were totally opposed to it, and this made some negotiations extremely difficult because any research into how the Scheme worked was seen as implying support for it or, at best, as giving publicity to something that they would prefer to see ignored. In its refusal to co-operate with the project, one LEA made this position explicit even though its director of education had publicly predicted damaging effects on the authority's schools. We question whether liking or disliking a policy is a good reason for either ignoring it or simply assuming its effects. Again, however, we benefited from headteachers' sense of territory and their consequent willingness to make their own decision about access and thereby commit their school.

Taking a broad view across the 40 or so schools in which we eventually undertook interviews, we found ourselves rather more welcome in the independent sector than in the state sector. Certainly their public relations were much better, and (at a time before "open" enrolment) their concern with image greater. Working under different and less intense pressures, most of the independent schools were able to give more time to being hosts, arranging the pupil interviews, and generally managing the impression they gave us. In some of the elite schools, where the staffroom still had some of the qualities of the sort of Common Room that once existed in universities, staff conveyed a sense of cultural affinity and collegiality with the researchers. In some maintained schools, the prevailing impression we received was of our own irrelevance to anything that mattered! Certainly ease of access was influenced by the broader context. An important reason why independent schools became increasingly willing to co-operate with our project as time went on was their renewed self-confidence in the aftermath of the landslide victory of the Conservatives in the 1983 general election, the Scheme being threatened with immediate extinction if Labour had won. Conversely, heads of some maintained schools were unwilling or unable to permit fieldwork in their schools during the teachers' industrial action of 1985.

Several methodological and ethical dilemmas arose from these experiences. Given the difficulties of access, especially at the start of the project, we were tempted to use subterfuge. Denied co-operation initially by an independent school, we occasionally contacted some parents through their child's primary school and then told the independent schools we already were getting some information about their pupils. Researchers sometimes face the temptation to facilitate access, or make informants more forthcoming, by indicating more or less subtly that they are on the same "side". Given the controversy surrounding the Scheme, we were questioned often about our own views, and there were times when to be viewed suspiciously from one side proved helpful in gaining access to the other. Having been denied access by an LEA was therefore, on occasions, quite useful.

Confidentiality was a problem because of the high visibility of some of our individual informants and of some of the independent schools. We decided that we would not name in any report those who could not easily respond and whose views were not already in the public domain. We therefore named politicians and representatives of national bodies, but we did not name civil servants, teachers, parents and pupils. Wanting to follow the effects of the Scheme on individuals, we included in our main report detailed "cases" drawn from interviews but did not, like Connell et al. (1983) construct "composite stories". Our stories belong to the particular, mainly anonymized individuals who told them. Anonymizing the schools proved difficult, not because we often forgot the pseudonyms ourselves while writing up the research (which we did) but because several of the independent schools were so distinctive in size or reputation.

Questions also arose about the use that the powerful can make of research findings. As mentioned earlier, one of the roles of the steering committee imposed upon our project by the SSRC was to guard against premature disclosure of findings. Nevertheless, the research team never adopted the classic positivistic stance of refusing to discuss the project with informants. This raised a number of issues. Clearly, talking about a policy can influence its development. This may be positively intended, as in action research with and by teachers, but it is even less clear than in relation to classroom practice what would constitute improvement in policy and its implementation. As political beings, we had serious misgivings about the Assisted Places Scheme. Yet our research might help to make it "work" better, at least in its own terms. For example, a discussion in one school about why advertisements in the *Daily Telegraph* were not eliciting many working-class applicants for the assisted places it was offering prompted the school to change its approach; and we were asked by a Bristol school to advise them on how to recruit more black pupils from St Paul's, an offer that we declined.

The reporting of research may also be taken as advice. When our first statement of findings (at the 1986 British Educational Research Association (BERA) conference) received considerable publicity, it was the very low representation of working-class pupils among assisted place holders that was highlighted. Both at the 1986 Headmasters' Conference (HMC) where we spoke about the research to heads of assisted place schools, and in a review of the subsequent book in the HMC journal, that finding was interpreted less as a criticism than as a challenge to the schools to attract more of the children who had most to gain from the opportunities being offered. In short, our research was seen as indicating a very different kind of marketing from that which elite schools, accustomed to their clients coming to them, normally found to be necessary.

Researching City Technology Colleges

The "pilot network" of City Technology Colleges (CTCs) that Kenneth Baker announced at the 1986 Conservative Party conference might be seen as a response to the failure of the Assisted Places Scheme to reach the working-class, inner-city children who had figured so prominently in the rhetoric used to justify it. Since it came within weeks of the Cabinet Office requesting a copy of our interim report on the Assisted Places

Scheme, it might even have been tempting (and disturbing) to see the new initiative as being in part a response to our report of the failures of the earlier one. That would have betrayed a naïvety about government's capacity to ignore inconvenient evidence, and the official view was and has remained that the Assisted Places Scheme has been a success. City Technology Colleges also had a very different provenance. Announced as a "new choice of school" to be created in inner-city areas with the help of business sponsorship, it was an overtly politicized initiative widely seen at the time as a harbinger of extensive restructuring of the system.

In the APS research, we may have taken a rather simplistic view of what multi-level research involves (Halpin & Fitz 1990). We started with policy development by the independent schools and within the Conservative Party during the 1970s, traced the detailed formulation of the Scheme in the 1980 Education Act and in specific regulations, and then looked at how the Scheme was implemented nationally and as it affected schools, parents and pupils in both private and public sectors. This approach to the research was not entirely inappropriate, given the individualistic approach to the Scheme adopted by its advocates and the dire systemic effects predicted by its critics. But it reflects a somewhat linear notion of policy-making and implementation.

In the CTC programme, national policy depended on persuading the locally powerful to sponsor colleges and gain support for them. We therefore found ourselves researching all levels at the same time rather than proceeding from the national to the local in orderly fashion. This is arguably a better model for policy research generally. It is certainly more appropriate for a policy where the initial conception bears little relationship to what is happens on the ground, and where local implementation can be seen not merely as mediating policy conceived elsewhere but as transforming it. In sharp contrast to the careful preparations that preceded the announcement of assisted places, the CTC programme was loosely sketched and poorly thought out at government level, leaving considerable scope for an educationist take-over of a highly politicized initiative. We return to that point later.

In getting the research under way, we experienced none of the difficulties experienced in the previous study. The project was approved by ESRC without delay and without conditions, though the initiative was perhaps even more controversial; we were even encouraged to request a small enhancement of the grant to study related initiatives in Germany and the USA. With the exception of Lord Griffiths, all the possible architects of the initiative at national government level agreed to be interviewed, as did the DES officials and HMI most involved in its implementation. Although only persistence beyond the call of duty on the part of one of our project consultants gave us indirect access to Kingshurst (the first CTC) and to information beyond his published profile of it (Walford and Miller 1991), most other CTCs we approached offered access willingly. One principal was much more co-operative "in principle" than in practice, and the first (and maverick) head of the Gateshead CTC proved as elusive to us as he did in relation to other CTCs, but the general openness to enquiry at local level was welcome. It was also apparent in relation to the CTC Trust, whose first chief executive was (rightly) searching in her questions about the research but informative in response to our own questions. If the CTC programme was controversial nationally, most CTCs were intensely unpopular with local secondary schools to which they offered direct (and apparently highly subsidized and unfair) competition, and with LEAs whose rationalizing of school places their appearance threatened. Yet we had no difficulty in obtaining interviews with LEA officers, or in visiting schools in the vicinity of a CTC. In all, 24 interviews were conducted with politicians, officials and industrialists at national level and about 60 with opinion leaders and gatekeepers at local and institutional levels.

It is not easy to make sense of this relative ease of access. We were able to claim in negotiating it that we had had no complaints about breaches of confidentiality during our previous project, nor had the schools involved received any complaints from parents about our requests for and conduct of pupil and home interviews. We referred to our self-restraint in not rushing to judgement, or to press, and might have considered citing as evidence of objectivity the fact that our book on the Assisted Places Scheme had been favourably reviewed from left and right by both Max Morris (*Education*, 30 March 1990) and Rhodes Boyson (*The Times Higher Education Supplement*, 18 May 1990)!

Yet although Thatcherite policies were, of course, much better established by 1986 when the CTC policy began, they were hardly less controversial. That particular initiative was intensely so, being widely attacked as a return to academic selection, as intensifying the problems faced by inner-city LEAs, as an attack on LEAs generally, and as a significant step towards privatizing educational provision. At the time when our research began in 1988, there was a real possibility that CTCs would be abolished within a few years by an incoming Labour government. In these circumstances, extreme defensiveness on the part of CTCs and the Trust might have been expected. Yet to counteract that and in contrast to the more fastidious and exclusive assisted places schools, there was an apparent sense of obligation to publicize the value for public money that CTCs intended to provide. They also felt committed, by inclination and by the repeated promises to that effect by the Trust's chairman Sir Cyril Taylor, to becoming (in his phrase) "beacons of excellence" for the system at large. Since the predominant attitude of schools and LEAs around them was hostile avoidance, then almost any publicity not created entirely from political opposition was to be welcomed. Simply, CTCs had a reputation to create whereas APS schools had only a reputation to lose. On the LEA side there was hostility looking for outlets, and individual education officers and school heads very willing to document the unfairness and the difficulties that the appearance of a CTC was creating for them. It was also clear in conducting interviews with CTC sponsors and project managers, though markedly less so in those with principals, that our informants could not conceive that any right-minded person could possibly have any reservations about what they were doing.

Our main difficulties of access, and even greater difficulties in using some of the information provided, came in relation to CTC sponsors. Although the programme's momentum depended from the start on the availability of backers for this unprecedented venture in using private money to create public schools, the scheme was announced before they had been secured. The high political investment in the programme, especially the personal investment of the then Secretary of State (Kenneth Baker), produced a desperate scramble to find sponsors in which both the recruitment of senior civil servants as heavy-handed persuaders and the use of threats and inducements apparently went well beyond normal practice. Understandably, the eloquence with which some of our informants described these methods was preceded by an insistence that none of the details were to be reported. On one occasion, our usual request to an executive of a major national company that we be allowed to tape the interview prompted the response that we could either record a series of bland responses or not record an account of what really occurred. We chose the latter, and the reporting of this aspect of the programme's implementation is a pallid reflection of the information we received (Whitty et al. 1993: 38–51). The reluctance of major national companies to back the programme produced among the eventual backers a predominance of the more entrepreneurial, and sometimes overtly Thatcherite, businessmen. Some of these tended to be markedly less disposed to be interviewed than more publicly minded senior employees of corporations were likely to have been, though others were keen to claim their place in history.

The slow and halting progress of the CTC programme meant that considerably fewer CTCs were open during the period of the research than had been anticipated. Those that we were able to visit were extremely co-operative, though like the independent schools in the APS project they organized those visits carefully and with an eye to impression management. Some tension occurred when we organized in Newcastle, as part of the BERA network series, a seminar on the project with the title "CTCs: Magnets, Beacons or White Elephants?" The question mark seems to have been ignored, the third alternative seems to have been taken as a conclusion, and a strong contingent from the CTC "movement" attended. Of particular relevance to this chapter is the response of members of that contingent, in particular the several CTC principals among them, to our analysis of the political origins of the programme of which they were part and our view that there might be something of an "educationist take-over" by those seeking in CTCs a context in which to be highly innovative in educational practice but who were uninterested in (and perhaps opposed to) the politicized objectives that they might be serving. Both points return our argument here to the various positions about "levels" of policy analysis with which we began.

We had no doubt from our analysis of origins that the CTC programme emerged from several and largely different sources. This heightened the difficulties mentioned earlier in assessing the credibility of supposedly key actors' claims to have had a decisive influence on its formulation. This was particularly difficult in relation to Kenneth Baker's view at interview that there was almost nothing in the way of "worked out" reforms in the DES when he took over as Secretary of State, and his obvious sense of ownership over the CTC initiative itself. Yet both Stuart Sexton, whom Baker had dispensed with as a political adviser immediately on taking office, and Robert Dunn, who had been the schools' minister for some time, reported a scheme already worked up if not in detail. There were also marked differences between the three of them in the policy objectives that they saw CTCs as serving. Briefly, Dunn seemed interested primarily in promoting a suitably modernized form of secondary technical education; Baker emphasized breaking the LEA "monopoly", and creating a bridge between what he called the "island" of private provision and the "continent" represented by the public sector; Sexton saw the value of "technology" as a gloss, but was interested in any measure that might contribute to his ultimate objective – an education system composed entirely of autonomous and competing units. We mention these contrasts, because they obviously raise questions about individual influence on policy and about the possibility that underlying "currents" may be carrying those individuals along.

Micro-politics and macro-theory

We indicated earlier our agreement with McPherson & Raab (1988) that a political sociology of education policy should involve the attempt to relate the "micro-politics of personal relationships to a wider analysis of power". Like McPherson and Raab, we have been criticized (at least implicitly) for not doing so (Ozga 1990: 359). Gerald Grace (1991) uses the term "policy science" to characterize studies that get trapped within the assumptions of the particular policy context being studied. Such studies become preoccupied with descriptive accounts of policy initiatives, or with the examination of financial, resource and logistical questions arising during their implementation. He recognizes that such work may not be unimportant, but "what can easily get lost in a culture of policy 'busyness' is analytical and evaluative study of a more fundamental kind" (p. 3). Following Fay (1975), he argues that policy science excludes consideration of wider contextual relations "by its sharply focused concern with the specifics of a particular set of policy initiatives" and is seductive in its concreteness, its apparently value-free and objective stance and its direct relation to action.

What risks being lost to view from this perspective is the examination of the politics and ideologies and interest groups of the policy-making process, the making visible of internal contradictions within policy formulations, and the wider structuring and constraining effects of the social and economic relations within which policy-making is taking place (Grace 1991: 3). All of that, he says, is the proper concern of "policy scholarship".

We see that distinction between policy science and policy scholarship as unhelpful in relation to recent empirically grounded work on specific education policies in the UK. In this context, our own work and a good deal of other current work on education policy straddles the boundary between Grace's two categories (e.g. Bowe et al. 1992, Halpin et al. 1993). Such work focuses on the origins, implementation and effects of specific policies, but it also explores how they are positioned in relation to other policies, and even how they can be understood in terms of changing modes of social solidarity and changing modes of regulation in contemporary societies.

We agree with Grace that it is better for research to be theoretically informed rather than naïvely empiricist, and that it is necessary to interrogate history with theory and theory with history. But there is an implication in Grace's work (and in Ozga's) that being theoretically informed means being informed by a particular form of theory. This is evident in their dismissal of work such as Kogan's many studies of the postwar settlement in England or McPherson & Raab's study of Scottish education policy as largely descriptive, when it is arguable that those studies are informed by a liberal pluralist theory. There is also a tendency in critiques of such work to regard micro-studies as descriptive and macro-studies as analytical, when in reality both can be either and either can be both.

Grace's approach and Ozga's critique are certainly important for reminding us of the political and ideological nature of policy, and the broader context of power relations within which specific policies develop. But we should be wary of dismissing too swiftly work that examines the empirical detail of policy formulation and implementation. The problem is surely that of making connections between theory and history and, in that respect, none of us has a very convincing record. If Grace (1989: 92) is right to argue that the attempt by McPherson & Raab to "relate the micro-politics of personal relationships to a wider analysis of power" is short on an analysis of power, they might well respond that too much other work on education policy is rather short on the micro-politics of personal relationships. The real problem is that all of us have difficulties in analyzing the relationship. Even Gewirtz & Ozga (1990: 47) end a fascinating empirical account of policy-making by identifying a need to relate the analysis of policy transactions to a state-centred theoretical framework, but they do not actually do it.

In practice, few of us get so obsessed with the detail that we lose sight of the need to locate it in the "bigger picture" and few of us engage in flights of pure theoretical fancy. We tend to occupy the middle ground, struggling to put it all together – except for those postmodern theorists who have decided there really is no bigger picture. Nevertheless, the detail is both fascinating and important and only in the detail is it possible to glimpse the complexity of power in its various manifestations. Both the micro-politics of policy-making and the micro-politics of doing research remain worthy of investigation.

It is probably true that, in reporting our own empirical studies, we have sometimes failed to make explicit the relevance of broader conceptions of power. However, Mary Darmanin (1991) has made the following observation on our study of the APS:

> Dale (1989) considers that in asking questions about processes of decision making, political questions are bracketed out. But this is demonstrably untrue . . . Though they have not made such a case in their analysis of the role of Stuart Sexton and his lobbying for his version of what the APS should be, Edwards *et al.* (1989) really bear out an old though important Althusserian (1977) position that if ideology interpellates individuals as subjects, it always does so within a system of narration . . . which constitutes the ideological field. (p. 62)

This is but one example of the ways in which social theory can have a symbiotic relationship to empirical studies of policy-making and thus help to illuminate both the nature of and the limits to the power of the powerful in education.

References

Althusser, L. 1977. *Lenin and philosophy*. London: New Left Books.

Bowe, R., S. Ball, with A. Gold 1992. *Reforming education and changing schools*. London: Routledge.

Connell, R., D. Ashenden, S. Kessler, G. Dowsett 1983. *Making the difference: schools, families and social division*. Sydney: Allen & Unwin.

Dale, R. 1989. *The state and education policy*. Milton Keynes: Open University Press.

Darmanin, M. 1991. National interests and private interests in policymaking. *International Studies in the Sociology of Education* 1 (1), 59–85.

Department for Education 1992. *Choice and diversity: a new framework for schools*. London: HMSO.

Edwards, T., M. Fulbrook, G. Whitty 1984. The state and the independent sector: policies, ideologies and theories. In *Social crisis and educational research*, L. Barton

& S. Walker (eds). London: Croom Helm.

Edwards, T., J. Fitz, G. Whitty 1989. *The state and private education: a study of the Assisted Places Scheme.* Lewes, Sussex: Falmer Press.

Fay, B. 1975. *Social theory and political practice.* London: Allen & Unwin.

Gewirtz, S. & J. Ozga 1990. Partnership, pluralism and education policy: A reassessment. *Journal of Education Policy* **5** (1).

Grace, G. 1989. Education policy studies: developments in Britain in the 1970s and 1980s. *New Zealand Journal of Educational Studies* **24** (1).

Grace, G. 1991. Welfare labourism versus the New Right: The struggle in New Zealand's education policy. Paper presented at the ERA Research Network, University of Warwick, 28 November.

Halpin, D. & J. Fitz 1990. Researching grant maintained schools. *Journal of Education Policy* **5** (2), 167–80.

Halpin, D., J. Fitz, S. Power 1993. *Grant maintained schools: Education in the marketplace.* London: Kogan Page.

Kogan, M. 1978. *The politics of educational change.* London: Fontana.

Lambert, R. & S. Millham 1968. *The hothouse society.* London: Weidenfeld & Nicolson.

Lambert, R., J. Hipkin, S. Stagg 1968. *New wine in old bottles: Studies in integration within the public schools.* London: Bell.

Lambert, R. with R. Bullock, S. Millham 1975. *The chance of a lifetime: A study of boys' and coeducational boarding schools in England and Wales.* London: Weidenfeld & Nicolson.

McPherson, A. & C. Raab 1988. *Governing education: A sociology of policy since 1945.* Edinburgh: Edinburgh University Press.

Ozga. J. 1990. Policy research and policy theory. *Journal of Education Policy* **5** (4), 359–63.

Ranson, S. 1985. Changing relations between centre and locality. In *Policy-making in education: The breakdown of consensus*, I. McNay & J. Ozga (eds). Oxford: Pergamon Press.

Sexton, S. 1987. *Our schools – A radical policy.* Warlingham, Surrey: Institute of Economic Affairs Education Unit.

Sexton, S. 1992. *Our schools – Future policy.* Warlingham, Surrey: IPSET Education Unit.

Walford, G. 1987. Research role conflicts and compromises in public schools. In *Doing sociology of education*, G. Walford (ed.). Lewes, Sussex: Falmer Press.

Walford, G. & H. Miller 1991. *City Technology College.* Milton Keynes: Open University Press.

Whitty, G., T. Edwards, S. Gewirtz 1993. *Specialisation and choice in urban education: The City Technology College experiment.* London: Routledge.

Wrigley, J. 1989. Curriculum development, teacher training and educational research: A view from the inside. *Research Papers in Education* **4** (3), 3–16.

CHAPTER THREE

Ministers and mandarins: educational research in elite settings

John Fitz and David Halpin

"Method is the road after one has travelled it"

(Ginsburg 1993)

Background

The research we report here was conducted between 1989 and 1991. It formed part of an investigation into the origins and effects of the grant-maintained (GM) schools policy, which was a central feature of the Education Reform Act 1988 for England and Wales (Fitz et al. 1993). In the course of our enquiries, we conducted interviews with politicians and civil servants and with other agencies involved in formulating the policy and fostering its development, as well others who were publicly opposed to it.

In this chapter we will focus on two groups of people whom we interviewed and who exerted considerable influence on the defining features of GM schools policy. The first set of interviewees comprises six civil servants who were directly involved in drafting the policy's administrative details, and who had the further responsibility for translating legislation into practice. The other comprises two Conservative education ministers.

The process of conducting the research was rather less organized and the various elements were less well articulated than we present in this account. Alongside researching policy-making at the centre, we were also engaged in fieldwork in local education authorities (LEAs) and in GM schools. Thus there were periods of intensive research in Whitehall, interspersed with travels elsewhere in the country, gaining knowledge at first hand about the initial impact of the policy on the ground. This, of course, fed back into the interviews we conducted in Whitehall. It is also fair to say that the decisions concerning what kind of research strategy we should adopt were less well thought through than we present here. Uppermost at the time were our perceptions, based on our previous experience, of what would assist in gaining access and what our likely respondents would tolerate and respond to and what we could do well. And those decisions were also influenced by the status and position of the intended interviewees, an issue to which we shall return in later discussion.

The contribution that qualitative research can make to an understanding of the processes, practice and substance of educational policy-making need not be elaborated here. A number of substantive studies have employed qualitative, interpretative methodology, within a variety of conceptual frameworks, which bear witness to the contribution this approach has made to the study of educational policy-making (e.g. Kogan 1975, Ozga 1987, Ball 1990, McPherson & Raab 1988, Edwards et al. 1989, Gewirtz & Ozga 1990). It was in that light that we sought access to, and conducted interviews with, key actors associated with the formulation and development of GM schools policy.

We undertook this element of our research with a number of objectives in mind. First, the interviews with people actively engaged in the policy-making process were intended to provide insights into, and details of, educational policy-making not otherwise available in documentary form and thus not in the public domain. Secondly, the interviews were intended to clarify, confirm or adjust existing published accounts of the formulation of GM schools policy and, as and where necessary, contribute to the construction of new and different narrative accounts. Thirdly, the interviews were conducted to assist the identification and understanding of the networks of individuals and agencies involved in contemporary policy-making in education and the relative influence they exercised. Fourthly, following McPherson & Raab (1988), we were concerned to familiarize ourselves with the "assumptive worlds" of policy-makers, and thus explore the ideas and values of key actors who were involved in setting the policy in motion and who had influenced its substance and the course of its progress. A detailed account of these influences on our work is reported in our study of policy-making in the DES (Fitz & Halpin 1991).

We have focused in this chapter on this aspect of our research because it took us into elite settings with which we were unfamiliar. For the purposes of this study we take elite settings to mean institutional locations in which national policy is devised and translated into directives. By virtue of their institutional locations and positions, therefore, our interviewees had a greater capacity to shape public events and meanings than either we, or other interviewees in our study, possessed. That situation had important implications for the manner in which we conducted this element of our research, for the nature of the data we collected and for our construction and narration of policy-making in education.

In this account of our research we will report on our experiences of data collection in elite settings and reflect on associated methodological issues and their implications for the analysis and reporting of policy-making in education. The chapter's focus on groups of administrators and senior politicians has the considerable advantage from the outset of suggesting that power is unequally distributed and differentially exercised, even amongst those described for the purpose of this study as "the powerful". In research terms it also enables us to report how we related in different ways to different groupings of powerful individuals and the relative effects this had on the research we conducted.

What follows broadly reflects the sequence of our research. The sequence itself illuminates the uneven pace at which this element of our research proceeded. The events unfolded not by design, but because this was the only path that we could negotiate. One attribute of the powerful is that they are able to make you wait and thus determine the organization and the pace of research.

In the next section, however, we discuss the general procedures we adopted in all of our interviews and the thinking that lay behind our methods of enquiry. The third section reports on our interviews with civil servants, all of whom were directly involved in taking the policy forward to legislation and some of whom were still engaged in transforming it into practice at the time we interviewed them. The fourth section discusses the data from our interviews with DES officials. The final section focuses on our interviews with ministers.

Methods of enquiry

When we commenced our research project, three factors guided our investigation of policy-making at the centre. First, we were convinced that those individuals involved in policy generation and implementation had a story to tell and thus we intended to provide an opportunity for them to tell it. In turn, it was also our concern, as Stephen Ball has put it, to move beyond "commentary and critique" towards a more complex, empirically based understanding of the policy processes associated with the Education Reform Act (Ball 1990). Through our interviews we aimed to ask individuals directly about their involvement in GM schools policy, about their motives, about their contributions to its construction and about the difficulties involved, and who else, to their knowledge, had been involved and their relative influence on the policy's development.

Secondly, we knew from the outset of our enquiries that we were researching a politically sensitive policy. The government had given GM schools policy a high profile in its 1987 election campaign (Thatcher 1993). In the run-up to, and during, that election, and throughout its passage from Bill to legislation, the policy met with hostile criticism from opposition politicians and from a broad spectrum of educationalists in local government, higher education and in schools. The government remained robust in its advocacy of the policy and at the time our research commenced, which coincided with the opening of the first group of GM schools, it was, alongside the National Curriculum, the most important of their reforms. It was against this background that we selected a methodological framework that one of us had employed previously in other politically sensitive policy research (Edwards et al. 1989).

Thirdly, the institutional location of our intended interviewees suggested that it would be unlikely they would agree to any intensive or long-term observationally based investigation. It was unlikely, we believed, that any request to observe policy-makers at work over an extended period of time would be granted. We knew of no studies of this kind. Indeed, the Official Secrets Act makes such research difficult if not impossible. We also anticipated that key actors would be unlikely to agree to off-the-record interviews in informal surroundings. We therefore requested interviews with individuals in their professional and/or party political capacity.

It was against this background that we also undertook not to identify any of our respondents in any reports of our research. Not all our informants were concerned to remain anonymous and indeed ministers spoke for the published record. From time to time, informants indicated that some information was not for publication although they had declared the interview itself could be attributed. We still think it is unlikely that civil servants would agree to be involved in policy research unless, or until, anonymity is assured.

We also limited the scope of our enquiries, in the first instance, to individuals who had been publicly identified as being involved in the generation and promotion of GM schools policy or, in the case of civil servants, those who had been directly involved with it in the course of their departmental duties. We did not approach retired policy-makers (as did Gewirtz & Ozga 1990) whose views might have contributed to placing GM schools policy in a broader historical and policy context. This was largely determined by the time we had available to pursue these enquiries. At this time we were located within a busy and demanding department of teacher education at Bristol Polytechnic (now the University of the West of England, Bristol) and for this element of the research we were without the valuable support of a research associate.

These considerations influenced our selection and use of the semi-structured interview as the main research instrument. The nature of the data we collected and their strengths and limitations were consequent upon this decision. The interview schedule was composed of a list of open-ended questions that were put to the interviewees. It was semi-structured in that the same schedule was used for all civil servant interviewees. Thus they were all asked the same questions in broadly the same sequence. The schedules devised for ministers reflected their different location within the policy process. Other researchers, such as Gewirtz & Ozga (1990) and Ball (1990), adopted a more open framework. Ozga and Gewirtz, for example, aimed for exchanges that resembled conversations and thus worked without a fixed schedule of questions.

However, in the fieldwork settings in which our research was to be conducted, the semi-structured interview offered a number of appealing features. Not only was it a technique with which we were familiar, it offered us the possibility of exerting some control over interviews conducted in difficult situations. Thus the existence of a schedule was intended to act as a foil to interviewees, many of whom were used to either being deferred and listened to, or "just talking" to their own agenda (Ostrander 1993). In other words, it was a device through which we could retain some control in situations where we wished to elicit information from individuals whose professional and institutional locations suggested that they were skilled at releasing very little. The schedule was also intended to supplement our documentary researches, which had identified gaps in the narrative of policy development. We hoped, too, that it would open up new issues to explore further and elsewhere. This preparatory work provided the substance of the open-ended questions on the schedule, which in turn were intended to provide opportunities for respondents to take the account forward, with the possibility of it moving in unanticipated directions.

The schedule additionally served as a prompt sheet. We also found it useful to give potential interviewees a copy of the schedule in order to indicate the areas we would explore in the course of the interview and to assure them that adequate opportunities existed to comment on a broad range of issues. This technique provided an opportunity for interviewees to organize their thoughts. The purpose of the semi-structured interviews, however, was not to validate or authenticate one account against another, but to hear about the policy features and processes from a number of perspectives and thus enable us to construct a more complex and more finely grained narrative account and interpretation of the GM schools policy's purposes, formulation and intended effects.

In addition to the choice of semi-structured interviews, two other decisions underpinned our method of enquiry. First, wherever possible we wished to have for the record a transcript of the interviews we conducted. We therefore requested, and in every case received, permission to make an audiotape of the interview for later transcription. The transcripts were to serve as a research record and as historical documents of the development of GM schools policy.

Secondly, in all exchanges reported in this chapter there were two interviewers. Curiosity was the principal factor here. We were each interested to hear the accounts at first hand and to observe the environments in which the interviewees routinely operated. Other benefits emerged as the research progressed. Working as a pair enabled one interviewer to be fully involved with the interviewee while the other superintended the tape machine, took notes and asked supplementary questions. In some instances it was a technique that facilitated a more conversational quality to the interview. The second interviewer also acted in effect as a second pair of eyes and ears, picking up details overlooked by the lead interviewer. In the field, it was an arrangement that also assisted the interviews to progress smoothly in situations where we were conscious that time was limited and always pressing.

The advantage of two interviewers, however, was fully realized at the conclusion of each interview. In the Festival Hall dining area (situated opposite the DES building) or in a local café or convenient public house we discussed and noted on the schedule the significance of what we had heard. Was it news? Was it at variance with other accounts? To what extent was there any correspondence in what each interviewer considered to be interesting and important? These informal conversations were the initial and often a most important stage in data analysis.

Working as a pair had one other advantage. We were not hard-bitten journalists with well-developed connections in London; we were researchers from a polytechnic working in settings somewhat unfamiliar and at times somewhat intimidating (one of us recalls sitting on his hands during one interview to hide the fact that they were shaking). The process of negotiating the way through an interview in these situations was considerably eased with a colleague in support. Working as a pair is also especially helpful in those circumstances where the interviewee is accompanied by advisers. In one case, for example, there were three other people in the room monitoring our meeting with a minister.

Looking back, and comparing and sharing our experience with other researchers, it was unusual to have had extensive access to politicians and policy-makers. Although it is difficult to identify the factors that made this possible, it is worth while to note, tentatively, some features of the research project that may have assisted, or at least did not work against, us.

Support from the British Economic and Social Research Council (ESRC), we believe, worked in our favour, contributing to our credibility as serious researchers under institutional obligations to do something with our material. One civil servant who organized our contacts within the Department of Education and Science, and who also in effect acted as a gatekeeper to ministers, had recently joined the DES from the ESRC. His assistance was vital to the project's further progress. The support of an external funding agency is an advantage if, like us, you are undertaking your first large-scale research project and do not have the benefit of professorial titles. Following established convention and practice also eased the progress of the research. We wrote to interviewees seeking permission to see them and telephoned to confirm arrangements. We indicated in our correspondence the nature of the research and identified the broad areas we would like to discuss. Before each interview we read through press cuttings and other relevant documents so that we were, and sounded, informed about the latest developments in a policy that underwent some fairly rapid adjustments during our time in the field. These research practices helped us in the field and, more important, to stay in it. One of the lessons of researching policy communities or networks is that the individuals in it communicate with each other, and about you and your research. Staying in is often dependent upon not making mistakes. How all the above elements came together as acts of research in the field will be discussed in further detail below.

Another country: interviewing civil servants

The door off Whitehall was somewhat inconspicuous, quite unlike the portals of the Treasury for example. The foyer was functional. At the reception desk the porters checked our names against the appointments log and then telephoned our interviewee. Prior to meeting our interviewee, however, we were each invited to step into what resembled a transparent plastic cylinder. Inside a stream of air flowed around us that, we later assumed, sniffed for explosives. We were greeted and then led down a long passage. The corridors of power were constructed of tudor brick. We turned off the corridor into a group of small offices where two or three people were at work at their personal computers. We were taken through the outer offices to a larger room where the interview took place.

Viewers of the television series *Yes Minister* will be familiar with Sir Humphrey's office, a replica, and an accurate one, of the room in which we stood. High ceilings, extensive wooden panelling, a writing desk, and a suite of plush velvet sofas and armchairs arranged around a large fireplace furnished the interview setting. Display cabinets of porcelain dominated one end of the room, and photographs of the Chief Secretary to the Cabinet and Head of the Civil Service with his predecessor were arranged on the mantelpiece. We sat in the armchairs, accepted coffee, explained the purpose of our research, sought permission to tape-record, and then began to ask our questions.

This episode is described in detail because it contains some of the key elements of the conduct of research interviews with powerful people in elite settings. One aspect of political and administrative power is that it is exercised behind the protection of gatekeepers and multi-layered gatekeeping processes. Although the experience we report here was somewhat unusual, those researchers who have recently visited the Palace of Westminster, and its associated annexes and civil service departments, will be familiar with uniformed porters controlling access to elected representatives and to administrators. But these are only the visible signs of a larger process. Gatekeeping, the process of sifting applications to interview policy-makers at the centre, extends well beyond the issue of passes at the lodges of government buildings, and is evident in the paucity of empirical educational policy research conducted in and around Whitehall.

This encounter, although somewhat untypical, nevertheless captures some of the experience of conducting research in unfamiliar and intimidating surroundings. It was the administrators' territory, a habitat with which they were familiar and in which they felt comfortable and confident. Thus the "reality" that was narrated and recorded was inevitably highly constrained. We glimpsed an unfamiliar world that was only ever partially revealed. We were not privy, for example, to situations in which the political skills and reputations of ministers were discussed, where civil service careers were forensically dissected.

Little has been said thus far about the substance of this and other similar interviews we conducted with civil servants. How these were conducted requires a further form of contextualization. As the research progressed, we became increasingly aware that in our interviews with civil servants we were involved in exchanges with individuals who were visible bearers of specific historical, cultural, linguistic and constitutional traditions that together constituted a discourse within which research becomes enmeshed and to a considerable degree reproduces. That was brought home to us in concrete terms in the first of the six interviews we did with civil servants.

This official was based, like the majority of our informants, at the old DES headquarters in Elizabeth House. He listened to our usual preamble in which we clarified some questions about the nature of our research. He then issued a very straightforward order, which was to cover this and subsequent interviews we were to conduct with other officials in the department. In plain, he said, we should not assume there existed, nor, therefore, should we seek to explore, any differences or divisions between himself, his ministers and other civil servants. When it came to policy determination, whatever advice might have been given, ministers and officials were at one as a department. We have already referred to gatekeeping and the variety of forms it took. Here was another – explicit, uncoded and in the form of a command.

Clearly then, there were avenues that we were unable to explore openly, with this or with less senior officials. Thus the policy options that civil servants put before ministers, and why this one course of action had been adopted and not others, were questions that we were able to pursue only obliquely. On the other hand, none of our respondents volunteered any comment on the options laid before ministers even when we suggested in roundabout ways that ministers in practice routinely devised policy in the light of several courses of action proposed by their officials. In consequence, we have been unable to say with any precision the extent to which the DES had muted the radical proposals for change advanced by agencies on the New Right. Stuart Sexton, for example, was convinced that civil service advice detrimentally affected the proposals that he and other advisers wished to see carried forward. These methodological constraints, however, have to be seen in the context of recent and ongoing struggles about civil service accountability (e.g. Ponting 1986). The important point here is that, when conducting qualitative, interview-based research, thinking about the nature of the data and the form of their analysis has to refer to a larger historical political and historical canvas.

What civil servants may disclose on a professional basis is governed by several overlapping frameworks. The first, the Official Secrets Act, can be interpreted to be so all-embracing as to cover all policy-related documents. According to one non-departmental informant, the DES was over-zealous in this regard. He recalled, for example, that the DES would regard as "secret" even low-level demographic statistics. Although the DES may have been over-scrupulous in these matters, the point is that officials work in an environment where they are predisposed to disclose very little.

They also work within conventions, notably the Osmotherly Rules, which state that the policy advice they provide is privileged information. Thus, officials have the right, notably exercised by Toby Weaver, a former Deputy Secretary in the DES, not to disclose, even to parliamentary committees, their professional communications with ministers. This has recently been complemented by guidelines drafted by Sir Robert Armstrong, a former Cabinet Secretary, in the wake of the prosecution of Clive Ponting and Sarah Tisdall, civil servants who made public material that caused some ministerial embarrassment. The Armstrong guidelines clarify the line of civil service accountability. In the first instance this was to be to ministers, not to Parliament or the general public.

In addition to these constitutional constraints there is a class cultural dimension that is central to a full appreciation of policy research at this level. This relates to attributes of individual, recruited into the civil service and who work within the conventions we outlined above. It remains the case that, of the fast-track civil servants, that is, those selected for future advancement to high office, and who have frequent direct contact with ministers, about half still come from Oxbridge and independent school backgrounds (Guardian 1993, Burnham & Jones 1993). We were not "public school", nor had we been to Oxbridge. In interview situations, we encountered individuals who, by selection and training, had the capacity to present their department's case clearly and persuasively. They were at ease with the demands made of them to present well-developed accounts of a policy's features and its intentions. We joked to one another that these were respondents who set out their case not only in correct, connected English sentences, but in paragraphs as well. These cultural features were articulated with our respondents' abilities to work successfully within the conventions of civil service life.

We have dwelt on these details because "studying up" inevitably involves researchers coming to understand the conventions that create and reproduce particular forms of policy-making practice, some of which are uniquely British. At the interpersonal level, and in the data we collected, in what form were these conventions manifest?

First, they appear as a distinctive civil service voice, evident in all our transcripts. Officials speak only for and on behalf of departments. In substance, then, they talk about policy features and intentions, but always within the context of government policy in general and departmental policy in particular. Asked to justify aspects of policy, responses begin, "Ministers would argue . . .". In these matters there is no distinction between their utterances and the ministerial and departmental view. The interviews, in character, read very much like fluent exegeses of government thinking at the time. Accordingly, in nine hours of such interviewing, we heard no expression of officials' personal opinions or dispositions, which contrasts with the way in which local authority officials chose to answer our questions.

Secondly, our interviewees readily talked about the processes of policy-making in the department, even though they refused to discuss either the substance of exchanges or the individuals involved. Thus they provide an interesting insight into the way departments respond to the demands of steering a major piece of legislation through Parliament. Indeed, two of our interviewees had been seconded to the DES from other departments to give them experience of the process and to strengthen in-house resources. In one sense, however, the conventions foster disclosures of the technicalities of policy-making but not discussion of its value assumptions or the various commitments of politicians and ministers and how these influenced policy outcomes.

The DES and GM schools policy

With these limitations in mind the questions must be posed: were the interviews worth doing, and what did we get from them? Our respondents were consistent in their claim that this policy was "political" rather than "administrative" in its origin. GM schools policy originated outside the DES. Other aspects of the 1988 Act, notably a National Curriculum and the devolution of school budgets (which became the Local Management of Schools), had been subject to considerable discussion and development within the department prior to the Act. In other words, although the officials were responsible for devising the detailed procedures that enabled schools to leave the control of LEAs, the idea of opting out was not one they had first thought of and subsequently championed. Even so, there was evidence in our transcripts that officials had come to believe that the policy would be effective in raising standards through the competitive effects of diversity and extended choice that it was intended to introduce into the school system.

In this instance, the interview data can also be interpreted as evidence of the extent to which an administrative elite has incorporated "choice" and "diversity" into its discourse on education. The policy was justified on the grounds that it would bring "competition" into the system and would "shake up" local authority education services, the beneficial effects of which would be higher standards.

We were struck also by the effort taken to place GM and local authority schools on a "level playing field" in respect of their funding and in terms of admissions. In order to demonstrate that autonomous schools, free of local bureaucracy, can deliver managerial efficiencies that translate into educational gains, it was argued that there had to be parity between different kinds of schools. Our respondents did not waver in this argument. Looking back over the policy, which has moved further and further away from this founding idea, these interviews thus stand as a valuable antidote to ministerial amnesia about the policy's official purpose and direction at the time the first GM schools were opened.

We also gleaned a great deal about civil servants' professional practice and, as we noted in an earlier paper (Fitz & Halpin 1991), the unparalleled access they have to ministers. Numerous opportunities therefore arise to determine policy details, if not the overall direction of education policy. As one of our informants noted, "ministers rarely put pen to paper"; he then proceeded to describe the circuit of minutes, meetings and redrafting through which policy develops. In this "policy loop", as we described it, other voices and other influences were largely excluded. Certainly, this would go some way to explaining why some neo-liberal educationists, such as Sexton, were disappointed that their proposals were not adopted in full.

Ministers talking

In our discussions with civil servants we made clear our intention to seek interviews with education ministers – those in post and their predecessors. We had written to Kenneth Baker, then Secretary of State for Education, in October 1989. Two years later we were granted interviews with Baker, who was then Home Secretary, and with Tim Eggar, Minister of State for Education.

The interview with Kenneth Baker was conducted at the Home Office. He was accompanied by his political adviser, who remained in the room throughout the interview. Prior to the commencement of the interview, for which we ran two tape recorders, Baker established that the interview was attributable. The interview that followed was dominated by Baker.

He produced a fat green file and, leafing through it, proceeded to tell us about the reform of education, the background to it, the need for it and his part in its history. There are two pages of single-spaced interview transcript before the first intervention into his monologue is recorded, and that came from the political adviser. The interview continued in similar fashion. We asked relatively few questions and exerted almost no control over the interview situation.

Baker's performance was skilled. The narrative was persuasive and engrossing. Here was a minister, on his account, persuaded by the prime minister to assume responsibility for, and do something about, education. He confronted a system, spotted with "bush fires", notably the teachers' action, that had rumbled on since 1984, which needed sorting out. In general, however, Baker saw himself as taking up the concerns first addressed in Labour Prime Minister Callaghan's 1976 Ruskin speech. He continued, "And so I started first on quality: what can one do? This led me to develop the idea of the National Curriculum, with standards of achievement. The rest is history, as it were, so I won't go in to that". In association with the DES, and Her Majesty's Inspectorate, the period prior to the 1987 general election was devoted to the preparation of the educational reforms announced in the run-up to the election. Baker explained, "A huge amount of work was done on that and I was aiming for a paper to Margaret [Thatcher] by December 1986. And in December, I sent her a blueprint, which I have here [in the green file], all of my educational reforms".

This account of events, as it was recounted to us, has also appeared recently in Baker's published memoirs. The blueprint setting out his proposals for educational reform appear as an annexe in that volume (Baker 1993). The excerpts above, however, also accurately reflect Baker's conception of himself as some kind of "policy hero". These were his reforms, authored by him and in seeming isolation from other participants in the policy loop. He was, for example, dismissive about the influence of the New Right "think tanks" on the educational reforms that were taken forward into legislation. Moreover, there was scant acknowledgement, reflected in the excerpts above, that considerable thought had previously been given to a National Curriculum and to local management of schools, by either the DES or Her Majesty's Inspectorate of Schools. Other evidence, in Ball (1990) for example, suggests that the reforms can only with difficulty be attributed entirely to Baker's initiative.

Any vision of policy-making as a rational process was undermined in this interview with a skilled, ambitious and relatively senior member of the Cabinet. It was a reminder that reforms happen for quite pragmatic, party political reasons. The importance of the political agendas of the government and the personal ambitions of ministers as aspects of the policy process came through strongly in this exchange. Educational reforms proceeded, not necessarily because they were needed or because they were right, but because the private opinion polls suggested educational reform was a vote winner. That this was primarily an interview with a politician was also made more apparent, however, when the interview was suspended so that we could follow the early evening news.

As Home Secretary, Baker had been at the House of Commons that day debating not only the "dangerous dogs" legislation but also arguments about Sunday trading, and responding to the release of the "Tottenham Three". For politicians, especially ministers involved in developing and defending policies on behalf of the government, the news is the best indication they have of the importance of their policies. Our interview was thus interrupted while the minister and his political adviser assessed the prominence given to Home Office matters.

At the end of the formal interview, the political adviser invited us to discuss any matters that the Home Secretary had raised and about which we required further clarification. This was a very different encounter, an off-the-record, more direct exchange of views about politics, policies and personalities. It contrasted very much with the Home Secretary's presentation of GM policy, its purposes and its antecedents. The adviser's contribution was a more robust defence of the Home Secretary's role in policy development, which included a less than flattering account of other individuals widely thought to be influential in educational policy-making. It also hinted at the effort required to impress on a sometimes reluctant DES the direction the Secretary of State wanted the reforms to take. Because these have since been graphically described in Baker's memoirs we can mention them here without fear of breaching confidentiality.

Overall, these meetings were more relaxed and expansive than the interview conducted with the then Minister of State for Education, Tim Eggar. The differences between them probably arise from civil servants' concerns to protect serving ministers in their department, compared with those who are no longer engaged in education policy (see Ponting 1986: 30–63). In addition, Eggar had not been involved in formulating the policy and so confined his remarks to his administration of a policy he had inherited and to some of the issues involved in taking it forward.

The interview took place in less than satisfactory circumstances for the researchers and the researched. Although we had arranged to see the minister for an hour, on arrival we were informed that he was likely to be called away at any time for consultations with the Secretary of State. The exchanges, therefore, were rather more hurried than we would have wished. We also edited the schedule as the interview proceeded, in an attempt to give priority to what we thought were the key questions. For our part, we were also conscious of three civil servants taking extensive notes of the questions and the minister's responses. That also put the respondent under pressure to get things right, to stick to the department's brief. The responses were similar in character and purpose to the civil servants' replies we spoke of earlier: hold the line and explain the departmental position. Judged from a civil service perspective, the minister's performance was admirable in so far as he held his brief and outlined the policy's purpose and direction with clarity and conviction. We learned very little that was new. This was disappointing, as the policy at that time was undergoing a very important review.

In research terms, the value of this interview lies in its contrast with Baker's. Their relative positions in government determined the interview context, and also the kind of account each was able to construct. On the one hand, we have Baker's narration of the policy's history and his part in its making. His seniority confers on him the power to provide a personalized account. On the other hand, Eggar is confined to an administrator's explanation of government policy in the company of civil service "minders". Again, this interview told us rather more about the arcane rules and regulations of Whitehall and its hierarchies than it did about GM schools policy.

Ponting has argued that "the real amateurs in government are Ministers" (Ponting 1986: 31). Their instincts, he noted, lead them to emphasize the short-term political aspects of the job. He concedes, however, that they are great talkers. The administrator's lofty judgement of ministers' involvement in long-term policy development emphasizes the difference between their respective aims and responsibilities. Throughout our research, however, we were struck by the similarities, at the interactional level, between the administrators and the politicians. The skills they exercised in research situations in their presentation of self, via language, dress and their orientation to the business of governing, had much in common. In our experience, and in contrast to Ponting, there were no "amateurs" at the level of policy-making we have described. And this is perhaps the key challenge of conducting qualitative research with the powerful in elite settings.

Conclusion

Although ethnographers may argue that their research gives a "voice" to the socially disadvantaged and politically under-represented, who are in effect silenced by the system in which they are situated, it is also the case, as Hunter argues, that their relative powerlessness is demonstrated by the frequency with which academics visit and record their lives (Hunter 1993). In contrast, the powerful – in this case the administrative and political elite – have considerable constitutional, legal and cultural resources that enable them to deflect or channel any research in which they are the object of enquiry. The power they exercise is reflected both in the paucity of studies about elites, in this case in education, and in the kind of research that is directed at them. The classroom or "street corner society" can be observed in minute detail, but the same cannot be said about the interactional exchanges in the Cabinet Office.

This chapter has discussed some of the problems of conducting qualitative research in elite settings. The barriers that have to be overcome are, in large measure, created by the formal and informal conventions that screen off the routines of education policy-making from the public and the academic gaze. The course of our enquiries demonstrates how contingent and conditional researchers' access is to those involved directly in the policy-making process at the centre. In our case, and without any claim to membership by birth, education or other affiliation to the establishment, it required sponsorship by a well-regarded research council and the help of key persons. It was also assisted by a research design based on conventional and commonly understood research protocols and methods, promises of confidentiality, and sufficient cultural and social awareness to know how to play the game well enough to remain in the field.

The obvious danger of the relationship of researchers to the researched in this context, as we earlier acknowledge, is that they simply end up reproducing the discourse of the powerful. This is likely to be the dominant discourse in the fieldwork phase of qualitative research in elite settings. Thus, there is always the problem of uncritically accepting elite narratives as the authentic, valid account of how policy was formulated and why. There are, however, resources within a well-established framework of qualitative research practice to ease researchers out of this difficulty.

First, interviews elicit accounts that provide transcripts of the utterances of individuals located in contexts that generate rules about what can and cannot be said. These accounts are helpful in the reconstruction of the processes of policy-making, and more so if they can be set alongside other sources. Interviews nevertheless express individual perspectives on events and, as such, carry with them undeclared interests. Interviews are unlikely ever to yield the whole story.

Secondly, and following on from the point above, the context within which interviewees speak must be described. In this chapter, for example, we have outlined the constitutional and conventional rules that gave rise to the civil servants' voice and that also regulated what they could say in a research environment. The context not only generates the nature of their accounts, including their mode of its expression, but also provides a basis for the evaluation of these interviews as evidence.

Thirdly, difficulties associated with access to administrators and politicians, the conditions placed on interviewers concerning the form and the kinds of questions that can be posed, and the conventions of politeness and deference within the interview itself are expressions of the boundaries between the administrative and academic fields. Policy research that involves qualitative methods of enquiry is thus likely to evoke contests over boundary maintenance, which are in themselves useful reminders to researchers to look again at the nature and purpose of the boundary and whose interests are best served by its existence. It can be argued, then, that the encounters are as important as the words in the transcript in terms of revealing the structures within which policy is formulated and developed.

The research experiences we have described above were not always comfortable for us, but, on the other hand, they were always seductively exciting. We would argue that it is worth doing and that it is a course of enquiry we will continue to undertake, and we would encourage others to do so. For, if nothing else, it gives rise to situations in which policy-makers are asked to render public accounts of themselves and their actions. In addition, research activities in elite settings have other beneficial effects. These encounters have the capacity to identify the rules generated by the elite concerning who may speak and who may not, which knowledge is for public consumption and which is not, and the values that are to be preserved and those that are not. Power, in these terms, resides in, and is exercised through, the classificatory framework that the elites have generated. Researching the powerful, or "studying up", therefore inevitably involves an analysis of the rules they create and reproduce, and the context within which they are generated.

References

Baker, K. 1993. *The turbulent years, My life in politics*. London: Faber & Faber.

Ball, S. J. 1990. *Politics and policy making in education: Explorations in policy sociology*. London: Routledge.

Burnham, J. & G. W. Jones 1993. Advising Margaret Thatcher: The Prime Minister's Office and the Cabinet Office compared. *Political Studies* **41**, 299–314.

Edwards, T., J. Fitz, G. Whitty 1989. *The state and private education: An evaluation of the Assisted Places Scheme*. Falmer, Sussex: Falmer Press.

Fitz, J. & D. Halpin 1991. From a "sketchy policy to a workable scheme": The DES and grant-maintained schools. *International Studies in Sociology of Education* **1**, 129–51.

Fitz, J., D. Halpin, S. Power 1993. *Grant maintained schools. Education in the market place*. London: Kogan Page.

Gewirtz, S. & J. Ozga 1990. Partnership, pluralism and education policy: A reassessment. *Journal of Education Policy* **5** (1) 37–48.

Ginsburg, C. 1993. Witches and shamans. *New Left Review* **200**, 75–85.

Guardian 1993. Whitehall favours Oxbridge. *Guardian*, 26 August, 2.

Hunter, A. 1993. Local knowledge and local power, notes on the ethnography of local community elites. *Journal of Contemporary Ethnography* **22** (1) 36–58.

Kogan, M. (1975) *Educational policy making: A study of interest groups and Parliament*. London: Allen & Unwin.

McPherson, A. & C. Raab 1988. *Governing education: A sociology of policy since 1945*. Edinburgh: Edinburgh University Press.

Ostrander, S. A. 1993. "Surely you're not in this to be helpful": Access, rapport and interviews in three studies of elites. *Journal of Contemporary Ethnography* **22** (1) 7–23.

Ozga, J. 1987. Studying education through the lives of policy-makers: An attempt to close the macro–micro gap. In *Changing policies, changing teachers: New directions in schooling*, L. Barton & S. Walker (eds). Lewes, Sussex: Falmer Press.

Ponting, C. 1986. *Whitehall: Tragedy and farce*. London: Hamilton.

Thatcher, M. 1993. *The Downing Street years*. London: HarperCollins.

CHAPTER FOUR

The Lords' will be done: interviewing the powerful in education

J. Daniel McHugh

Introduction

As Director of Religious Education in a large Catholic diocese, with some 220 primary schools and 40 secondary schools, I have overall responsibility on behalf of the Bishop for advising on and inspecting religious education and worship in those schools. Further, I must ensure that there is suitable inservice training for teachers not only in RE and collective worship but also in the approaches teachers take to the spiritual, moral, social and cultural development of pupils. Being involved in the church–state schools partnership in England and Wales carries with it a responsibility to work within the arrangements that have been arrived at in legislation and the guidance offered in circulars issued by the Department for Education. However, just as the Catholic Church is regulated in its schools by educational legislation, so it has the opportunity to influence the policy government adopts and the legislation it enacts to carry that policy forward. There, like other responsible bodies, the Church will be concerned about other schools as well as its own in the maintained sector, whether they are Anglican, Jewish, county or non-denominational grant-maintained schools. It is also true that the Church is concerned not only about RE and worship, but about broader issues in schools, and may seek to influence government and ministers on a range of educational issues.

But how can the Church as a whole, or a diocese, which is the body with responsibility for supporting the Catholic schools in its area, influence government in policy-making, particularly in the legislative process? This has been one of my concerns as I have experienced the impact of legislation and have sometimes felt powerless in the face of its implementation. Surely the Church should not only be reacting to policy, but be more actively involved in forming it. It was in this context that I set out to research the way policy is made in the legislative process.

The 1988 Education Reform Act

I chose the sections on religious education and worship of the 1988 Education Reform Act for detailed study. There were of course many other aspects of that Act with which the Church was particularly concerned. For example, the Catholic Church saw the provisions for grant-maintained schools as potentially undermining the overall planning of school provision in an area, and as giving powers to a transient group of parents at the expense of the broader interests of the local community. In a similar way, the Church saw the proposals on admissions of pupils, which require schools to take up to their standard number, as possibly opening the way to a situation in which the popular reputation (possible temporary) of some schools could result in the draining of pupils and resources from other local schools, consequently impeding development in those other schools.

However, my particular responsibility in the area of religious education led to my choosing the sections on religious education and worship in the 1988 Act for a "case-study" approach to researching the legislative process. The research was undertaken towards a PhD, but I wished to make use of the research not only for its own sake but as a means to influence future legislation. It was thus important that I choose the area where I was anxious to see the Church being active.

Approaching the research

Documentation is of course to be found in *Hansard*, and its record of the debates in both Houses of Parliament was the primary source of written information concerning the passage of the Bill. A reading of *Hansard* indicates clearly that there was concern in many quarters about the lack of emphasis in the Bill on religious education and worship, but also that a coming together of Churches, interest groups and members of both Houses of Parliament led to long debates on issues concerning religious education and worship and to major amendments to the Bill that were accepted by the government. The main areas of amendment involved:

- giving religious education a more prominent place in the curriculum through the creation of the Basic Curriculum, which included RE and the National Curriculum;
- making explicit the prominent place of Christianity – as part of our heritage and culture – in the content of religious education and worship;
- legislation requiring Standing Advisory Councils on Religious Education (SACREs)to be established in each local authority. SACREs were to involve members of the different denominations and faiths, and to have an important part to play in raising the status and quality of religious education and worship.

I concentrated on the first two areas above, considering the policy that emerged, where it came from, and how it was legislated for. It was in the second area, on the place of Christianity in religious education and worship, that most tension and conflict emerged. This contributed considerably to far more attention being given during the passage of the Bill to the issue of religious education and worship than was ever intended. This of course leaves the researcher with many questions:

- In the consultative process leading to the publication of the Education Reform Bill in 1987 concerns were expressed about the lack of emphasis on religious education in the papers issued for comment. Why were these concerns not allowed for in the Bill?
- As the Bill went through the second reading and committee stage in the House of Commons a number of issues were raised: some the Secretary of State responded to in a positive way and promised to support amendments, others he rejected. How did this come about and why? Who were the people with influence?
- In the House of Lords the unthinkable (apparently) happened when the government agreed to the word "Christianity" being placed on the face of the Bill: RE should be "in the main" Christian. Since the Secretary of State had rejected this earlier, why was there a change of mind? How did this come about? Who was influential? Why did it happen?

It was clear that it would not be possible to find answers to these questions in any existing documentation; indeed, different groups and individuals involved in the process were not necessarily aware of all the activities of each other and would have differing interpretations of events. It seemed to me that the best way forward was to ask those involved or at least to identify and ask the principal characters involved – the "powerful" as far as this piece of legislation was concerned.

The central research instrument for this study was therefore to be the personal interview. The value of the interview in revealing who the key people were, their roles and influence in the policy-making process is emphasized by Anthony Seldon and Joanna Pappworth (1983: 42) in their book *By Word of Mouth*. They quote Brian Hanson (1972: 34) where he writes "interviews can shed light on elusive but important problems such as how decisions are reached, how influence is exerted . . . and how organizations are run". Seldon and Pappworth argue that documents often hide the real reasons certain events took place and you can get to them only by speaking to those who know. They claim that the contribution of interviewing to the understanding of government has been critical (Seldon & Pappworth 1983: 179).

The interview

Access

A particular concern in undertaking such research is of course "access", and, as many of the principal actors in the legislative process were members of the House of Commons or the House of Lords, I was going to be seeking interviews with busy people on whose goodwill I would have to rely. I began however with the Churches. I felt it would be important to begin where I had ready access and in a situation where I could obtain further introductions.

I found members of both the Catholic Education Council (now Catholic Education Services) and the Church of England Board of Education ready to give time despite busy schedules. The Churches had indeed been very active during the passage of the Bill: the Catholic Education Council had been involved in lobbying on schools' opting out, open enrolment, and the National Curriculum, especially as it affected the status of religious education; the Church of England had been involved in the lobby about the National Curriculum too, but went on to play a much greater part in drafting amendments on RE and worship when the Bill reached the House of Lords. Both sets of interviews were complementary, helping me to obtain an overview of the concerns of the Churches and detail of involvement in certain issues by each Church. These interviews led to my identifying key people for the Churches, particularly in the Commons and the Lords, but also other groups and individuals. For the Catholic Church, the roles of Sir Hugh Rossi in the Commons and the Duke of Norfolk in the Lords, to mention just two, were particularly important. For the Church of England, Michael Alison in the Commons and the Bishop of London, in the Lords, again to mention two, were especially significant. There were other leading personalities the Churches looked to as well, and these were in close touch with Church leaders and officials at different stages in the passage of the Bill. At the same time I was able to begin to assess the role and influence of the Churches, their wider connections in Parliament and government, their power when acting in unison, and their weakness when divided.

While the Church education officers pointed to key parliamentary figures in the legislative process, I obtained introductions to most of them from among their colleagues in the House of Lords or the Commons – I felt that was an important way to go about seeking interviews. However, the door opened for me via a Jesuit priest who knew the Earl of Lauderdale in the House of Lords. The priest wrote to the Earl explaining what I was doing and asking him to assist me. The Earl invited me to tea in the House and it was from there that the interviews began. Just as Jarol Manheim and Richard Rich (1991: 142) write that we often learn whom to interview by interviewing, so it was in my initial interview with the Earl. He was not himself the leader of the moves to bring about policy change in the Lords, but he was very much a supporter. Therefore, he knew the key people personally and was prepared to write to them on my behalf. I would agree with Lewis Dexter (1970: 33) that it is an asset to have important people (like the Earl) writing to other important people introducing the researcher. Dexter himself obviously had persistence in gaining access to interviewees, and used all means possible to achieve it. It seems to me that gaining access is not a neat process, any more than social research as a whole is, and, as Robert Burgess wrote, "the project and methodology is [sic] continually defined and redefined by the researcher and in some cases by the researched" (1984: 31).

It was through the Earl of Lauderdale that I was introduced to the leading figure in a very important phase of the Bill's passage in the House of Lords, the Baroness Caroline Cox. Lady Cox in turn guided me to some of the other leading figures in the moves to place "Christianity" at the centre of religious education and worship in county schools. This was one of the most controversial phases of the legislation: it involved Members of the Commons as well as the Lords and senior figures in government past and present. What became clear in the interview with Lady Cox was the important role played by a network of concerned parents, teachers, Christians and others outside and inside both Houses of Parliament. It was through the Baroness that I met the authors of the booklet *The Crisis in Religious Education* (Burn and Hart 1988), which was recognized in interviews as having a great deal of influence on the policy that was eventually backed by government.

It has been said to me that my position as a priest helped me to gain access. I have no doubt that this is true – it might be expected that those concerned for matters like religious education and worship would relate well to a priest or minister of religion. Also, as one having a special position, being Director of Religious Education in a diocese, it was clear that I would have a certain responsibility and authority on educational issues. I suspect having the title "Monsignor" also indicates a recognized status in the Church, which would help a busy Member of Parliament to decide whether giving valuable time would be justified. It would be true to say, I think, that once I had gained access to certain key people, and they had found my approach and motives acceptable, it was easier to move on to others, supported by further recommendations. As one MP said to me in the bar of the House of Commons, "If you say whom you have met, they'll know you are not a way-out person, who will distort what they say."

My initial approach to a Member of the Commons or the Lords was by letter: this explained that I was seeking an interview in the course of research into policy-making through the study of the religious education and worship clauses of the 1988 Education Reform Act. I explained my position in the diocese and the fact that the research was authorized by my Archbishop. I felt this would give sufficient information to enable the person I sought to interview to prepare for it, and at the same time showed that the research was supported by the Church. Quite deliberately the letter was not too detailed or demanding in case it might deter the person concerned from giving an interview. I think Sidney and Beatrice Webb were correct in *Methods of Social Study* (1932: 135) where they wrote, "Do not ask for too much at the first start off; you can always ask for more; and an inch given is better than an ell refused!" In a similar way, a little more recently, Lewis Dexter (1970: 49) suggested when soliciting an interview, "Do not be any more precise than you absolutely have to be about what you are looking for." I also gave dates when I would be in London in the hope that one of them might be suitable, but I offered to go to London on another date if that was more convenient. Obviously, I wished to fit in two or three interviews in a day: travel to London is expensive and time is precious, so I wished to get the most from my journey. On the other hand, I was conscious that it was better not to exceed three interviews; the immediate preparation for an interview is important, so it is not advisable to rush from one to another. In fact, over the course of the research, I obtained interviews with nine members of the House of Commons and nine members of the House of Lords who were associated with the clauses on religious education and worship. There was just one member of the Commons who would have found it difficult to meet me, and he wrote, "it does seem to me that you have covered all the people who are concerned in the shaping of this policy". So my approach at the very least had not put off those I sought to interview.

The response to my letter to a Member of the Commons or the Lords was frequently a telephone call from his/her secretary confirming that the person concerned was willing to see me, and arranging the date and time. At this point I normally explained to the secretary that I wished to take a tape recorder along and I hoped that would be in order. The secretary said she would let the member know – most were familiar with researchers using a tape recorder. I must say I was glad this presented no difficulty, because I found the use of a recorder a great asset: nothing was missed; some of the points I had not even detected in the course of the interview, I noted when I played back; some issues raised that seem unimportant at the time can become quite significant in the light of later evidence; on tape you catch the intonation, the way things were said (cf. Seldon & Pappworth 1983: 71).

A conversation with a purpose

Preparing thoroughly for the interviews was most important. Though Sidney and Beatrice Webb describe the interview "as a conversation with a purpose" – and that describes it very well – they do not intend to make light of its scientific purpose. They also describe the interview as the "unique instrument of the social investigator", "the eliciting of facts from a competent informant by skilled interrogation", and "a device of scientific investigation" (1932: 130, 135). They go on to note the importance of being prepared for the interview, knowing the published material and knowing terminology (1932: 136). My preparation for the interviews can be seen as having two stages: remote preparation and proximate preparation.

Remote preparation involved reading the official account of debates in *Hansard* – when the person to be interviewed was a member of the Lords or Commons – to brief myself on what he/she had said in the course of debates in the House or in committee; reading newspaper reports related to the time in question; reading articles and other material by the interviewee; as time went on, checking tapes and transcripts of interviews that had already taken place to inform myself about the point of view of others involved in the same situation and, where relevant, the earlier interviewees' views on the role of the person I was about to interview. Then there was the preparation of questions for the interviewee. My intention here was to try to get to the heart of the situation: who did what; how they did it; who supported them; why they thought this was important, etc. However, although I had prepared questions well, I also wanted the person to have the freedom to recall the event as he/she saw it and to expound on that freely. Moyser & Wagstaffe (1987: 18) write about three major variants of the interview: the structured, the semi-structured and the unstructured. I think the semi-structured interview probably describes best what I was aiming at in my preparation. In the course of an initial recollection of events I found the respondent frequently answering more than one of the questions I intended to ask, so there was no point in being a slave to the questions.

Proximate preparation, in the main, involved going through the questions carefully and making any last-minute preparations just before the interview. The purpose was to have a good recall of the major aims and main questions for the interview so that there was no need to refer to notes too frequently. My intention was to be so well prepared that I would be free to follow the train of thought of the interviewee; to respond to him/her; to draw in the questions I had in mind in an easy way without disrupting the conversation. Robert Burgess (1984: 108) discusses the agenda of topics/issues he wished to cover in a series of interviews and says, "This agenda acted as an 'aide-mémoire' which I could use to ensure that similar topics were covered in all interviews." The agenda in my case had topics/issues for all interviewees, and topics/issues specific to a particular person, but the proximate preparation was in the main preparing my *aide-mémoire*. There was also the need to do a final test of the tape recorder. When I was visiting the Lords and the Commons this phase usually took place in Grandma Lee's, a cafeteria on the right as you emerge from Westminster underground station. I wonder how many other researchers use it as their base too!

It cannot be emphasized too much that a full preparation for the interview is most important. Lewis Dexter (1964: 557) discusses the increased requests for interviews that elite interviewees faced in the 1960s. He found that between 1953-4, when he first conducted interviews with Congressmen in the USA, and 1959 their attitudes had changed. Originally, they did not seem to distinguish between a journalist doing a serious piece and an academic. By 1959 however they were complaining about "the frequency and 'stupidity' of academic interviewers". There are a number of issues here of course – such as who the "academics" were the Congressmen were referring to – but it is clear from the article by Dexter that thorough preparation for the interview could avoid some of the problems that might lead to "destroying the willingness of subjects to be genuinely co-operative".

Then came the conduct of the interview itself. It was important to be on time of course and to arrive feeling well and ready to go to work. Travelling can be tiring, and allowing time for a cup of tea or coffee before the interview was important. However, I was frequently fortunate to be invited for tea or for a drink in the House of Lords/Commons tea room or bar. Some would say neither of those places would be suitable for an interview with the noise of conversation, people coming and going, and so on. I did not find that; in general I found the conversation over a drink or a cup of tea was relaxed, and on the whole I preferred it to an interview in an office, for example, where a telephone could ring and work was all around the desk. I found the interviewee was more relaxed too, and I imagine that, in a busy life of divisions, debates, lobbying and so on, an interview over a cup of tea might not be unpleasant. Occasionally, I was not so fortunate and I ended up doing an interview seated in one of the niches along the corridors of the House – invariably I found those interviews were shorter and the interviewee had very limited time to give me. It is important of course for an interviewer to make maximum use of the time available and not to be "thrown" by the situation he/she is in.

As soon as I was face to face with the person I was to interview, I explained – as I had done more briefly in the letter seeking the interview – who I was, what I was doing, and the purpose of my research. I feel Manheim & Rich (1991: 143) are right when they say that you cannot assume that the interviewee remembers all the facts about the interview as communicated by the personal letter and telephone call to the secretary noted above. It was at this point that I introduced my intention of quoting the interviewee in my research report. It was my policy not to mention this earlier in case the person being interviewed had any doubts in the first instance about giving the interview. I found when I was face to face with the person I was interviewing, explained my work in more detail and said I wished to quote them, they usually agreed. However, some said there could be times during the interview when they would request that the recorder be switched off, or they would simply ask me not to quote certain matters, which they would indicate as we went along. On one occasion only did I find an interviewee who did not wish to be recorded: he said he did not wish to be quoted and therefore I was not to record him. However, when the interview was only a few minutes old, he saw that I was having such difficulty making notes that he relented and allowed me to use the recorder. He still did not wish to be quoted, but he was happy that I should use the interview as background information, as a guide to other sources of information, as an aid to interpretation of events, and so on. Wherever I conducted the interview – the bar, tea room, interview room, office or corridor – I always placed the tape recorder well and tested it with the interviewees. I found they did not mind – they knew how important it was for me to get the recording, since I had travelled from Birmingham to London in the winter!

In the course of the interview it was essential to be flexible: first, the interviewee may take you along unexpected paths, so it is important not to continue with your questioning as if he/she has not taken that direction at all; secondly, the interviewee may not actually answer the question you ask – they may not wish to, for various reasons, and you will need to go along with them and find a way of coming back to the question on which you want a response; or, again, the response to a question may not go as deep as you would wish and you may need to return in order to probe further. Seldon & Pappworth (1983: 75) note: "Every interview is unique: some informants will expect and need constant questions; others will not allow you to get questions in." And they quote Bernard Crick, a respondent from their Oral Questionnaire 1981, "One simply has to be very clear oneself beforehand what questions one wants to put, but completely opportunistic and patient about when and how one puts them." Sometimes interviewees do not wish to answer a question because they do not know the answer and may not wish to reveal this; for example, if they make a claim in support of their argument in a debate in Parliament and in fact there is little evidence for it, or they are unsure of the evidence, they will not wish to take the matter further. Again, an interviewee may not like your line of questioning. One peer I interviewed clearly felt this way, as the following extract indicates:

I. On the 18th of April, the second reading here in the House of Lords, you come back to this point [on Christian religious education] and your points are most interesting because you give secular reasons, as you say there, for having Christianity in religious education. First of all you relate Christianity to the basis of morality, and then morality to right and wrong and the very fabric of society. I am wondering whether you could say a bit more about that?

R. Well, I'm not sure of the purpose of your questions. I thought you were asking about what had happened.

I. Yes.

R. Rather than my comments on a theme.

I. Well, I'm interested in the philosophy behind what you actually did and what happened. The thinking behind what happened.

R. Well, I'm a Christian and I wish to advance the teaching of Christianity in schools which I see to be being eroded, as it is in society as a whole. And it struck me that since we were addressing a secular audience, largely only nominally Christian people – the audience is much wider than the House of Lords, you will understand – it was important to put the points in a way that would appeal to people, who were not already convinced Christian, and that's what I did.

I. In that debate you speak about the question of culture and the need for our young people to have an education in their own culture, which includes of course the religious dimension, and the fact that is needed in order to relate well to the multicultural society that we live in. I am interested in whether you would be prepared to comment on that at all.

R. Well again, as I understand it, you are doing a piece of research on past events.

I. That's right.

R. So, if you are interviewing me now on a multicultural British society, that is something quite different. So, when you're saying would I comment on that you are not asking me to comment on my views on multicultural society but why I raised it at that point. Is that right?

I. Yes, that's right.

R. Well, quite simply because the relationships between the ethnic groups in the country are of critical importance and interest and I was anxious to show that the question which was before us on how religion should be taught in this country was to remain central to that issue and it was likely to be best, come to a best conclusion. If the broadly Christian population, if I may use the term somewhat nominally, that the indigenous society, which has been brought up in a Christian tradition, if they found themselves rooted in that tradition and adopted its attitudes then we were more likely to come to a settled self-respecting, sovereign society than if they were left at sea in materialism and you name it.

As might be deduced from this brief conversation, that particular interview required some persistence if I was to get to the underlying values and issues. David Riesman (1964: 523), discussing interviewing the elite, argues that the interview should be not non-directive "but probing and intensive". To achieve this, it is essential to engage with the interviewee. Seldon & Pappworth (1983: 127) give an interesting illustration from the field of English law, where evidence cannot just be volunteered, it must be based on question and answer – cross- examination does not allow the witness to present evidence just in the way he/she wishes. If the findings of research are to have credibility, then the interview methods should in some way parallel the rigour of the law of evidence, which is an established field of law. On the other hand, an interview is of course not a courtroom. It seems to me from experience that the personal relationship that evolves with the interviewee in the course of an interview is also important. If the researcher is to see things as the actor sees them, then it seems to me a certain "empathy" is important (Blumer 1969: 56). The interviewee responds to a sincere appreciation of his/her concerns and convictions. The interviewer needs to have the balance Riesman (1964: 523) writes of in "The sociology of the interview": knowing enough of the insider's semantics, and yet having an outsider's detachment; not appearing too innocent in case the interviewee feels there is no point communicating with him, and yet not appearing too knowledgeable in case the interviewee thinks there is little point in instructing.

An interviewer who expects a Member of the House of Commons or the House of Lords to remember every detail of the discussions, the behind-the-scenes lobbying and other related activities is going to be disappointed. These are frequently people with many commitments and very busy schedules – they cannot be expected to remember all the details, even if they have been intimately involved with the passage of a Bill. I remember Sir Hugh Rossi saying at the start of our interview:

> As I am saying, it is many months since these events took place and, although I have a filing drawer full of papers, I haven't had an opportunity of going through them and refreshing my memory as to detail, but clearly if there are any outstanding questions after we've talked I'd be happy to do a bit of research – now that we've reached the recess and I'll have a little more time on my hands.

On the whole, however, the more committed they have been to working on a particular piece of legislation, the more they will remember about what was achieved and also where they failed. It was important to allow them to recall the highlights of the work on the Bill. In fact that was frequently my opening question, giving them the freedom to recall the key moments and issues. It was possible then to build on the opening remarks in terms of motives, key supporters, influence inside and outside Parliament. If a researcher is able to interview a number of people on a particular piece of legislation, as I have done, it is possible I think to obtain a very full picture and to cross-check the different accounts. McPherson and Raab discuss how the researcher arrives at the truth of the situation in terms of "triangulation", which they say is "the common answer to this question, the view, that is, that if one sets out different perspectives on an event according to the different vantage points of the participants, then the truth of the matter will emerge in the round, at the intersection of these perspectives" (1988: 63ff). There is a major question here for sociologists and historians as to how you arrive at the "truth of the matter". The fact is that any human situation can be seen from a number of perspectives, and the researcher can hope to come closer to the whole picture only by seeking out those different perspectives; interviews with a variety of key people undoubtedly help to build up the overall picture (Burgess 1984: 154–6).

An example of the differing perspectives of those involved in the debate on Christianity in religious education and worship during the passage of the 1988 Act comes from my interviews with Lord Peter Thorneycroft and the Bishop of London, Graham Leonard. In response to the suggestion that some would claim that moves to place Christianity on the face of the Bill were "fundamentalist" or an attempt to "force Christianity on people", Lord Thorneycroft said:

> Our view was, if you don't teach the child about religion, how on earth can the child ever learn about religion and the beauty of it . . . A lot of this is about how you do it and the tone of voice; we weren't asking that religion be taught absolutely dogmatically; they didn't say it should never be questioned, but that we should say there is a lovely story to be told, why not tell it.

The Bishop of London saw matters differently. He said:

> it is the attitude within those who think you can make . . . education Christian by legislation, by enforcing it, and really ignoring the fact that we are really in a multicultural and multi-religious society, and that the issue is how far in fact do we preserve the Christian provision for education in this country while at the same time making reasonable provision for those of other faiths.

There is a realism when you tell the story from "the lips of the people themselves" (Burgess 1984: 102). Frequently you can also get behind the written law to the values that inspire those who make the policy enshrined in it (see Kogan 1975: 71).

After the interview

The final phase in the interview cycle is of course returning home and transcribing the interview, but I also found that it was valuable to note some of the snippets of conversation after the tape recorder was turned off. I remember one influential peer saying, "I look forward to hearing the outcome of your research. I had not realized I was in such an important position in all of this." Others I had interviewed drew attention to his bridging role between the different groups at a difficult stage in the negotiations; I pointed that out to him.

Considering the number of researchers who must be troubling Members of Parliament, I found them almost always kind and hospitable. On one occasion a retired minister who had held very high office invited me to his home and, together with his wife, made me most welcome. I believe it is important that the researcher in return respects confidentiality and takes the trouble to write and thank the person who gave the interview. Both of these matters are courtesy of course, but they are also important for the sake of future researchers; these are not unimportant considerations, as McPherson & Raab point out in *Governing Education* (1988: 62).

Conclusion

As I indicated at the beginning of this chapter, part of my purpose in setting out to do this research was to discover ways in which the Church might influence the legislative process. The contacts I was making in the course of the research enabled me to play a part in the thinking, discussions and lobbying leading to amendments in the Education Act 1993. Although this was not part of the research I intended to write up on the 1988 Education Reform Act for a PhD, the fact that I was engaged in this process of formulating policy in the area of religious education and worship in the 1993 Act enabled me to see things as they happen. Manheim & Rich discuss "direct observation" in the research process and say it "can serve as a foundation for using inductive logic to devise testable theories which provide a scientific understanding of the phenomenon in question" (1991: 174). Patricia T. Clough in *The End(s) of Ethnography* writes of the social scientist learning from listening to the world "a way to look at it, so as to see it as it really is" (1992: 29). The involvement in the policy process is an experience enabling me to see the earlier research against the backdrop of the real world of policy-making as I have seen it; ethically, I could not report the policy process in the 1993

Act of course, but I can theorize about the 1988 Act in a way that is confirmed by experience.

References

Blumer, H. 1969. *Symbolic interactionism: Perspective and method*. New Jersey: Prentice-Hall.

Burgess, R. G. 1984. *In the field : An introduction to field research*. London: Allen & Unwin.

Burn, J. & C. Hart 1988. *The crisis in religious education*. London: The Educational Research Trust.

Clough, P. T. 1992. *The end(s) of ethnography*. London: Sage.

Dexter, L. A. 1964. The goodwill of important people: More on the jeopardy of the interview, *Public Opinion Quarterly* **27**, 556–63.

Dexter, L. A. 1970. *Elite and specialized interviewing*. Evanston, Ill.: Northwestern University Press.

Hanson, B. 1972. Oral history and recent political history. *Oral History* **1** (3), 34.

Kogan, M. 1975. *Education policy making: A study of interest groups in Parliament*. London: Allen & Unwin.

Manheim, J. B. & R. C. Rich 1991. *Empirical political analysis: Research methods in political science*. London: Longman.

McPherson, A. & C. D. Raab 1988. *Governing education: A sociology of policy since 1945*. Edinburgh: Edinburgh University Press.

Moyser, G. & M. Wagstaffe (eds) 1987. *Research methods for elite studies*. London: Allen & Unwin.

Riesman, D. 1964. *Abundance for what and other essays*. London: Chatto & Windus.

Seldon, A. & J. Pappworth 1983. *By word of mouth*. London: Methuen.

Webb, S. & B. Webb 1932. *Methods of social study*. London: Longmans, Green.

CHAPTER FIVE

Researching the powerful in education and elsewhere

Maurice Kogan

Introduction

In making studies of education and other policy zones that have involved researching the powerful, I have produced several kinds of work, and each of them has given rise to different methods of approach.

In a series of books written with former ministers of education (Boyle, Crosland & Kogan 1971) and with directors or former directors of education (Kogan with van der Eyken 1973, Bush & Kogan 1982, Bush et al. 1989), we invited our interviewees to explore in their own words the part they had played in key roles. In the 1982 and 1989 books we also included data from questionnaire surveys, but all of these were largely collaborative studies.

In another series of works, less collaborative in mode, interviews, together with documentary evidence, were the main sources, but the interview material was collated and usually not quoted directly. In one book on education policy-making (1975), for example, I interviewed former ministers and senior officials, MPs, interest group leaders, and officials, and also made detailed analyses of debates and Parliamentary Questions. Here the collation was essentially that employed by a conventional historian, piecing together evidence from a range of sources. Similar in method, but not in objectives, have been a long series of evaluative studies conducted for the British Department of Health, for the Swedish and Finnish governments, and for OECD in the course of three educational policy examinations. A particularly interesting exercise was a review of the OECD review system, which involved me in interviewing ministers, officials and MPs in several member countries in order to establish the impact of OECD examinations.

Yet a further kind of study was on the commissioning of research in the Department of Health and Social Security (DHSS) in the period of the implementation of the Rothschild Report (Kogan & Henkel 1983). We studied the actions of powerful people within a government department and their scientific advisers. We not only interviewed them over a seven-year period, but also observed the Chief Scientist's scientific review teams in visitation to research units, and interviewed the reviewers and those reviewed before and after the visits. This work was academic in outcome but collaborative at the outset.

Finally, there were two political or polemical works, one on the Labour Party and one on higher education policy (Kogan & Kogan 1982, 1984). The first involved interviews with MPs and trade unionists, but we also had several caches of documents. The second involved interviews, study of documentation and liberal use of *The Times Higher Education Supplement*.

This wide range of projects and research approaches, for different purposes and with different types of interlocutors, raises the question of how far research objectives affect methods and outcome. Because the first set of books, with ministers and directors, involved collaborative forms of exploration, the interviewees had complete power of veto over the dialogues to be published. The second kind of research was more distanced, and sought to objectivize, as far as is ever possible, the evidence derived from multiple sources. That applied to the Department of Health study where, although the book was formally cleared with them, they respected our need to publish our own version of events and also to address issues on such conceptual dimensions as the relationship between different forms of knowledge generation and the modes of its reception within the policy system. The more polemical studies were again driven by other motives.

Discussion of these connections between research objectives and modes of enquiry follows here under the headings of access, the framing of the interview content, interview behaviour and bias, ethical considerations and the problem of truth.

Access

My own career as an academic interviewing the powerful began in the late 1960s, a different era of political behaviour, and in circumstances that certainly would not obtain now. I had an advantage in seeking access for *Politics of Education* (Boyle, Crosland & Kogan 1971) in that I had been Edward Boyle's private secretary and had been just about close enough to Anthony Crosland at least to engage him in negotiations about what he might get out of the exercise. My prior acquaintance with these interviewees, together with the fact that the publishers were then still a good imprint (Penguin), enabled me to make an easy approach and start on what turned out to be a successful book. The fact, too, that it mainly received rave reviews and that large chunks of it appeared in a Sunday paper may have helped me gain access in other projects that followed.

These special circumstances did not obtain when a new political era dawned. Sir Keith Joseph refused to participate in a successor volume, and, indeed, his private office failed even to acknowledge successive attempts to get a reply out of him. A further hazard occurred at an attempt to update *Politics of Education.* Shirley Williams suggested to me, more than once, that a successor volume ought to be attempted; she said she would be a principal contributor, and that was, of course, an enticing prospect. She is probably one of the most perceptive, interesting and succinct interviewees whom I have encountered. But no attempt of mine to move an inch towards starting this exercise was successful. I still do not know why she urged the possibility of a joint venture in which she did not want to participate.

The most notable refuser (for *Educational Policy-Making*, 1975) was Margaret Thatcher, just then elected to lead the Opposition, who did at least reply promptly to say that she was just too busy. There was also a former junior minister who wrote, "Why should I help you with your money making?" (I probably earned from each book about what he took per week as a solicitor.)

Tony Bush and I, and later Tony Lenney, had virtually no difficulty in securing interviews with chief education officers (Kogan with van der Eyken 1973, Bush & Kogan 1982, Bush et al. 1989). One of the ablest, and potentially most interesting, interviewees, Sir William Houghton, died three days before the date agreed for the interview session.

Chief education officers, then, contributed willingly to the three books on local government. Interest group leaders, policy-makers and, with the exception mentioned above, former ministers and MPs all contributed without stint to *Educational Policy-Making*. One junior minister and a former Secretary of State agreed to be interviewed for *The Attack on Higher Education*. The ease with which I secured access to political leaders in education is curious because, in my experience, education is not the most open of public sector fields to independent research. The health service is far more used to being raked over by researchers and consultants, yet there is very little written about the politics of health. The relatively closed nature of education to research may be due to the large numbers of Her Majesty's Inspectors (HMIs) and local authority advisers, who have tended to crowd out other forms of disciplined enquiry. In 1992 we were, however, refused access to HMIs on a study of patterns of governance in education (Cordingley and Kogan 1993). But in earlier days that did not inhibit political leaders at the national level and those close to them from responding to requests for interviews in the earlier studies. Perhaps there is a finite quantum of openness in any public sector, and it is condoned by different groups within each sector.

The most delicate tests of access came not so much with those in or near the political arena in education as in the study conducted, over seven years in all, in the Department of Health and Social Security on their Rothschild research commissioning system. We had been invited to act in effect as consultants to the Department, and they could not have been more open. But if we were admitted as consultants, on the extremely liberal understanding that we were allowed unrestricted access to internal meetings, research review visitations and confidential files, it was also agreed that we could later publish our account of the exercise as independent researchers. This we did (Kogan & Henkel 1983). Our subjects may not perhaps have qualified as ultra powerful; they were senior officials, leading academics on the research advisory committees and researchers running and working in research units. We were later attacked for having such easy access in a review by Martin Bulmer; his line of argument still evades me.

Far less sensitive were interviews conducted in a more recent work on graduate education and research policy (Becher et al. 1993). Here, too, leading policy-makers in funding and research councils, though not ministers, who by then had become virtually unapproachable, gave us time without stint. So did senior academics in the universities. Indeed, interviewees never restricted the time set aside for meetings, except for hard-pressed consultants in the health service.

So, too, for my two polemical books (Kogan & Kogan 1982, 1984), we received excellent co-operation from everybody approached, although in the case of the book on the higher education cuts, some of those interviewed must have known that our account would be critical. This is incidentally a good opportunity to apologize to one interviewee, Edward Parkes, on whom our comments were indeed well over the top.

Why did interviewees agree to be interviewed? Certainly not for the money, except in one case of a former minister who insisted on what at the time seemed an enormous fee, and who also sold extracts to a Sunday paper without reference of any kind to the other contributors. It is not easy now to divine whether it was an altruistic desire to contribute to knowledge or a narcissistic desire to get into print that persuaded them; it was probably a reasonable mixture of both.

Framing questions

Once access was achieved, my collaborators and I took great care, in all of our studies, in framing our questions. Here we faced technical issues. It is in the nature of political or organizational studies that interlocutors with distinguished records and minds of their own are not likely to accept too much control over the questions they answer. Indeed, it is precisely because one wants to capture their individual construction of events and relationships that it often proves best to explain what one is after and let them structure the answer. One would then employ a checklist to make sure that important zones of enquiry or important factual issues are not left out. Thus, in the cases of Boyle and Crosland, I drafted (but with skilled advice from my editor Willem van der Eyken) a fairly comprehensive list of questions, but Crosland – a better academic than me anyway – looked carefully at the questions and redrafted some of them. His changes were made to improve clarity and relevance, and in no sense to guard himself against challenge. This was a special case because the questions were to be part of the published text anyway, and detailed attention was necessary because they were an integral part of the revealed discussion.

Collaborating with interviewees in the very framing of the enquiry could be regarded as a risky venture given the high priority accorded to theory in mutual evaluations of academics. Those books were certainly atheoretical, and at least one academic reference (Dunleavy 1980) obliquely criticized them as such. Be that as it may, on the whole they seemed to be received with gratitude by other scholars either as teaching material or as primary sources that they could take or leave. On looking back over 20 or so years, it seems odd now that so few political scientists were seeking to secure extended interviews of this kind. Were I to do them again now I would certainly, however, want to put them into a more theoretical and critical framework.

One must also ask whether the collaboration with, and, indeed, complete dependence on, the interviewees restricted critical questioning. Probably it did to some extent, although it is relevant that none of those interviewed was in ideologically different camps from me or my collaborators. The real test would have come had Thatcher and Joseph consented to be interviewed. I certainly did not feel restricted in the interviewing and writing up for the non-collaborative books.

Quite different procedures apply when interviewing for evaluative research. There it is necessary to apply controls over the questions in order to ensure responses that help comparisons to be made with the declared objectives of the programme and, often, to compare perceptions of impacts in a time series of evaluations. On the whole, interviews with politicians are concerned with unique statements about unique events, and controls are not so possible or appropriate.

Yet it is always necessary to be tough with oneself in framing the key research question, although there is no orthodoxy about the formality and order with which one seeks the answers. There has to be a balance between logic and comprehensiveness and dynamic development of the theme in collaboration with the interviewees.

The questions most obviously difficult to ask are those that might reveal a sense of failure or incompetence on the part of the interviewee. This may be construed as cowardice or more likely as simple prudence on the part of an interviewer, but it is better to get an incomplete interview than none at all. For the most part, failures of policy will be on the public record, which can be used to supplement the interview data, but the gap between the public persona of a minister and what, say, civil servants know to be the truth about his or her feet of clay may have to be insinuated rather than explicated. Nor can one do much about interviewees who in effect lie dead in the water – denying or simply not mentioning the fact that there was ever a problem, while presiding over one of the most politicized and problem-wracked of educational systems. At least one of our interviews with directors of education was of that kind, and he survived to get even more important quango jobs by the year. Of course one challenges blandness as best as one can. And, more among the professionals than the politicians, one may find that interviewees may be defensive at first but then feel that the interview is in effect helping them to resolve or at least face up to a problem that they have never before fully explicated.

Interview behaviour

There is an extensive literature on interview behaviour, which tackles such issues as whether tape recorders should be used (e.g. Headey 1974, Williams 1980). At one OECD interview, a leading academic in Chicago removed his cigar to snarl, "turn off that damn machine". I have used tape recorders for interviews that were to be published verbatim, where preservation of the *verba ipsissima* was of sovereign importance. On other occasions, I have done so but also kept a full written record, because tape recorders or incompetent recordists such as myself go wrong. The principal objection to them is that they might inhibit the dialogue, and one has to take care to reassure the interviewee on the precise use to which the material will be put.

A further and more mundane argument for writing full notes is that this reduces the obligation to maintain eye contact for long periods at a time. In the same area of concern is the need to attend to body language. At the end of a long day of interviewing in Sweden recently, I was told by the seasoned Swedish person accompanying me that I was plainly signalling disapproval of the last person I had seen that day. Fortunately this may not have mattered because he was an interminable monologist who avoided all eye contact himself.

The researcher has to behave so as to make the interviewee feel an important contributor to a worthwhile exercise. This is consistent with regarding the interview as a dynamic and not a stable and clinical experience, while preserving as much control as is needed to meet the objectives of the research.

The relationship with the interviewee is complex and variable, but some common characteristics might be noted. In all face-to-face empirical research there is what a former colleague, John Furlong, called the ritual humiliation of the researcher. Some of us are not as demure as we have to appear to be. We often have to pretend to know far less than we do and resist the temptation to correct errors of interpretation or to over-edit responses in the course of an interview. On one occasion, when we were sitting in as non-participant observers at a Chief Scientist's review visitations to a research unit, we had to remain silent and impassive through incompetent interrogation on a subject we knew quite well.

A somewhat different issue arises from the intimacy that arises between interviewers and subjects, particularly when one person is interviewed more than once. The interviewers are, after all, asking them to surrender quite a lot of information about themselves, to reveal their characters and to stand up to questioning of their motives and, perhaps, life history. Perhaps a kind of love, said to develop with those whom one is going to betray, then develops. This is not a spurious or false relationship because there may be a mutual entry into each other's psyche, ambitions and anxieties. The same affection develops in biographers of the most unlikely subjects. The researcher must, however, eventually withdraw into objectivity.

Interview bias

Generally, I undertook a lot of my work on education at a time when there was a consensus about expansion and about such issues as comprehensive schools. In those days, too, it was difficult to find a journalist who was not on the side of progressive education, equality and expansion. For the most part one was dealing with relatively uncontroversial issues, and the reader of my encounters with Boyle and Crosland would be able to detect only a few – if key – substantive differences in policy between them. The exception was a book on the 1981 cuts in higher education (Kogan & Kogan 1984), where my view of the cuts could easily be inferred by those interviewed. I had thought it acceptable to step out of the academic role to defend my own profession. But my explicit biases in that book were later punished when it was brandished at me by a distinguished former public servant, acting as a member of an interviewing panel for a key job for which I had applied. He thought I was a Jekyll and Hyde character for both analyzing government impartially (in *Government and Research*, 1983) and attacking it in *The Attack on Higher Education*.

The problem of bias cannot go away. Whenever I have taped an interview I have found that my own assumptive world peeps through the supplementary questions. The bias need not be on overtly ideological issues. We can hardly escape emitting a view of how society and organizations work, and questions are contaminated by the kind of theory one is addressing in the project. Thus I know that I have difficulty in applying the key actor presumption to my analyses, but instead look for more structural manifestations of the use of power and authority and of policy outcomes. I know I lean towards functionalism. For example, in studying the role of research customers in a government department, it seemed obvious that their behaviour was moulded to a large extent by the job they were doing, and that they took on the values and preoccupations of the area of policy they were administering. Nor have I ever been comfortable with conflict theory or the assertion of interests as a leading explanatory frame – although the style and actions of government in the last decade have to some extent turned us all into Marxists.

Ethical considerations

If one cannot avoid an element of betrayal of one's subjects, there are formal ethics that it would be immoral and self-defeating not to observe. If an interviewee says "Don't quote me on this", one should not quote. But one should make every effort to clear a usable version with the informant. In one case, a completely frank discussion with an academic about the virtual destruction of subject disciplines in her/his university was not flagged as confidential during the interview, but I thought it appropriate to check back to make sure that its publication would not do him/her any harm, even though the identity of the university was disguised. Once the question was put (over the phone), I was asked to cut out the whole of the statement. This would have seriously damaged the range of examples of how higher education was responding to pressures to adapt to what government thought were the needs of the economy. We reached a compromise eventually that seemed safe to the interviewee, although the difference in the two versions would not be greatly visible to a third person.

People have a right to be sensitive to the effect of what they are recorded as saying, and their apprehensions do not have to be fully rational to be legitimate. In interviewing Crosland, he recounted – on tape – that he had come back on his first night as Secretary of State for Education and had said to his wife that "we must do something about those f—g grammar schools". The typist employed by Penguin Books to transcribe the texts thought fit to cut out this obscenity (this was 1970), and Crosland refused to restore it. It re-emerged posthumously in his wife's delightful account of her husband's life and career. This perhaps not very interesting story was not mine to reveal until the author, or his proxy, gave in effect the order of release.

The truth problem

The largest technical problem encountered is what our research students at Brunel University call the "Problem of Truth". We can all try to triangulate accounts from different sources, but in the end we may be able to do no more than present as completely as we can the contrary versions. Indeed, much of the purpose of social science enquiry is to uncover ambivalences, different perspectives and epistemologies. The problem, if that is what it is, is only partly alleviated by use of corroboratory or conflicting printed sources that might straighten up ambiguous matters of record. Le Carré remarks somewhere that for his hero, Smiley, there was no greater truth than the file, but written accounts may have been based on no more than exactly the kind of conflicting material that is the problem in the first place. The fact of publication does mean, however, that the author may or should have gone through some kind of verifying process, and the additional version must help by simply adding to the corpus of evidence and witness scrutiny.

The most vexing problem is that of incomplete truths. One example that I could not publish was that of an episode in which civil servants were being blamed by a Select Committee for refusing to allow a perfectly innocuous official exercise to be published. It was, in fact, the minister who put the gag on, a possibility obvious to anybody who has mixed enough with the vain and paranoiac personalities who sometimes get to ministerial office. The point is not trivial in view of the sedulously disseminated assumption that it is ministers who are open to the people while civil servants are defensively opposed to freedom of information. It is also a point made about local government in a study of three local authorities in the 1970s (Jennings 1977), which noted how interest groups were being kept out of policy formation by the politicians rather than the bureaucrats.

In these cases we can only do our best; that which we cannot know we can hardly disclose, and ethical constraints cannot be overridden. These problems are sometimes overcome by the elapse of time, but, perhaps because we are dealing with a mass of ephemera, we do not spend enough time on treating our accounts as provisional and revising them as new facts or interpretations come to light. In my own field of educational politics I have been very impressed by an account (Knight 1990) of right-wing conservative resistance (from the 1950s) to consensus progressive policies that certainly did not emerge when I was interviewing some of the people involved nearer the time. One problem might be that of publication outlet; only the biggest fish are thought worth repeated revisiting.

If the researcher faces a truth problem, so does the reader, particularly in accounts of interviews conducted with officials. If the research is financed by a government department it must be cleared with them, and for the most part I have found this to result in constructive critique rather than restriction or obstruction. But that very helpfulness could be interpreted as cosiness. All I can say, and readers could judge for themselves, is that, in our large study from within a government department, they allowed through a rigorous critique of their own policies. A somewhat different approach was shown by a government department when I attempted to clear an account of the behaviour of one minister on taking office. They politely asked me to remove a comment by a civil servant to the effect that he sat in his room like some little clerical officer, instead of getting down to the big policy issues. Obviously, the department did not like it to be thought that its officers criticized ministers in that way. Crosland, however, did not yield to a request to delete his account of a decision to appoint a chairman of a key committee, and it is, indeed, difficult to see why the officers ever thought it inappropriate to publish it.

The reader's trust in the interviewer's account can be safeguarded in several ways. First, of course, the book will be reviewed, and some reviewers are knowledgeable enough to challenge the version given. Secondly, the news presumably gets round if a researcher is seen by some of his or her subjects to be unreliable. Thirdly, there are referencing conventions that one can adopt. In works relying heavily on anonymous interviews, my colleagues and I have taken to numbering each interview and referring to them by those numbers in the published version. The notes are kept for at least two years after the book is published in case of challenge. Although confidentiality is usually offered, an accredited researcher ought to have access to the data to sustain a challenge, although not for purposes of use in further research without the permission of the interviewee as well as the original researcher. None of these circumstances has arisen, possibly because the bulk of the research has not been of a dramatically interesting nature. It is perhaps a pity that so much hard work is not used for more than one research project, to establish some kind of time series of exploration and build up an accumulation of knowledge. Most of us have to be content with the second rendering of the material produced by others.

Other problems

Those who research with the famous or powerful encounter particular problems not experienced in work with more commonplace samples. First, famous people are known about and one's own interpretation of the person and his or her policies or practices will be up for challenge by others who also have knowledge, some of which did not emerge from the research. Secondly, serious journalists may get irritated by what they regard as encroachment into what they regard as their territory. Often now they, rather than academics, review books about the famous. Two books applauded by academics were panned by serious journalists (but also reviewed fairly by others). A distinguished journalist published a condescending review of our book on conflict in the Labour Party (Kogan & Kogan 1982) and then, the very next week, without acknowledgement, published an article in the same journal quoting at some length the text of a key interview with Ken Livingstone. This was hard-won material, gained because my co-author had good access to Livingstone. I wrote politely but pointedly to enquire after his source and was told in reply: "Touché, but the cobbler should stick to his last", an attitude that must have come from associating sympathetically with too many trade unionists.

Certainly one is in direct competition with journalists in certain fields, and the differences in outcome can be described only as the academic having and taking the time to fit the data into some kind of analytic and referenced context, and in a form that can be tested against any available other evidence and theory – all sometimes a tall order. Journalists' detachment tends to be expressed through irony rather than multiple analysis. The distinction breaks down in the case of the best: Hugo Young could easily step into a distinguished academic post, and Peter Hennessey has done so; and not all academics are careful to triangulate and test.

Conclusion

In this chapter reference has been made to interviewing in more than one zone and at more than one level. There are many features of the mode of research that are uniquely responsive to the zone of enquiry and to the individual being interviewed. But they all have in common the decrees of ethical behaviour and of trying to keep a balance between structured and controlled enquiry and dynamic interaction with the matter being researched. That balance changes as one encounters unwillingness or demands for degrees of control by the interviewee, and one may have then to ask whether, if the task is worth doing, is it worth doing badly?

That then raises the question of what differentiates scholarly from other kinds of work with the powerful. The simple criterion is the extent to which the process of enquiry produces materials that are testable by other evidence or by its own internal logic, and whether, too, it addresses, tests and perhaps modifies existing theories relevant to it. On this spectrum, there can be overlaps between the four modes of enquiry that I have pursued. The polemical books contained elements of triangulation. Some kind of theory about the decline of authority and deference peeped out in our analysis of struggles within the Labour Party. The collaborative works were not theoretical, but no less so than many other descriptive works of a previous era. Qualities and characteristics of studies may therefore depend not wholly on their objectives, but more on the seizing of opportunities or, of course, on the ability of the researcher to theorize.

References

Becher, T., M. Henkel, M. Kogan 1993. *Graduate education in Britain*. London: Jessica Kingsley.

Boyle, E., A. Crosland, M. Kogan 1971. *Politics of education*. London: Penguin.

Bush, T. & M. Kogan 1982. *Directors of education*. London: Allen & Unwin.

Bush, T., M. Kogan, T. Lenney 1989. *Directors of education – Facing reform*. London: Jessica Kingsley.

Cordingley, P. & M. Kogan 1993. *In support of education: The functioning of local government*. London: Jessica Kingsley.

Dunleavy, P. 1980. *Urban political analysis*. London: Macmillan.

Headey, B. 1974. *British Cabinet Ministers*. London: Allen & Unwin.

Jennings, E. J. 1977. *Education and politics*. London: Batsford.

Knight, C. 1990. *The making of Tory education policy in post-war Britain 1950-1986*. London: Falmer.

Kogan, D. & M. Kogan 1982. *The battle for the Labour Party*. London: Kogan Page.

Kogan, M. 1975. *Educational policy-making*. London: Allen & Unwin.

Kogan, M. & M. Henkel 1983. *Government and research*. London: Heinemann.

Kogan, M. with D. Kogan 1984. *The attack on higher education*. London: Kogan Page.

Kogan, M with W. van der Eyken 1973. *County hall*. London: Penguin.

Williams, P. 1980. Interviewing politicians: The life of Hugh Gaitskell. *Political Quarterly* **51** (3), 303–16.

CHAPTER SIX

Ethics and power in a study of pressure group politics

Geoffrey Walford

Introduction

In this chapter I wish to discuss a few of the ethical and power issues that I have encountered within an ongoing research project concerned with a campaign to obtain state funding for private evangelical Christian schools. The Christian Schools Campaign itself, although national, was small scale, never having more than a handful of active workers. However, it has been able to achieve considerable success by working together with other groups campaigning for funding of their own schools and by closely associating with several powerful and prominent individuals on the political New Right. Although there is no necessary overall ideological agreement with those on the New Right, the aims of the Christian Schools Campaign coincided with the Right's wider project of encouraging a greater diversity of schools and a more market orientation towards schooling (Sexton 1987). As a result, the Christian Schools Campaign has been able to ensure legislative changes in the 1993 Education Act that enable these Christian schools to apply to become a new form of state-funded grant-maintained school. Before discussing some of the ethical and power problems encountered in the research, the next sections will summarize the background issues and the methodology used in the research.

Background to the research

Since the 1944 Education Act, the vast majority of religious denominational primary and secondary schools in England and Wales have been an integral part of the state-maintained system. Religious schools within the state system have the status of voluntary schools, where all of the everyday running costs and teachers' salaries are provided by the state. In the case of voluntary aided schools, the church organizations pay 15 per cent of any new capital expenditure required. At present about 28 per cent of primary-aged pupils and 17 per cent of secondary pupils are in voluntary schools. In short, unlike in the USA, religious schools are a well-established and central part of the English and Welsh state-maintained educational scene.

However, the vast majority of these voluntary schools are Church of England or Roman Catholic schools, with a very few Methodist and Jewish schools. The current arrangements thus reflect the social and religious character of the 1940s rather than the 1990s. As Britain has gradually become more multi-ethnic and more diverse, there has been growing pressure to establish new schools to serve these new groups. In theory it is open to followers of other Christian denominations or religious faiths to establish schools that could then be taken into the state-maintained system. Yet, in practice, in spite of clear demand for such schools, there are currently no state-supported Muslim schools or Hindu schools in Britain. Neither are there any state-supported schools representing any of the smaller Christian groups or denominations.

The 1993 Education Act for England and Wales opens the way for new state-supported grant-maintained schools to be established that reflect particular religious or philosophical beliefs. Existing faith-based private schools will be able to apply to become re-established as grant-maintained schools. The legislation that permits these new faith-based grant-maintained schools is the direct result of continued campaigning from an interlocking network of pressure groups that represent a range of "reluctant" private schools (Walford 1991a). The most prominent groups that have campaigned for such schools are several Muslim pressure groups (including the Muslim Parliament and the Muslim Educational Trust; Dooley 1991) and the Christian Schools Campaign, which represents about 65 private evangelical Christian schools. The legislation came into operation in April 1994 and several private Christian schools and Muslim schools are already preparing applications for submission to the Department for Education.

The development of a research project

My original interest in the new Christian schools developed from my long-standing research focus on the private sector. During the 1980s I had written about elite private boys' boarding schools (Walford 1986, 1987), and I had followed that with several articles and books about the private sector (e.g. Walford 1989, 1990). I began to recognize that there was great diversity within the private sector and that very little research had been conducted on the smaller and more idiosyncratic schools. I attended some meetings of various groupings of small private schools and began to visit a few, but my interest intensified as a result of attempts in the House of Lords to amend the 1987 Education Bill such that "opting-in" was included as well as "opting-out". The amendments had little chance of success and were duly rejected, but they generated considerable publicity. It was evident that many of those involved would continue with their campaign.

I decided that I would attempt to follow the campaign and also find out more about the new Christian schools, which are a group of small private schools that share an ideology of biblically based evangelical Christianity that seeks to relate the message of the Bible to all aspects of present-day life. These schools have usually been set up by parents or a church group to deal with a growing dissatisfaction with what is seen as the increased secularism of the great majority of schools – including the religious voluntary schools already within the state system. The schools aim to provide a distinctive Christian approach to every part of school life and the curriculum and, in most cases, parents have a continuing role in the management and organization of the schools (Deakin 1989, O'Keeffe 1992). In general, these schools are not well provided for in terms of physical facilities; fees are modest, with teaching staff often on low salaries. They do not serve the "traditional" private school market and are often in a financially precarious position.

Once I had decided to investigate the schools and the campaign, the research project passed through several stages. At first it was very much a "background" project while I conducted and published research on a rather different form of private school – the City Technology Colleges (Walford & Miller 1991, Walford 1991b). However, I collected newspaper cuttings, visited a few schools, attended some meetings (including a three-day meeting of the schools), conducted some interviews, and published an early article based on this work (Walford 1991a). But intensive activity did not really start until I obtained a small two-year grant from the Nuffield Foundation in early 1992. Following the award of this grant, further schools were visited, headteachers, principals, politicians, officials and academics involved with the pressure group were interviewed and a further crop of meetings attended. A questionnaire survey of the schools was also conducted, which eventually drew a response rate of 83 per cent (Poyntz & Walford 1994). Further articles have now been published (Walford 1994a, 1994b).

This high response rate to the questionnaire is indicative of the level of support that I received from the schools. Access to schools was always granted, and all the headteachers asked agreed to be interviewed. The director of the Christian Schools Campaign and those most closely concerned with the Campaign were particularly helpful throughout the research, being prepared to give access to documentary data as well as respond to long interview sessions. There are several possible reasons for this level of support. The first is simply that, being Christians, they felt some obligation to help others where they could. The second probable reason for helping me with the research was that they wanted publicity. If a group is trying to campaign for change, almost any publicity is seen as potentially beneficial. This poses obvious problems of possible "incorporation" of the researcher.

The ethics of the interview

All research brings ethical decisions, but these decisions are particularly difficult if the researcher has political, ideological or religious views that are in opposition to those being studied (Klatch 1988). One of the most difficult decisions to be made by interviewers is the degree to which their own views should be explained to interviewees. To what extent is it right to allow others to believe that you agree with them?

When I visited schools and interviewed headteachers and principals, they were welcoming and helpful but, quite understandably, wanted to know something about me. I could, of course, explain my research interest in terms of my previous work on private schools and a parallel concern with educational policy-making. But this was not really what most wanted to know – they wanted to know whether I was a Christian. The easy (and correct) answer to the question is "yes", and at first I simply stated this. However, my own Christianity is a very liberal version, such that David Jenkins, former Bishop of Durham, looks to be almost conservative in comparison. To those involved with the new Christian schools, such a liberal interpretation of Christianity is definitely *not* Christian, and many would see it as potentially more dangerous than atheism.

Where I did just reply in the affirmative to the question about my own belief, I found the resulting interview both difficult and embarrassing, for the interviewee believed that we shared a whole ideological view that we did not. I gathered good data, but at some cost to my own self-respect. I decided that in future interviews I would be more honest and explain that my interpretation of Christianity might be some distance from their own. In some cases this led to severe suspicion of my motives, and corresponding reticence, whereas in others the interviewee clearly did not fully comprehend my explanation of "liberal Christian" or, at least, forgot what I had said once the interviews progressed. As I did not generally challenge anything that was said, interviewees appeared to believe that I was in agreement with them. This was far from always true, as I found some of their literalist interpretations of the Bible simply perverse and simplistic. Neutrality caused me some severe ethical doubts.

In general, although I did not always agree with my interviewees, I found them to be congenial, thoughtful and reasonable people. But a few were not. A very few had extreme views that I found abhorrent. The following extract gives an example. It is noticeable that, in this case, I have not simply allowed the interviewee to state his own views unchallenged, but the challenges are still very weak indeed.

G.W.   Are there any bits of the National Curriculum that you are unhappy with?

A.   No.

G.W.   You're happy with the whole thing?

A.   Well except for the idea, I mean, I would be unhappy with the lunacy of AIDS idea, because AIDS is basically a homosexual disease . . .

G.W.   Mainly, and it depends where you are actually.

A.   . . . and it is doing a very effective job of ridding the population of undesirables. But, it is basically, according to the statistics, and I've got them, it is basically homosexual. Out of 600, 6000 . . .

G.W. In this country, that may be true, but not in . . .

A. In the States, it's drug related. In Africa, it is basically a non-existent disease in many places, but the statistics have been grossly distorted because they find Western countries will give them money.

G.W. Some of that may be true.

A. It *is* true, but the ignorant West doesn't want to know that . . . And you take the figures as they really are, and not as the Trust, what is it, the Higgins Trust, wanted to put over, it's a woofters' disease. If you're a woolly woofter, you get what you deserve. And that's the end of it, as far as I'm concerned. I know in America, intravenous drug users and sharing needles has caused it. I just feel that politically they are not telling society the truth, because they don't want to. They don't want to face up to it, because they don't . . . I would never employ a homosexual to teach at my school. I do not believe it's a lifestyle that is alternative – I believe it's evil, intrinsically.

This man was actually a minister of a church that supported a school. He also showed what I thought was an horrific attitude towards women and used the term "welfare state" almost as a swear word. At one point he launched into a tirade against socialist and communist teachers. According to him, most teachers were socialists and communists – that was the trouble. "They teach the kids that there is no point in working because there are no jobs. In one junior school the teachers told them that there was no point in working because there were no jobs for them anyway."

At this last point, I agreed with him that this was not an appropriate thing to say. Technically, I agreed only with what I truly agreed with, but he probably interpreted this as meaning that I was against socialists and communists, and that I agreed that "most teachers" were such, and that this was the problem.

I left that interview with some very "good data", but with great anger at myself and at the irreconcilable difficulties that interviewing sets up. The interview had been a long one, and had been very informative about divisions between schools themselves and within the Campaign. I obtained information that I had not been able to obtain elsewhere. To have challenged his understandings would simply have brought the interview to an abrupt close, yet my lack of challenge meant that he probably had the feeling that a university academic specializing in education policy studies actually agreed with his crude bigoted views.

Observing meetings

During the research, at the invitation of the director of the Christian Schools Campaign, I attended several meetings where strategy was being discussed and information shared between interested groups. The director obviously had some apprehension about this, for I had been clear with her about my overall political position, so I agreed with her that I would not use any information gained through interviews or meetings to act politically against the campaign. This was a self-imposed agreement more than a negotiated one, but it certainly made my sometimes ambiguous position easier to deal with. After all, here was an academic who had written passionately against privatization in education (Walford 1990), and who had been critical of the increased diversity of schools inherent in the City Technology College initiative (Walford & Miller 1991), actually at a meeting where the wording was being discussed of an Amendment to an Education Bill that was designed to encourage further diversity! (This amendment failed.) Amongst those present at that particular meeting was Stuart Sexton (see below), who clearly did not link me with anything I had written.

One particularly interesting series of meetings was the "Educational Issues Group" held irregularly in the House of Lords under the auspices of Baroness Caroline Cox. At the beginning of each meeting Baroness Cox would remind the 60 or so people gathered that the meeting was not an official meeting of any kind, and that the House of Lords was the location merely because of its convenient geographical position. But the location was clearly of more than passing convenience. It allowed busy politicians to spend some time at meetings and gave a spurious authority to the proceedings. The meetings were officially non-party-political and open to anyone interested in educational issues. However, the method of announcing the date of the next meeting (through the post to those on a list) meant that the vast majority of those present appeared to be supporters of the New Right. The meetings were designed to "share information about matters of common interest" and the format was that various speakers who were active in various pressure groups would, in turn, explain their recent activities to the meeting. Few questions were asked, and only very rarely was there any open disagreement. The assumption was that everyone there was of "like mind" about the problems of education and possible remedies.

I attended only five meetings, but others present included John Marks (who was secretary for the meeting), Stuart Sexton, Nick Seaton (Campaign for Real Education), Martin Turner, Fred Naylor, Professor Anthony O'Hear, Professor Antony Flew, Katie Ivens, Jennifer Chew (English Curriculum Association), Anthony Freeman and Chris McGovern (History Curriculum Association). This is very like a roll-call of the educational New Right, and a group with whom I had little affinity.

Baroness Caroline Cox, for example, is a key figure in the New Right. She was made baroness in 1982, and from 1983 to 1985 was director of the Centre for Policy Studies. She is a committed Christian and has also been a key member of several small but influential right-wing educational groups, including the Academic Council for Peace and Freedom, the Educational Research Trust, the National Council for Academic Standards (NCAS) and the Parental Alliance for Choice in Education (PACE) (Griggs 1989). She was a contributor to one of the early Black Papers (Cox et al. 1977) and to the Hillgate Group's two influential pamphlets *Whose Schools?* (1986) and *The Reform of British Education* (1987). Along with John Marks, she is firmly in favour of selective schooling (Marks et al. 1983, Cox & Marks 1988).

Stuart Sexton also had a key position in the New Right. He was policy adviser to two past Conservative Secretaries of State for Education and Science (Mark Carlisle and Keith Joseph), he was the guiding hand behind the controversial Assisted Places Scheme and he was later a leading proponent of City Technology Colleges. He has been a key figure in the Institute of Economic Affairs and director of its Education Unit. Over the years, Sexton (1987, 1992) has made clear his desire for a fully privatized educational system, preferably financed through vouchers that can be "topped-up" by parents. In 1987 he set out his "step-by-step approach to the eventual introduction of a 'market system', a system truly based upon the supremacy of parental choice, the supremacy of purchasing power" (Sexton 1987: 11). His ultimate plan is to have per capita funding from the state that would be the minimum sum to be spent on each child's education. Schools would be allowed to make additional charges to cover any extra provision beyond the basic level of schooling. Sexton further envisages that, eventually, the proportion of taxpayers' money spent on education would reduce from its present level as parents pay more and more for the schooling of their own children.

With the regular attendance of such key people at these meetings, I found them extremely informative. They provided me with a host of background material that I would have been unable to obtain any other way. Because the assumption was that everyone was "of like mind", a wide range of comments were freely made by the participants that indicated their beliefs, long-term aims and ideologies. As most people present did not speak, I shall never know if there were other "spies" present at these meetings. They were certainly not as evident as Klatch (1988: 80) found in her study of American New Right women.

At the meetings, I simply sat near the back and took notes, but it was not always easy to remain quiet. I often wanted to shout out that the information a speaker was giving was simply incorrect, or that the interpretation or argument was specious. After one irregular attender gave some information about forthcoming changes in higher education, I felt compelled to tell him that his was the only speech of the day with which I had agreed. He, and others nearby, looked aghast.

In October 1992 the National Commission on Education published my Briefing Paper on "Selection for secondary schooling" (Walford 1992), which was widely circulated and reported in the national press. These Briefing Papers were only 3000 words and were designed to summarize research in particular areas. I included a very brief comment on some work by Caroline Cox and John Marks. I received a letter from John Marks informing me that he thought that my summary misrepresented their findings and that I should circulate a correction to all those who had received the paper. I sincerely believed that the summary was a reasonable one given the space limitations and wrote back in that vein. I heard nothing more, but also, and maybe coincidentally, I never received any more invitations to attend the "Educational Issues Group". I also became ultra-careful about what I wrote concerning the powerful.

This little incident illuminates several important points. First, the powerful have the ability to exclude researchers – in this case simply by limiting the supply of information about future meetings. Further, of course, any of the members of this network could have made it very difficult for me to obtain access to the whole group of similar people. Exclusion by one could easily lead to exclusion by all. Secondly, although the importance of academic work should not be overestimated, publishing comment that is even perceived to be critical may inhibit future access and co-operation. Thirdly, in many cases, research about those with power necessitates naming those people. As they are in powerful positions and have made significant contributions to particular policies, they are widely known and it is usually impossible to conceal their identities. It is not only what was said that is important, but who said it. However, if academic reports are to name individuals there is always the potential problem of perceived libel, and, being powerful people, the possibility of libel writs has to be taken very seriously. This means that self-censorship becomes an ever-present problem. If there is any doubt at all about a comment or interpretation, the researcher of the powerful may tend to omit discussion of it in any publications.

Whose side are you on?

Howard Becker has exhorted us to be clear about "whose side we are on" (1967). But, in this case, at first I simply did not know whose side I was on. I could see that those campaigning for state support for these new Christian schools had a good case. There was something deeply unjust about the Church of England and the Roman Catholic Church being able to have their schools funded by the state, yet Muslims and new Christians being forced to pay for their own private schools if they wanted their children to be taught as they wished. However, I was also aware that the New Right's support for these schools was an indication that a growth in the diversity of schools would suit their long-term aims and could be instrumental in leading to greater inequity throughout the whole educational system.

When I first started visiting schools and interviewing headteachers and others I did not have a clear understanding of how the Campaign might be seen as a piece in the New Right's jigsaw. At first, my interest focused on an unusual group of private schools more than on the campaign that was linked to it. I thus was unable to tell interviewees what viewpoint I might take in any subsequent publications. This might be conceived as a form of "objectivity", but it is doubtful whether the interviewees actually believed my indecision, and it certainly made interviewing more difficult. Many of those involved with the schools saw state support as a simple question of "righteousness", and argued that they were currently "paying twice" for the education of their children.

They often did not consider the wider issues of what the changes might mean to the whole of the education system as being their concern. As they saw the question of state funding as a relatively simple one, and clearly expected me to have already come to a conclusion on the issue, they became suspicious if I said that the issue was more complicated than they seemed to feel.

Once I had begun to uncover the extent of the links to and involvement of key actors in the New Right, I became clearer about where my support should be given. My visits to schools also had an effect as I became concerned about the potential effects on children of the extreme views being voiced in a few of the schools. The interview quoted and discussed above, for example, made me recognize that there was a need, in some cases, for the state to protect children from the ideas of their parents. As a result, I became convinced that a compromise was needed where faith-based schools should be supported, but only within a strong framework of local education authority (or similar) control that would enforce minimum standards and ensure equity between schools.

As the research progressed, I became concerned about the extent to which those linked to the Campaign might not be fully aware of the ideas of those on the New Right with whom they were working. It became clear from my research in the schools that many of those involved would not wish to be associated with any plans for an inequitable educational system. Indeed, the schools themselves often have fee policies that attempt to redress inequalities by charging according to financial means. Many of the schools try to offer open access, irrespective of ability to pay, and their curriculum is one that emphasizes the Christian virtues of sharing and caring for others. They are not natural allies of the New Right, but had become enmeshed within this wider political programme as a result of their own individualistic desires to obtain funding for their own schools.

This does not mean that those involved were naïve, or that they were being "used" by the Right. They saw it as a matter of God's law and justice that parents should have control over the education of their own children. They pointed to other countries such as Denmark and The Netherlands where it is relatively easy for groups to establish their own state-supported schools. But it was clear that those involved had not read Sexton's ideas about privatization, or fully understood the Right's vision for the future. Should I provide a "reader" of relevant extracts or a booklist?

I decided that I should at least tell some of those involved about particular books that I thought they might wish to read, but I did not provide any books myself. Strangely, it was Dale Spender's *Man Made Language* (1980) that probably had the most effect on the Campaign, for the female director of the Campaign resigned in 1992 – in part owing to problems over "women in positions of authority in the Church". She moved to another campaigning organization instead (Christian Action Research and Education, CARE), and the final campaigning on the 1993 Education Act was done from there.

Acknowledgements

I am most grateful to those who have helped in this research and, in particular, to Ruth Deakin, director of the Christian Schools Campaign, who provided a wealth of information and kindly gave me access to several meetings and documents. The research was funded by the Nuffield Foundation and the Strategic Innovation Research Group at Aston Business School.

References

Becker, H. S. 1967. Whose side are we on? *Social Problems* 14, 239–47.
Cox, C. & J. Marks 1988. *The insolence of office*. London: Claridge Press.
Cox, C., K. Jacka & J. Marks 1977. Marxism, knowledge and the academies. In *Black Paper 1977*, C. B. Cox & R. Boyson (eds) London: Temple-Smith.
Deakin, R. 1989. *The new Christian schools*. Bristol: Regius.
Dooley, P. 1991. Muslim private schools. In *Private schooling: Tradition, change and diversity*. G. Walford (ed.). London: Paul Chapman.
Griggs, C. 1989. The new right and English secondary education. In *The changing secondary school*, R. Lowe (ed.). London: Falmer.
Hillgate Group 1986. *Whose schools?* London: Hillgate Group.
Hillgate Group 1987. *The reform of British education*. London: Claridge Press.
Klatch, R. E. 1988. The methodological problems of studying a politically resistant community. *Studies in Qualitative Methodology* 1, 73–88.
Marks, J., C. Cox & M. Pomian-Srzednicki 1983. *Standards in English schools*. London: National Council for Educational Standards.
O'Keeffe, B. 1992. A look at the Christian schools movement. In *Priorities in reli-

gious education, B. Watson (ed.). London: Falmer.

Poyntz, C. & G. Walford 1994. The new Christian schools: a survey. *Educational Studies* **20** (1), 127–43.

Sexton, S. 1987. *Our schools – A radical policy*. Warlingham, Surrey: Institute of Economic Affairs Education Unit.

Sexton, S. 1992. *Our schools – Future policy*. Warlingham, Surrey: IPSET Education Unit.

Spender, D. 1980. *Man made language*. London: Routledge & Kegan Paul.

Walford, G. 1986. *Life in public schools*. London: Routledge.

Walford, G. 1987. Research role conflicts and compromises in public schools. In *Doing sociology of education*, G. Walford (ed.). London: Falmer.

Walford, G. (ed.) 1989. *Private schools in ten countries: Policy and practice*. London: Routledge.

Walford, G. 1990. *Privatization and privilege in education*. London: Routledge.

Walford, G. 1991a. The reluctant private sector: of small schools, politics and people. In *Private schooling: Tradition, change and diversity*, G. Walford (ed.). London: Paul Chapman.

Walford, G. 1991b. Researching the City Technology College, Kingshurst. In *Doing educational research*, G. Walford (ed.). London: Routledge.

Walford, G. 1992. Selection for secondary schooling. *National Commission on Education*, Briefing Paper 7. London: National Commission on Education.

Walford, G. 1994a. Weak choice, strong choice and the new Christian schools. In *Parental choice and education*, M. Halstead (ed.). London: Kogan Page.

Walford, G. 1994b. The new religious grant-maintained schools. *Educational Management and Administration* **22** (2), 123–30.

Walford, G. & H. Miller 1991. *City Technology College*. Buckingham: Open University Press.

PART II

Interpreting interviews

CHAPTER SEVEN

Political interviews and the politics of interviewing

Stephen J. Ball

In this chapter I shall be exploring some aspects of elite interviewing through a fine-grain analysis of extracts from interviews conducted in the UK with political actors involved, in one way or another, with the 1988 Education Reform Act. I recognize that many of the points I have to make could equally well be written of other kinds of research interviews. That is significant in itself. But there are some peculiarities and peculiar difficulties involved in interviewing and interpreting the interviews of actors operating within the arena of public politics (see also Ball 1994). For example, it is trite, but none the less valid, to point out that many political actors are skilled interviewees. For various reasons political actors have an investment, public and personal, in being interviewed. But they also have particular reasons for being careful about what and how they say things in interview. Scheurich's (1992: 24) point about interviewee resistance is especially true of the political interviewee.

> Interviewees do not simply go along with the researcher's program. I find that they carve out space of their own, that they push against or resist my goals, my intentions, my questions, my meanings.

More than in any other kind of interviewing I have experienced, interviews with political actors highlight the struggle both to control the event and to control meanings. Scheurich again makes the point that interviewees "often validate themselves in the process of telling their stories" (p. 24). Thus, one key point that runs through the chapter is the multi-faceted uniqueness of each encounter and thus each interview transcript. In relation to this, I shall argue that, in the analysis and interpretation of interview data, researchers routinely neglect the significance and the analytical possibilities of difference, and that we tend to focus too much on the content and too little on the form of our interviews. Transcripts are typically processed as a transparent medium of another world or culture. And yet crucially the interview is a confrontation and a joint construction; "It is not the unmediated world of the 'others', but the world between ourselves and the others" (Hastrup 1992: 117).

The study being drawn upon here was an attempt to "get inside" the UK educational state by using ethnographic interviewing to explore recent developments in educational policy. The analysis was aimed at the development of a conceptual field via which the state and education policy could be theorized (Ball 1990). I conducted 49 such interviews over an 18-month period in 1988–9. They were conducted at the respondents' convenience, on their "home territory". I conducted interviews in the House of Lords tea room and bar, in a House of Commons canteen, in the Athenaeum club, in the Northern Ireland Office, in a Merchant Bank, at the Confederation of British Industry, in a Cambridge College lodge, and in many offices (on several occasions at Elizabeth House, then home of the DES) and in several people's homes. All but two people allowed me to tape the interviews. And only two of the people I originally wrote to were unwilling to be interviewed. The interviews were individually prepared for and constructed, but where relevant I tried to cover the same ground and to triangulate and cross-check accounts and interpretations. In the case of politicians in particular I "read up" on the respondents in advance. In effect each interview had a specific and general purpose. All of this fits quite comfortably in my background as an ethnographer. In the ethnographic interview the aim is, as far as possible, to hand over control of the content of talk to the interviewee – always bearing in mind the purposefulness of the interviewer. And the ethnographer will attempt to accommodate the setting, mode, style and pace of the interview to the preferences of the interviewee – to create, bearing in mind the inherent peculiarities of the interview, as naturalistic an encounter as is possible. But, as noted already, political interviews are themselves highly political. In many, but not all, cases, the interviewee has specific aims for and in the interview: to present themselves in a good light, not to be indiscreet, to convey a particular interpretation of events, to get arguments and points of view across, to deride or displace other interpretations and points of view. Furthermore, dispositions towards the content of the interviews differed. Some respondents were disillusioned, some were angry or bitter, some were defensive, others were off-hand, others were willingly indiscreet, others were celebratory. In other words, the differences between interviews, the idiosyncrasies of each, were not simply the product of setting or content or the position of the respondent. They were also the product of the demeanour of the respondent. And, as I realized when I began the analysis, they were also the outcome of differences in style. This is something I discuss in more detail below.

I quickly learned that interviews with the retired and "out of office" were often more revealing, interesting and frank that those with incumbents. With this in mind, I decided not to approach serving ministers and relied instead on their press releases, Commons' answers, speeches, etc. The interviews with civil servants were particularly interesting as research events. Given that they are subject to civil service rules and the Official Secrets Act, there were certain types of questions that they were unable to answer (although that did not mean that the questions could not be asked). The civil servants are the only respondents not named in the book and were the only ones to whom I showed the interview material I intended to use. All the other interview material remained entirely within my control, although one or two people expressed the hope that I would treat their more indiscreet contributions sensitively.

Only a tiny proportion of the 1200 pages of transcript material appeared in the book and many of those interviewed did not make an appearance. But that did not mean that their interviews were unimportant. Part of the process of conducting the interviews was my immersion in the culture and community of policy influence and policy struggle (past and present). Some of the interviews provided a kind of surrogate acculturation into the assumptions, ways and means of policy-making. This was particularly the case in understanding the shifts in educational policy thought that took place during the 1980s. During this time the policy community was thoroughly reconstructed and many long-standing participants were firmly removed from the "context of influence".

What I attempt here is made particularly difficult by the limits of space. I shall take some extracts from interview transcripts and use these to point up some of the various differences I have adumbrated above.

This will, I believe, serve two purposes. First, it may serve as a vehicle for the development and enhancement of interviewing skills. Secondly, it may challenge the "simple realism" that dominates most interview analyses in educational research.

Struggles and assumptions

One of the distinguishing characteristics of ethnographic interviewing is that it both makes possible *and* trades upon a significant degree of cultural sharing. My interviews "inside" the educational state were intended to provide insights into and understanding of the new assumptive world of education policy. But I found myself treading a fine line in the interviews between knowledgeability and naïvety. That is, between being seen as understanding "the field" and its main issues *and* still having something to learn. In a sense, the interviewees had to feel that I was informed enough but that there were still things that they could teach me. I would deliberately present myself as more or less knowledgeable or more or less naïve as seemed tactically appropriate. Accordingly, the extracts used here are filled with cultural "taken-for-granteds". I will try to unpack some of these for the non-native reader.

We might begin with Philip Merridale – at the time of the interview, a Hampshire county councillor and chair of the Education Committee and chair of the Council of Local Education Authorities since 1974 and long-standing member of the Burnham Committee (which was responsible for teachers' pay negotiations). As an interviewee, Philip Merridale is a story-teller. Here is a part of one of his stories related to the negotiations over teachers' pay and conditions in the mid-1980s and his relationships in this matter with Keith Joseph. This is part of an eight-page uninterrupted account; the interviewer is seen only once here. The interviewee is in total control of the topic and is able to change, develop, elaborate (and exclude) as he sees fit. This is what Scheurich (1992: 25) calls the "chaos/freedom" of the interview.

P.M.   I'm probably teaching you to suck eggs.

S.B.   No, no, it gives a lot more flesh.

P.M.   . . . so Carlisle who was still trying, I think, to operate within the system and by consensus was perceived to be too soft and disap-

peared; and you can never tell. This is the sort of thing, where somebody like myself who at that time would be in and out of what are
described as the corridors of power. You might be in the corridor, but
you haven't opened the door of the sanctum . . . so when you go to
see somebody who isn't there, nobody tells you why he isn't there,
you have to form your own conclusions. But you'll remember that
Carlisle was replaced by Keith Joseph. And Keith Joseph was your
sort of zero budgeting philosopher. His view was that you shouldn't
accept anything until you have dissected right the way through the
whole proposition that was being put to you; back to first principles,
and he, of course, spent quite a considerable period of his early time
at the DES engaged in philosophic exploration, seeking to find out
what was wrong with the education service and what was wrong
with the way we administered the education service. Sadly I think
that when I had the longest period of close collaboration, at the high-
est level of government, with Keith Joseph, because I was by that time
the chairman of the Council of Local Education Authorities, the chairman of the ACC (association of County Councils) Education Committee and the leader of the employers' negotiating body, the Burnham
Committee, so I was, as it were, the commander in chief of the armies
of the Philistines. And I found him vastly interesting. He was a man
who was hugely committed to the welfare of children, and a patriot
deeply committed to the welfare of the country. A very, very likeable
man too, although not with the superficial social graces that go with
ease of social converse, like Carlisle had. He found small-talk difficult. And of course as you know he was a man in far from robust
health. But he was one of the nicest people to deal with that you
could ever meet because there burned out from the man a tremen-
dous sincerity. I mean he was personally lampooned, vilified, more
than perhaps any minister of his time, by those who only saw the
public image. But I have yet to meet anyone who didn't regard Keith
Joseph with affection, with real affection . . . We got on like a house on
fire. You could say almost anything to Keith, as long as you were prepared to stand by it and argue it through, and he loved to talk, he
would have me in his room late at night, arguing this, that and the
other. The proposition that I put to him was, that unless we did something to stop this constant beating to and fro, every time, just recover-
ing and getting the sort of dis-masted ship back into the vertical and
manage to erect a little bit of jury rigging and scrambling on for

another few knots and then another storm, the ship was getting completely waterlogged, and we were going to founder for good and all unless we could get the thing on to a permanent seaworthy sort of basis. And so he said, well, what have you got in mind, sort of thing. And I said, well really we've got to have a partnership, a really working partnership which is actually significant and not just a lip-service to the fact that when you talk about your partners, you mean people who you're going to tell what to do. And if they don't do what you tell them, then suddenly they're no longer your partners . . . If on the other hand what you want is a government which actually controls the education service, and we are merely your agents, then you have got to legislate to make us your agents, and not your partners, and this is really the constitutional dilemma that confronts you on the management side of this business, never mind the economics of it. As the Thatcher government became more high profile in respects of other parts of its legislation, and as problems like unemployment grew and so on, so the Labour Party withdrew within the fortresses of its municipal ramparts and sought to set up enclaves of defiance, within the autonomy of their local authority strongholds . . . . That of course brought about a state of affairs in which Margaret Thatcher would ride round the fortifications and say, will none rid me of this turbulent pest. And the people inside the fortifications were less and less inclined to lower the drawbridge and come out to parley with Keith Joseph, so that made that aspect of the thing more difficult than it might have otherwise been, but I believe that the Rubicon which we could perhaps have crossed, was on the touchstone issue of teachers' salaries – what to do about the career structure for teachers and how to organize teacher negotiations? And I remember him throwing his glasses down on the table in front of himself, something like 11 o'clock at night in his room in Elizabeth House, when we were holding this conversation and saying, you know, Philip, the trouble with you is, you're a crusader. I rather like crusaders. If we could bring this off together, we would do for this nation a great public service together and we said, okay, that's it, we'll do it, and his civil servants of course were wetting their trousers, because the idea of having their minister night after night alone with a politician like me, negotiating executive conclusions, without civil service advice, they were very bothered by this. And they felt that he was making concessions, being carried along by the golden tongue of councillor Merridale into the realms of the very greatest peril . . . He said, if you can bring me, and this was the agreement we had, he said if you can bring me an agreement which all your colleagues, 'cos he was aware of the problem of the Holy Roman Empire, if you can bring me an agreement which all your colleagues will subscribe to and which the teachers will accept, I will go to the Cabinet and seek to get the money to fund it. Because I told him that such an agreement would have to be bought, it could not be had for the rate of inflation, or any of that nonsense. And he said that would be the deal. So away I went and I negotiated with my local authority colleagues . . . Broadly speaking there was a tendency on the part of the Conservative shire authorities to want the agreement to be more rigid and a feeling amongst the Labour authorities that they wanted corporate professionalism in schools; the group responsibility of the staffroom for the school to be the dominant theme of the agreement and that there should be the minimum of assessed progression. Well, a compromise between those two propositions was arrived at, and it was universally supported, by all the employer authorities, a miracle in our time that everyone from the ILEA to the most orthodox East Anglian Tory subscribed to that agreement, and we then took it to the teachers. All the teachers unions agreed to it, said yes, okay, that could provide a basis for a Burnham agreement, with the sole exception of the National Union of Teachers, and they were the majority, they had a majority of one vote over all the others and Jarvis didn't even bother to read our proposals. He said no, they were not having these . . .

This extract rehearses the background to a key period of educational politics in the UK in the mid-1980s. The teachers' pay negotiations and industrial action of 1984–6 ended in defeat for the teacher unions and, in effect, brought to an end the "partnership" politics between DES, unions and LEAs that had been such a central feature of postwar policy-making. In Philip Merridale's account, we have a mixture of anecdote, narrative, personal comment and commentary. The language is often flamboyant, full of metaphor and wide ranging. The metaphors are interesting in themselves. They draw upon the imagery of battle and confrontation – fortifications, strongholds, armies and ramparts. In a sense, the metaphors also place the teachers and LEAs "on the defensive" and outside the prevailing discourse – they were "the philistines", a disunited alliance of resistance to the conquering hordes of Thatcherism, the decaying vestiges of a once great empire of educational administration. (Analytically as researchers we tend to neglect the poetics of language.) But the story also has a strong analytical thread. He is telling us not only what happened but how to understand it. He is doing the work of analysis for the research, to some extent. Platt (1981: 81) has referred to this second-order accounting as generating "bad" interviews:

> those where the people interviewed implicitly defined themselves as informants rather than respondents; rather than offering raw data for me to interpret, they told me their interpretations and the conclusions they had reached. This solves the status problem by redefining relative statuses or by bringing in statuses from outside the interview situation.

But much of the interpretational work done by Philip Merridale is reflexive and instrumental, as observer of and participant in state decision-making. The analysis here is situational and substantive – related to teachers' pay negotiations. There are, however, a number of more general analytical possibilities for the researcher arising from this material. For example:

- All of this highlights the increasing "ministerialization" of policy during the 1980s. More and more education policy came to be inflected by or directed by the personal beliefs and prejudices of the Secretary of State. And the Secretary of State became a prime actor in policy negotiations and decision-making.
- The changing relationship between local government and central government – from partnership to agency- and thus the changing patterns of interest representation are articulated. And we see something of LEA and union politics, and their repositioning in the political field.
- These comments open out the analysis of educational politics to relate them to national politics and new modes of political regulation and new discourses of policy under the Thatcher government.
- We also have some insight into a changing role for the DES civil servants in relation to policy-making and decision-making.
- The particular significance of Keith Joseph is pointed up in a number of ways. Of particular interest is his approach to the role of Secretary of State. As a philosopher rather than politician he was to rethink the system of administration (control) in education rather

than, as is more usual, tinker with the system currently in place. This rethinking did not produce major legislation but had profound implications for state–teacher–LEA relationships and for the future direction of Conservative Party education policy.

The interviewee is centre stage in the narrative. He is offering an account of himself as well as of policy activity. Perhaps not surprisingly, many respondents "claimed" key roles or telling influence in the dramatics of policy. Policy-making is thus portrayed as an interpersonal process, as constituted by relationships, by encounter and by argument. This is the politics of smoke-filled rooms and late-night deals. The interviewee offers the researcher a surrogate presence in the scene. The characters and settings are described; the general issues are related to specific events. Policy also emerges as being indeterminate, in the sense that different outcomes were possible, different things might have happened. Thus, within the substance of the account a particular imagery of policy-making is conveyed.

All of the above could be developed further but I want now to contrast this with an extract from an interview with Keith Joseph himself. This comes from close to the end of the interview and is a kind of mopping up and summing up, and I was running out of my allotted time. As well as being interested in Keith Joseph as Secretary of State for Education, I was interested in his role as party ideologue. The preparation done for the interview should be evident.

S.B.   Going back to . . . I must let you get away . . . the first question I asked, people I think will also see your, if you like, intellectual and political contribution to redirecting Conservative thought, if one puts it in that way.

K.J.   Yes, but it was far easier you see to do this in the economy . . . where things like abolishing wage controls and price controls and foreign exchange controls, dividend controls . . . were obviously justified . . . trade union law, and council house sales . . . all straightforward . . . done by a simple decision and it happened . . . not so in education, a lot of sensational policy, much more complicated, much more difficult. So I can claim credit for being part of a team that made changes in the economic framework, and that was un-do-able . . . and once done, very hard to change back, invert . . . far harder in social policy.

S.B.   Can I be impertinent and ask whether you would have liked to have pursued those policies as leader of the Conservative Party, and Prime Minister?

K.J.   That's not impertinent, it's a perfectly legitimate question. The answer is an unqualified no . . . I don't have the skill, I don't have the political judgement.

S.B.   I mean political analysts writing about the period in '74, suggest that you were on the verge of standing . . .

K.J.   Oh I might have been . . . I might have stood, and it would have been a calamity for me and a calamity for the country, but standing and failing would have been virtually impossible . . . but no, no, no . . . I'm not, I'm nowhere near the stature or skills. . . or . . . courage . . . you need these. You won't get everything right of course, but she's [Margaret Thatcher] got a superb fund of moral courage . . . overwhelmingly . . . that's the key characteristic you need . . . had it all too rarely.

S.B.   But again people commonly suggest that you were, in an intellectual sense, the architect of many of the . . ..

K.J.   She's got instincts, you see. She didn't arrive by intellect . . . analysis . . . and instinct is even more glorious than intellect. Reagan's got instincts. He's not intellectual, which we all know.

S.B.   But that which people call Thatcherism . . . I mean, could very well be called Josephism . . .

K.J.   Look, it was obvious to many, there are people like Enoch, and John Biffen, and Bruce Gardine and Nicholas Ridley, who were proclaiming all these truths . . . it's most unfair to give a name to them, but the point is that she has the moral courage . . . and never forget that characteristic in politicians. No good having the right ideas if you don't have the stomach.

This section of the interview is about the relationship of education policy to the broader framework of Thatcherist policy in the 1980s, founded upon neoliberalism, monetarism and the reduction of public sector spending, and Keith Joseph's role as organic intellectual of Hayekian economics within the Conservative Party. The interview has a game-like quality. There are a set of harry and evasion exchanges that end with Joseph's assertion of his agenda. He clearly wants to overplay the role of Margaret Thatcher and underplay his own. There is a complex interplay being constructed between personality and radical party ideology and intellect and instinct.

In contrast to other interviewees, Joseph is reluctant to place himself straightforwardly in the centre of the policy-making process and rather makes underclaims for his role and his effect. Here, though, there is also again a powerful imagery of policy, although a problematic one as far as analysts are concerned. This is a political imagery resting on particular qualities of personality and things like courage and instinct. This is a powerful corrective to those analyses of policy and policy-making (my own included) that rationalize and reify policy or look for simple relationships between ideology and structure.

The issue of style is important here, in relation not just to the interviewee but also the interviewer. They are of course tied together. My style changes across the interviews in response to the interviewee (but also in relation to my own purposes). Thus, the curt and evasive responses by Joseph produce a tendency to dogged pursuit on my part – a "let me put it another way" approach. Even so, what is elicited remains in one sense "thin". We have glimpses rather than thick descriptions. I use the term "glimpse" here to indicate the partialness of the views that are elicited. Important "intractable uncertainties" (Mishler 1991: 260) about and aspects of "diffuse texturing" (Ryan 1989) in what is said and meant remain. The interview is rarely clear and obvious. Substantive details are few and far between and often emerge almost accidentally. This contrasts starkly with Phillip Merridale's unprompted, detailed narrative. My point is that, at least within the tenets of ethnographic interviewing, the interviewer must respond to and adapt to the style adopted by the interviewee – that is, among other things, their mode of response to questions, their directness or evasiveness, their use of language, their use of concrete or abstract forms of account, their pace and coverage of issues, their ability to recall specific events, their willingness to refer to and account for others in "the field". The variety of styles is potentially enormous. It may not be impossible, but it is unlikely, that the interviewer will be able to push or seduce an experienced respondent into a style of interview with which they are uncomfortable or unfamiliar within the confines of a one-hour exchange. But it must also be doubtful whether this would be methodologically worth while or sensible. However, of course, this is exactly what some types of interviewing aim to do.

Clearly the interviewees can and do assert subtle control over what they are willing to talk about; because they regard some issues either as inappropriate or irrelevant. And in this regard the tactic of self-deprecation, above, is both disarming and effectively evasive. But sometimes the resistance of the interviewee is all too evident and the interviewer is left frustrated. I will give an example of one such dead-end. This illustrates again the importance of the difference in the style of interview given by different respondents and the still further increased differentiation between the interviews that results. Keith Joseph offered no anecdotes, and was reluctant to deal in the concrete matters of decision-making or policy dispute. He was clearly happier and fairly determined to deal with issues and ideas in fairly abstract terms.

S.B.   Was there a particular group . . . or particular individuals in the DES who collaborated closely with you on the development of the GCSE?

K.J.   Yes, the . . ... is wide.

S.B.   I was thinking whether there would be anybody I could talk to, you would recommend I talk to . . . to pursue that a little further.

K.J.   Yes, but I don't want you to go and think that I'm blaming an individual, I'm blaming myself.

S.B.   No not at all, not at all.

K.J.   It's the job of ministers to take the decision, knowing what they're doing. You know the names of the key officials, don't you?

S.B.   I don't know who would be involved in . . .

K.J.   Well the particular person concerned with that was a very clever and nice man called Walter Ulrich, now retired I think . . . just about to retire. A very high-quality man, who as far as I know shares entirely my passion for stretching.

S.B.   Was Stuart Sexton advising you at that time?

K.J.   Stuart Sexton and Oliver Letwin were my advisers.

S.B.   I mean I know Stuart Sexton was particularly interested in the Assisted Places Scheme, and was very involved. Was he involved in the . . .

K.J.   He was involved in everything. And seldom content with what I did, seldom content.

S.B.   Did you rely heavily on your advisers in terms of . . .

K.J.   . . . perhaps more than now.

S.B.   Oliver Letwin in particular tends to be associated with . . . again with groups like the Hillgate group, not so much Stuart Sexton.

K.J.   Oh I think Stuart Sexton very much . . .

S.B.   Yes, I suppose the Institute of Economic Affairs somewhat more.

K.J.   Yes, as an ally. Right, anything else?

Clearly, Joseph is unwilling to discuss his advisers and confidants and, after successfully avoiding my series of questions, he indicates that the topic is closed and it is time to move on. He is clearly in control of the interview at this stage. However, although thin on realist descriptions, this style of response in interview was certainly amenable to discursive analysis and an understanding of the play of power/knowledge upon the possibilities of policy. In other parts of the interview, Keith Joseph sketched in some of the assumptive landscape over which policy ranged and the ideological touchstones that informed "policy talk" and "policy thought" (see Ball 1990: 62–4). Here, we can cease to treat the respondent as author of the interview text. "Instead of constituting the language that creates the world, the speaking subject is constituted by its place within a linguistic system" (Taylor 1986: 13–14).

I want to consider briefly an extract from an interview with Rhodes Boyson, another key "New Right" ideologue, and one-time junior education minister. Under pressure of time – Rhodes Boyson was waiting in his rooms in the Northern Ireland Office for a division bell to ring – I was keen to pick up the issue that I had explored in several other interviews: the role of vocational education within Conservative education (or DES) policy. Here I was looking for another view of DES/DoE (Department of Employment) relations and influence and the impact of the MSC (Manpower Services Commission) on DES credibility. There was a point in the mid-1980s when it seemed likely that a joint ministry of employment, education and training would be created. The response again illustrates the role of respondents' "claims" but also something of the relationships between the departmental culture of the DES, legitimate interest representation and education policy.

S.B.   One omission in a sense . . . particularly if you look at the things, the Hillgate Group, the Centre for Policy Studies . . . are talking about, which is interesting in relation to say some of the interests of Keith Joseph . . . is vocational education.

R.B.   Yes, Yes.

S.B.   There doesn't seem much said about the role of vocational education. It seems much more straight-down-the-line liberal curriculum . . . position . . . would that be accurate?

R.B.   Yes, I think so, I mean . . . the academic . . . the old school master, who went from school..to university, and then back to school, knew and still knows very little about life outside there, particularly now national service has ended. But he does know the liberal curriculum, and . . . I mean, the teaching profession has very little enthusiasm for vocational education, and still hasn't. That's why the TVEI had to be done from outside. I was involved in bringing that in, with the Department of Employment . . . as the Minister of Education responsible when it came in.

S.B.   Oh . . . [Unintentionally here I seem to convey my scepticism about RB's strong claims about involvement and advocacy of vocational education and he appears to respond by toning these down.]

R.B.   So I mean I accepted it, because . . . I accepted it because the less able child will only work if there's going to be a carrot at the end which will get him a job. But the . . . my colleagues, who are less earthy than I am, since my first experience . . . secondary modern schools, are the actual after the liberal curriculum . . . very strongly . . . they are basically . . . you could almost say classical liberals.

S.B.   Right, but one thing people often say about . . . particularly TVEI, that there was a lot of resistance from DES officials, because this was seen to be a . . . [Here the interviewer searches for a diplomatic word and interestingly the interviewee provides his own, and thus gives strong confirmation of the point being made.]

R.B.   A take-over.

S.B.   Yes.

R.B.   Well I mean, DES could have done it, but the DES had no intention of doing it. And the pace was made elsewhere, so then it had to run after it for a bit, otherwise it was going to lose the whole of its schools . . .

This extract highlights the possibilities of joint construction within the interview. In contrast to the Joseph extract, Boyson is more willing to take on the interviewer's agenda. My allusions and line of questioning seem to be accepted and understood. Again here the antiquated and "Conservative" language use tells us something about the assumptive framework within which education policy is "talked" about. Again we glimpse the struggles for influence and control taking place inside the state and education policy-making. Very little of this sort of material appeared in the book, but it played a very important role in the development of my understanding and eventually my attempts to explain education policy.

Policy subcultures

Apart from issues of language and style, noted above, the mode of interviewing and the form of question and answering realized in any encounter was related to the professional and work "culture" of the respondents. The arenas of policy are populated by very diverse policy communities. The modes and forms varied noticeably between politicians, trade unionists, civil servants, business people and members of the educational establishment. There were marked differences in degrees of forthrightness, stubborn belief, and surety between the groups. For example, New Right advocates typically spoke as uncompromising "true believers" (See Baroness Cox in Ball 1990: 50).

One striking and unique work culture is that of civil servants (see Hennessey 1989 ch. 9). As noted already there were particular constraints in play within these interviews. And, in contrast to the "claims" made by other respondents, civil servants are socialized to present their absence from the processes of policy-making. They are clearly often decisively influential but are almost always unwilling or unable to account for such influence.

Again I will illustrate with examples. I tried to pursue the issue of "the personal" in relation to policy in interviews with civil servants. They after all could compare very directly the impact of different ministers on policy orientation. But this kind of questioning points up the very peculiar difficulties that can arise in such interviews. I was in fact surprised by how candid the civil servants were. But let me illustrate some of the limits and specifics of these encounters.

S.B. Kenneth Baker does seem to hold a more traditional sort of liberal humanist view of the curriculum, whereas Keith Joseph was interested in experimenting in the sorts of areas like Records of Achievement, GCSEs and ... where Kenneth Baker seems much more orthodox.

CS1 Again I wouldn't want to be drawn on things like that ... I only ever see over the shoulders of colleagues.

S.B. I talked to Keith Joseph and he was very interesting and helpful. But yes, it's difficult, it's always difficult to pick out the impact of individuals. It's just looking generally at the sort of emphasis that they've given to particular areas of development, there seems to be an overall difference in orientation.

CS1 I'm uneasy about venturing comparative comments on my political masters, but if you want an off-the-record comment, I'll give you one. My off-the-record comment is that ...

Here we have the interviewer in dogged pursuit of the issue. I was aware that I was unlikely to get a response, but thought the mention of my previous interview with Keith Joseph might disarm or legitimate the questioning. I did get a response, a very interesting one, but not for the record. We had not discussed any ground rules for the interview in advance and here common practice when talking to journalists is invoked. What was offered again served as background and provided further triangulation of views and perceptions on the role and perspective of the two Secretaries of State. Clearly, part of the interviewer's skill here is finding a formulation for a question that makes it answerable from the point of view of a civil servant. The civil servants were clearly much happier when talking in generalities than being pinned down to the specifics of the policy process. They often preferred to speak in the formal language of civil service clichés, a form of prose that had to be understood as both evasion and allusion. Only after a series of such interviews does one begin to "read" and understand the meaningfulness of some of these formulaic expressions. However, sometimes they were willing to go further and offer clues rather than answer direct questions. One way of doing that was for them to ask the interviewer questions. The following comes from an interview with the most senior civil servant I interviewed.

S.B.   . . . one of the interpretations particularly of the background to the current Education Bill is that supposedly Stuart Sexton, in particular, had considerable influence on its form and its writing.

CS2   Well . . . [No response was forthcoming.]

S.B.   And that's something he is ready to claim.

CS2   Oh yes sure. Well I think you have to . . . we're now getting into territory where I don't think I could . . . if I produced as it were, all the things that I knew, I would I think be going beyond the constraints that I have imposed, but let me try to be helpful. You've got to look at the timing of it. You have to ask yourself whether you think that the Education Act is Baker or is Joseph. What do you think actually?

The example above also indicates the usefulness of making statements that you know your respondent will disagree with. In doing so, one hopes that they will explain their position. Again the game-like quality of the interviewing is apparent and a set of complex rules are being invoked by the interviewee. This sort of complexity in the interview exchanges, involving my multiple agendas and interests and the interpretation and selection work done by respondents, points up some of the generic difficulties involved in interviewing that have been addressed by postmodernist researchers. Thus, Scheurich writes: "my perspective is that the researcher has multiple intentions and desires, some of which are self-known and some of which are not. The same is true of the interviewee" (1992: 5).

Conclusions

All of this has serious and important implications for the art and skills of interviewing, for the processes of analysis and for the interpretation and deployment of data within research reports. Certainly few of the complexities, uncertainties and idiosyncrasies of the interviewing, touched on above, were detailed in *Politics and Policy Making* (Ball 1990). My use of the interview material in that text traded heavily upon an assumption of "simple realism" – that the meanings and status of the extracts were clear, bounded and stable; that a single reading of the extracts was possible, and that meanings did not slip between different interviews. And within the process the interviewer himself is an invisible presence, a shadowy but omni-competent figure who slips effortlessly from setting to setting, subculture to subculture. My difficulties, mistakes and off-days remain invisible. Qualitative researchers feign to be skilled at and attentive to the particularities of events, but the vast majority of reported qualitative research trades upon an unproblematic common-sense version of "the interview" when accounting for data collection. We are to assume that we know what is meant and that it means the same for all cases. Thus, the complexities of data collection become detached from the analysis and interpretation of data. See Walkerdine (1990 Ch. 19) for a notable exception; "the problem with ethnographic work", she notes, "is how to take adequate account of the psychic reality of both observer and observed" (p. 197).

As regards elite interviewing, especially when this touches upon issues of public concern, we need to recognize and explore more fully the interview as an extension of the "play of power" rather than separate from it, merely a commentary upon it. McPherson and Raab (1988: 64) were certainly aware of this in their careful discussion of interviewees' motives in their Scottish civil servant interviews; "it quickly became apparent that a variety of considerations lay behind prospective interviewees' offers of assistance." Perhaps we need to reverse our social scientific common-sense and re-problematize the interview. It might be helpful to begin from the position argued by Scheurich and see interviews routinely as events of struggle, as a complex interplay of dominance/resistance and chaos/freedom. The skills and vested interests of the political actor highlight this struggle particularly, but it is in evidence in many other types of interviews to different degrees.[1] The objectification of the interview and of the informant within method is essentially a means of obfuscation; "methodology may often be a locus of displacement for the anxiety provoked not just by the data but by the investigator's confrontation with the subjects of research" (Crapanzano 1977: 69).

My point here is not that the interview is irretrievably flawed as a research instrument for elite studies but rather that it is actually both richer and more difficult than is typically acknowledged by researchers. In trying to scientize and objectify the interview we have tended to ignore some of the important difficulties and also to underestimate some of the potential. The interview is both an ethnographic (idiosyncratic and responsive) and a political event. In accepting that we do not need to abandon the struggle for rigour but rather we need to reassess the sorts of the claims we make about our interpretations and accounts and strive for a more epistemologically sophisticated self-reflection.

Note

1. In very different ways, two pieces of research in which I am currently engaged indicate the importance of this kind of reflexive analysis: one interviews working-class and middle-class parents about choice of secondary school; the other interviews parents of children with cancer. In the latter in particular many parents have strong personal agendas for submitting themselves to interview, which, inside the event, are very difficult to resist.

References

Ball, S. J. 1990. *Politics and policy making in education*. London: Routledge.

Ball, S. J. 1994. Researching inside the state: Issues in the interpretation of elite interviews. In *Researching educational policy: ethical and methodological issues*, D. Halpin & B. Troyna (eds). London: Falmer.

Crapanzano, V. 1977. On the writing of ethnography. *Dialectical Anthropology* 2, 69–73.

Hastrup, K. 1992. Writing ethnography: State of the art. In *Anthropology and autobiography*, J. Okely & H. Callaway (eds). London: Routledge.

Hennessey, P. 1989. *Whitehall*. London: Secker & Warburg.

McPherson, A. and Raab, C. 1988. *Governing education*. Edinburgh: University of Edinburgh Press.

Mishler, E. G. 1986. *Research interviewing: Context and narrative*. Cambridge, Mass.: Harvard University Press.

Mishler, E. G. 1991. Representing discourse: The rhetoric of transcription. *Journal of Narrative and Life History* 1 (4), 255–80.

Platt, J. 1981. On interviewing one's peers. *British Journal of Sociology* 32 (1), 75–91.

Ryan, M. 1989. *Politics and culture*. London: Macmillan.

Scheurich, J. 1992. A postmodernist review of interviewing: Dominance, resistance and chaos. Paper presented at the Annual Meeting of the American Educa-

REFERENCES

tional Research Association, San Francisco (and forthcoming in the *International Journal of Qualitative Studies in Education*).

Taylor, M. C. 1986. Introduction. In *Deconstruction in context: Literature and philosophy*, M. C. Taylor (ed.). Chicago: University of Chicago Press.

Walkerdine, V. 1990. *Schoolgirl fictions*. London: Verso.

CHAPTER EIGHT

The power discourse: elite narratives and educational policy formation

Peter W. Cookson, Jr

Reclaiming the radical imagination

As someone who has taught research methods for a number of years and has conducted research among educational elites for even longer, I am struck by the paucity of research about the critical role that educational elites play in shaping and implementing educational policy and a similar paucity of information about how to gain access to educational elites for research purposes. Reflecting on the first issue, I have tried to unpack the reasons why I believe researchers underestimate the importance of elites in creating educational policy by developing the concept of the "power discourse". Essentially, the power discourse is coded language. Decoding the power discourse requires a series of understandings about the nature of language as a verbal expression of social relations. Words do not exist in a disembodied form; they have meaning within a social context that is class bound, conflictual and power driven. Those who control this symbolic world are able to shape and manipulate the marketplace of educational ideas. The first part of this chapter will examine the elements of how this symbolic dominance occurs. The second part of the paper provides a methodological overview about how to gain access to educational elites, how to gather data and how to interpret these data through the methodology of power decoding.

The purpose of this chapter is to demystify the processes by which the powerful disguise power relations and cloak class interests in the mantle of universal values. Elites create a public conversation that sets the legitimate boundaries of discourse. In the United States this conversation places the responsibility for school failure on the shoulders of students and teachers and avoids confronting institutional failures that are the direct result of inadequate resources and insufficient public support, which, in turn, are the consequences of a class system that perpetuates huge disparities in wealth. Power arises from material advantages and is often legitimated through individualistic ideologies that place the burden of the class system on the shoulders of its victims. It is important to demystify the social scripts used by the powerful against the powerless and to provide methodological strategies for researchers who wish to analyze current conditions in educational policy and to liberate themselves and others from the intellectually and politically stultifying effects of language that appears value free, but is, in reality, a form of symbolic violence.

Research without critical consciousness is weak knowledge because it lacks a strong sense of purpose and because it is disconnected from social structure. The radical imagination begins with a critical consciousness that human social suffering is not brought upon by non-human factors. It was never written in the cosmos that women should be subservient to men or that non-whites should labour to makes whites wealthy. It was never written in the cosmos that poor children should attend unsafe, under-equipped and intellectually deadening schools while wealthy children should attend safe, well equipped and intellectually alive schools. These conditions were created by individuals and groups through social institutions. Critical consciousness begins with an understanding of social relations based on class interests and proceeds to illuminate the consequences and ramifications of structural inequality in the lives of subordinate groups. The radical imagination grows out of critical consciousness and includes not only a critique of present conditions but a call for action. Analysis without prescription renders the pursuit of grounded knowledge a game of intellectual hide-and-seek. Thus, the larger purpose of this chapter is to stimulate readers to think critically about educational policy and to encourage them to imagine an educational world where all children have the opportunity to learn, irrespective of their family backgrounds.

Sources of information

Since the mid-1970s I have been engaged in the study of elite educational institutions and their effects on students and of the larger social and educational environments. In the last six years I have studied the educational reform movement in the United States and very recently had the opportunity to study the legislative process in the United States Senate. Specifically, during the 1980s, my colleague Caroline Hodges Persell and I conducted research in elite secondary schools throughout the United States (Cookson & Persell 1985). This research included site visits to private secondary boarding schools and day schools, interviews with administrators, teachers, students, parents and alumni, surveys of students, and visits to similar types of schools in Great Britain and Israel. This experience provided a rich background in understanding how those who lead the most elite private schools use special forms of discourse that legitimate privilege. It was in the study of the elite schools that I began to understand the importance of the power discourse. Still, the world of elite private schools is small compared with the world of national public policy-making.

In the last six years I have studied school choice in the United States (Cookson 1994). This educational reform movement is highly politicized; those who promote choice and those who oppose choice are sophisticated players in the game of public opinion. The shaping of public opinion is a complex process based on resources, access to media and the capacity to create an aura of disinterest through the use of social science. The school choice movement has been enormously successful in placing this reform on the policy agenda and in the public eye. I had the opportunity in conducting this research to interview nearly 100 educational policy-makers. These individuals came from government and the private sector (for details concerning the sample, see Cookson 1994). What I learned from this research was that in the world of educational policy the winners and the losers were separated not so much by the coherence of their arguments, but by their capacity to influence public perception. The power discourse at the national level is a carefully orchestrated symphony of apparent fact, ideological argument and concerted political effort.

Very recently I had the opportunity to be a participant observer of the legislative process in the United States Senate. There are few institutions in the world as elite as this branch of Congress. Fashioning education legislation is balancing the opinions and interests of educational lobbying groups, and political friends and foes, and the needs of constituents located throughout the United States. There is nothing routine about writing Bills and passing laws. Each Bill has a legislative and political life of its own. A Bill succeeds or fails depending on how much political support its authors can command. Thus, the significance of the power discourse at the national legislative level cannot be underestimated. At some point policy becomes politics, and politics is not only the art of the possible, but also the art of packaging small victories in the ideological wrappings of grand accomplishments.

In sum, I have had three distinct opportunities to interview and observe educational elites and educational policy elites as they go about the business of shaping American education. I did not begin my research with the concept of the power discourse; it developed through experience and observation. The importance of symbolic signalling through socially contextualized discourse emerged in my thinking as I wondered why it was that, after 20 years of educational reform, one-third of all American schoolchildren attend schools that track them for failure.

Unpacking the power discourse

Building on the work of Basil Bernstein, Caroline Persell and I in an earlier work developed the concept of the "super-elaborated code" (Cookson & Persell 1995). Although elements of Bernstein's work are controversial and subject to empirical test, there is little doubt that his application of linguistics to social structure has been a key element in uncovering the means by which class reproduction occurs. The super-elaborated code can be thought of as the social linguistic method by which the upper class transmits its social authority and signals to other members of the class system a series of social relations that involve dominance and subordination. In this regard the classical curriculum can be thought of as a form of intellectual conspicuous consumption – a cultural extravagance, if you will, that symbolically demonstrates the leisure that is associated with aristocracy. In order to be socially significant, however, the super-elaborated code should signal a form of cultural superiority that legitimates the resources devoted to the cultural pastimes of the upper class. Thus, elites argue that the classical curriculum provides the mental discipline necessary for leadership. Whereas to the casual observer the chain of causation seems ambiguous, to the upper class the linkage between the classical curriculum, social superiority, moral elevation and social leadership seems obvious.

The power discourse has its origin in the super-elaborated code of the upper class, but it has been commandeered, so to speak, by other members of the power elite, and it has been expanded and to some degree debased so that it "speaks" to a larger audience of listeners. Power is the ability to coerce others to do what they might not do otherwise. Power can be direct and demanding or indirect and suggestive. Those who wish to wield power in American society are required to master the rhetoric of democracy and the reality of vested interest. The power discourse is the classical curriculum with a sword. Discourse implies communication; in American society, however, communication is no longer limited to oral and written mediums. The electronic revolution has expanded not only the possibilities of discourse but the very nature of discourse itself. The electronic revolution is a social revolution as well as a technological revolution. At the heart of the electronic form of communication is imagery. The image has placed the written word in the shadows of public discourse. Years ago the historian Daniel J. Boorstin wrote about pseudo-events that were in effect media created spectacles that appeared to be socially important, but in fact were of no significance beyond the immediate experience. A press conference that is meant to transmit a particular point of view and is treated by the news media as genuine news is a pseudo-event according to Boorstin.

Much of public discourse is a matter of creating images that resonate with spectators and give the illusion of content when, in fact, they are self-stimulating pseudo-events. Political elites have been extremely adroit at mastering imagery and portraying their political agendas as being compatible with the general welfare. Evidence of how important imagery is in power politics is close at hand. The tactics of creating an image include paid advertisements, controlled speaking events, disinformation campaigns against opponents, press releases, self-interested research, media engagements, and a carefully calculated creation of the self. The fact that American politicians spend much of their time with their cosmetologists and plastic surgeons tells us much about the nature of public discourse at the end of the 20th century.

The power discourse then has its roots in the class structure whereby the culture of the upper class is accorded deference. But it has developed into an expanded form of symbolic signalling that can be defined as social coercion through the manipulation of imagery. Virtually all elites in the United States speak in the language of the power discourse, although the content of the message varies according to its intended audience. To unpack this discourse is to separate out its particular elements. I have chosen four elements to examine, although there may be more. These elements are the ideological field, the institutional setting, the individual actor, and syntactical style.

The ideological field

In the marketplace of ideas there are few rules of good behaviour. When public opinion is the adjudicator of veracity, then those who wish to have their ideas heard become immersed in shaping public opinion regardless of the "facts". An ideological field comprises those institutions and individuals who are capable of shaping public opinion. They must have social authority and access to the media, and express themselves in a manner compatible with American pragmatism. In America, social authority is granted to institutions that are wealthy and traditional. Thus it is not surprising that publishing mega-corporations such as The *New York Times* and The *Washington Post* are considered to be authoritative. Large foundations such as the Ford Foundation, the Rockefeller Foundation, and the Carnegie Foundation are considered to be authoritative. In the last 15 years a whole group of new foundations have arisen within the Washington DC Beltway. These foundations tend to be openly ideological and publish many reports, monographs and books that purportedly are independent and scholarly. Certainly, major political personages are considered authoritative, although their authority is particularly vulnerable to shifts in public opinion. Prestigious universities and well-known churches are also authoritative in their pronouncements. In the last 20 years, corporations and multinationals have entered into the power discourse and have played a particularly important role in shaping public opinion.

In effect, there are a small number of institutions and individuals attached to those institutions that shape public opinion. By definition, elite narratives must be sanctioned and repeated by these institutions and individuals if they are to seem credible. This last point is important because in the area of educational policy-making the agenda is set by the ideological field, composed of authoritative and elite institutions.

Groups and individuals attempting to compete with the dominant ideo-logical field are at a distinct disadvantage because they are defined as lacking credibility by the very institutions they wish to criticize. Thus, in the area of educational policy, non-mainstream critics have a very diffi-cult time reaching a large public.

The institutional setting

Part of being authoritative is to have an institutional setting that impresses and intimidates. A college professor working in a remote office of a large university may be far more brilliant than a federal bureaucrat sitting in a large office on the top floor of a marble-lined building; the chances are very great, however, that the college professor will have little opportunity to engage in the power discourse, whereas the bureaucrat will be seen by the press and the public as being authori-tative.

Part of the power discourse is framing the interaction in such a way that dominance is demonstrated through the physical setting. For instance, most headmasters' offices are the largest and most elegant office in their respective schools. There was a time when headmasters such as Frank Boynton of Deerfield Academy had his desk in the hall, but those days are long gone. Spartan simplicity has been replaced by romantic images of the English study, complete with leather furniture, wood panelling and fireplace. These accoutrements of authority are meant to demonstrate the understated, but none the less real, power of the American upper class.

At the national level the institutional settings become even more criti-cal. Virtually all authoritative institutions require buildings that demon-strate social power by their size, their beauty and the number of staff required to maintain them. We are accustomed to thinking that power is somehow invisible and that we have socially evolved beyond the time of the Pharaohs and the Roman emperors. Yet a tour through the United States Capitol, or the offices of major foundations and corporations, or the campuses of the most prestigious universities should suggest that social power still requires a physical setting. Grandeur and size still impress the public and perhaps the researcher.

Individuals who speak for authoritative institutions require offices that transmit the not-too-subtle message that they are powerful and somewhat protected from ordinary life, and control their social and professional interactions. Secretaries, security guards and assistants protect the authoritative individual from random interactions. This form of control promotes a sense of mystery and specialness and underscores the importance of the individual and his or her message. Authoritative individuals create a drama in which they are the star and those seeking audience must demonstrate their worthiness.

If one is fortunate enough to have been permitted into the building of an authoritative institution and allowed an audience with one of its senior officials, one is likely to encounter an office space that is similar to a headmaster's office, only larger, more elegant and, in Washington, decorated with an American flag. The elite narrative is conducted in elite surroundings and these settings are critical for advancing the elite conception of educational reform. The person behind the polished desk assumes that they speak with authority about the problems of American education even if they themselves have little or no direct contact with schools. The power discourse requires a setting as well as an ideological field if it is to dominate other competing discourses that may arise from rebellious or marginal groups.

The individual actor

One way to think about the power discourse is to imagine an extended conversation among a relatively small group of individuals. These people are the "movers and shakers" of policy and politics. The composition of this group varies by issue and institution – but, in general, they share similar characteristics. Like the buildings they occupy and the offices they sit in, authoritative individuals must possess those social credentials that allow them to speak with authority. Until recently, being white and male was a necessary but not sufficient condition for authority. This demographic profile has changed somewhat in the last 15 years as more women and minorities play a role in the power discourse. On balance, however, white males are still the dominant actors in the policy-creation field.

These influential individuals almost inevitably possess credentials from elite educational institutions and come from family backgrounds where, as Randall Collins has written, they acquire the "habit of command". Creating a commanding presence in American society includes manner of speech, dress and a body language that is meant to show personal strength and social gracefulness. In American society, a commanding presence is not pompous; in fact, among the power elite an effort is made to appear humble and receptive. Democracy implies egalitarianism, and those who understand the power discourse recognize that demonstrations of overt social superiority run against the American grain and are politically counter-productive because they draw attention to the obvious – American society is decidedly not egalitarian except in folklore and contemporary mythology.

The presentation of self among those who lead authoritative institutions and thus define ideological fields is a carefully calibrated mixture of seeming humility, pragmatism and a desire to resolve problems. This is particularly true in the area of educational policy because all policymakers must, for political reasons, profess their concern for the "kids". This is not to say that these highly credentialized, affluent, powerful individuals are hypocritical; on the contrary, they are almost utterly sincere. They believe themselves to have been chosen to lead and they take their leadership role seriously and with a sense of moral purpose. This righteousness is an ideal defense, against the obvious observation that they are the beneficiaries of other people's lack of opportunity. The educational policy arena has more than its fair share of moral crusaders who deeply believe that they are in the vanguard of a great educational evolution while, at the same time, reaping the benefits of the status quo.

Syntactical style

Earlier the power discourse was defined as the manipulation of imagery in the service of political ends. What is the actual style of the power discourse? I would suggest that the power discourse can be thought of as a series of assumptions and inferences that are communicated through coded imagery and language that signals the following qualities: the benefits of hierarchy, social authority, moral righteousness, reasoned judgement and the reliance on facts. There is, I should say, a latent threat to the power discourse that signals to the listener and the observer that, if they do not accept the message of the discourse, it is because they have failed to understand and not because the message is flawed.

The ideological fields, the organizational settings and the characteristics of the individual actors all reinforce the perception that hierarchy is the glue of society. The overt message of the elite narrative is the celebration of democracy; the covert message is the reinforcement of status. Images of plurality are no substitute for genuine social sharing. The power discourse is sophisticated rhetoric; for instance, market-oriented school choice advocates make strong claims that markets create more equality than democracy, yet the evidence for this claim seems singularly skimpy. None the less, by repeating this claim with conviction, it acquires a social credibility that is unrelated to its empirical believability.

The text of the power discourse must be seen as socially authoritative if it is to be believed by its intended audiences. Thus there is a great deal of effort to bolster the position of the educational power elite by calling on the authority of other elites to underwrite particular positions. This is more than complicated name-dropping; it contextualizes a finding, a plan or a policy in a social web that gives it credibility. If all these influential people believe that school choice is the magic bullet that will save American education, how can I, as an individual, challenge their beliefs? Boards of trustees are selected for their social status and wealth. It is difficult for the average citizen to challenge their social authority without appearing to be "irresponsible".

There was a time when the power elite believed that God was an Englishman. Whether or not the American power elite believes itself to be the chosen people, there is a strong belief among elites, whether they write educational policy or not, that they command the moral high ground. Rectitude is an important element in portraying the power discourse as above politics. Former President George Bush repeatedly referred to the struggle for school choice as "the Lord's work". In an era of apparent tolerance, rectitude may not be expressed as fire and brimstone, but a sense of moral superiority pervades those who participate in the power discourse because, ultimately, the final justification for their assumption of power is that they represent righteousness and even, on occasion, the Lord Herself.

Contemporary social styles, however, tend to minimize moral fervour, at least among the power elite. Because much of the power discourse is designed to create an image of the world that is compatible with the status quo, it is important that the discourse should appear to rely on reasoned judgement and facts. Ultimately, reform, including educational reform, is portrayed in the power discourse as a technical problem requiring expert attention. By transmuting deeply political issues into technical problems the power discourse shifts the debate from who benefits from the present educational arrangements to how we can marginally improve schools for the poor so that they can become competent workers. There is the assumption that competence results in compensation that results in escaping from poverty. Unfortunately, the facts do not bear out this assumption, although these facts virtually never appear in the power discourse.

In sum, the power discourse is a complex, socially dense form of communication that relies on imagery and suggestion. To demystify this form of communication is an important task for the social scientist. For those who are interested in improving education, it is imperative that the elite narrative not be the only narrative about how to improve schools. If knowledge is power, then social science ought to be in the service of those most in need of knowledge – that is, those who do not participate in the power discourse. How does one study elites and decode the power discourse, while at the same time preserving a sense of ethics and promoting the best possible social science?

Methodological suggestions

Clearly, there are many ethical and scientific issues related to studying the powerful. I have focused on the power discourse as one element of studying elites because I believe that the mystification caused by the power discourse is one of the major reasons so much research on elites and educational policy is naïve and often unintentionally presents an inaccurate picture of the social world. In comments below I suggest ways of conducting research among elites, especially educational elites, that will not be systematically biased by the acceptance of the power discourse as the authoritative narrative.

Before discussing these methodological issues, however, I would like to mention that research among elites presents many thorny ethical issues. On the one hand, is a desire for truth and the refusal to be intimidated by power. On the other hand, elite respondents deserve to have their observations and comments treated with respect, accuracy and, if they wish, confidentiality. There are several ethical safeguards when planning a study of elites. It is prudent that the researcher makes sure that his or her hypotheses are scientifically rigorous and free of bias. Hypotheses should be field tested with experts in the field, not all of whom should agree with the researcher. It is important that potential elite respondents be aware of the study's scope and fundamental purposes. It is my belief that whereas respondents have fundamental rights concerning the ethical treatment of the data they contribute to a study, they do not have rights concerning the interpretation of the data. Researchers should be careful to get their facts straight, but should not be intimidated into avoiding conclusions because they do not wish to offend their powerful respondents. The key ethical issues are honesty in approaching the respondents, careful and systematic data collection and reporting the results in as unbiased a manner as possible. Elites are never likely to congratulate researchers for revealing certain social processes. I believe that the path of true ethics lies in revealing social processes no matter whom such revelations offend.

In studying the powerful, it is critical to understand the ideological fields and institutional settings of the respondents. This requires a great deal of preliminary research and a sincere attempt to get the "big picture". Because of the sensitivity and importance of power structure research, it is critical for the researcher to have a comprehensive understanding of previous research and new methodological strategies. Researchers should attempt to keep abreast of recent developments in ethnography because the study of the powerful almost inevitably implies ethnographic strategies. Some network analyses may be statistical, but, in attempting to create accurate descriptions of the powerful and to understand their world-view, field studies are required.

Sampling

Elite samples should be large enough to cover the scope of opinion on whatever issues the researcher is studying. One or two interviews or observations are insufficient when attempting to understand complex social phenomena. The best way to avoid systematic bias is to draw a sample that represents the range of opinion. This requires a great deal of preliminary work to understand the nature of the population that is under investigation. This information can be obtained through a literature review and/or discussions with social scientists knowledgeable of the area.

Initial contact

When Caroline Persell and I were conducting our study of elite schools we laboured mightily over the letter that we sent to headmasters. We wanted the letter to be informative, literate and interesting. This letter was our introduction to most of the headmasters in the sample and they would decide whether or not to participate in the study on the basis of this letter. One English headmaster told us that the only reason he granted us an interview was because of our letter. I suggest that the initial letter be followed up by a phone call requesting an interview. One must be patient in this process; the powerful are busy and can easily overlook a phone call from a social scientist. Initial rejection should never be taken personally and gentle persistence is more likely to win the day than avoidance or aggression. Researchers should be prepared to answer all questions thoroughly and accept the fact that in most cases the timing of the interview and other research events will be done at the convenience of the respondent.

I believe that it is critical to be highly organized when approaching the powerful because organization implies that the researcher is not a time-waster and can be relied upon. The powerful are used to dealing with the public and they take their cues from a few indicators when considering their time use. Clearly, the powerful want to know how much time the research project will demand of them and those for whom they are responsible. The presentation of self by the researcher is also very important because the powerful have certain expectations about the meaning of professionalism and they tend to gossip with each other. There is a very high likelihood that researchers who have been successful in interviewing and observing the powerful in one institutional setting will become known to others in the same ideological field. The researcher's professional reputation is his or her best insurance for gaining access to elites.

Triangulation

As in most research it is methodologically unsound to rely upon only one source of information when collecting data. When studying elite schools, Caroline Persell and I made great efforts to interview as many of the participants and graduates as we could. We used survey data, interview data and observation in drawing our conclusions about the elite schools. In studying school choice, I interviewed pro- and anti-choice advocates in government and outside government. In that study I used a "snowball" technique in determining the size of my sample. In time, the same names appeared so often that I felt comfortable that I had interviewed most of the major players in the school choice drama. The same principle applies when studying educational policy elites. By using previous research and a snowball strategy the researcher can, in time, develop a reasonably accurate picture of who the major individuals and groups are in shaping educational policy.

Analysis of data

I suggest that when analyzing the data the researcher remain very close to the words of the respondents with a minimum of interpretation. The objective at this time is to understand the views of the respondents before jumping to conclusions. A research study is more akin to making a good soup than eating fast foods. Good research takes time to develop, and examining the results of one's research should be a thoughtful process, punctuated by a great deal of hypothesis testing and counter-hypothesis testing. Sharing one's thoughts with others familiar with the field, including the powerful, may be very helpful at this juncture.

Reporting the results

The struggle for objectivity is ongoing. Ideologies shape our perception at levels we may not even be aware of. I have found it useful to identify my primary intended audience because it focuses the writing and provides an honest platform for disagreement. It is important that the researcher share the results with respondents even if the respondents are dismayed or angry at the findings. The powerful need not be protected and, if the researcher has done his or her job, the powerful will recognize themselves in his or her work even as they protest.

Conclusion

Since its inception social science has had a social problems orientation that has focused on the weak and not on the strong. The victims of society are often treated as if they were pathological. To my way of thinking, social pathology is structural and the most productive kind of research is that which examines and uncovers the processes of social reproduction and the pathology of power. I have examined the power discourse in depth because it shapes the world-view of not only the powerful but those who wish to study the powerful. If social scientists are to illuminate social processes they must first liberate themselves from unacknowledged mystifications. In the coming years it would be a great step forward in the social science if more men and women placed on their intellectual agenda the world-view and the vested interests of those who reap the greatest benefits from society.

References

Cookson, P. W. Jr 1994. *School choice – The struggle for the soul of American education.* New Haven, Conn.: Yale University Press.

Cookson, P. W. Jr & C. H. Persell 1985. *Preparing for power: America's elite boarding schools.* New York: Basic Books.

Cookson, P. W. Jr & C. H. Persell 1995. Knowledge for power's sake: Bernstein's theoretical contributions to the study of elite education. In *Knowledge and pedagogy: The sociology of Basil Bernstein*, A. R. Sadovnik (ed.). Norwood, NJ: Ablex.

PART III

Feminist perspectives

CHAPTER NINE

A feminist approach to researching the powerful in education

Roslyn Arlin Mickelson

Is a feminist approach to researching the powerful in education an oxymoron? One hallmark of feminist research is its focus on the dispossessed, the marginalized and the oppressed, and particularly on women in these categories. Another critical feature of feminist approaches to social enquiry is scholars' identification with their research subjects and advocacy of their interests. For these reasons, the very notion of a feminist approach to researching the powerful in education would appear to be a contradictory, incongruous enterprise. To state the obvious, the powerful are rarely women and, by definition, never are they the dispossessed. Even in education, power beyond the classroom is rarely in the hands of women. Moreover, feminist scholars seek to empower the dispossessed, not aid the already privileged. Nevertheless, in this chapter I will argue that research on the powerful in education, or in any location in the political economy, is possible within a feminist methodological framework.

To accomplish this, I will discuss and analyze my own research on school reform, which I have conducted within a feminist paradigm. The visible participation of national business and educational leaders, policy experts and federal state actors in the efforts of Charlotte, North Carolina, to reform local public education offered me what Robert Merton called a "strategic site" for research on the powerful in education. Because of the unique circumstances of school reform in Charlotte, North Carolina, my case study of one community's efforts to reform its schools became, in part, research on the powerful in US education.

In this chapter I discuss essential elements that distinguish feminist approaches to research and illustrate them with examples from my interviews with various powerful actors in education. I conducted these interviews within the context of massive efforts to reform education in the United States and in Charlotte.[1] The interviews I cite will, in addition, provide substantive data regarding the ways powerful people in the United States define the problems with education and shape the reforms instituted to address these. The interviews also demystify the powerful by revealing, in their own words, the slender reeds upon which many of their pet policies rest and, occasionally, the rather pedestrian nature of their thoughts.

The entire project has been a complicated intellectual and emotional enterprise for me as I attempt to integrate scholarship, feminism and activism. My two children attend the public schools in this district and various reforms have a direct effect on my family. As a feminist activist who participates in a community organization charged with ensuring that equality of educational opportunity for all children is not compromised by current reforms, I work for social justice, the end of educational privilege and the improvement of education. As a critical sociologist engaged in scholarly research, I strive for ethical and scientific clarity in the production of socially useful knowledge. In the sections that follow, I will discuss the ways, as an activist and a scholar, I have attempted to use the research process and the information I gather to struggle against class, race and gender inequality in schooling.

Feminist social science research

A number of feminist scholars have raised the question of what, if anything, is a feminist methodology (Smith 1984, Harding 1987, Harding & O'Barr 1987, Reinharz 1992). Feminist methodology is a very broad concept: it is partly about technique, partly about correcting the incomplete canon of substantive knowledge; it is partly a question of epistemology, and partly about political goals of social transformation. Dale Spender (quoted in Reinharz 1992 p. 7) observes that "at the core of feminist ideas is the crucial insight that there is no one truth, no one authority, no one objective method which leads to the production of pure knowledge". Yet, there are crucial features of feminist social research that distinguish it from more traditional, even critical, approaches to the production of knowledge. First, the subjects of the enquiry are usually the forgotten and the less privileged, often women. Secondly, from a feminist perspective, the choice of problems that animate research are very different from traditional approaches. Thirdly, the epistemological basis of feminist knowledge is quite distinct from and in opposition to modes of thought found in traditional social science, which are often androcentric, patriarchal or mysogynistic. Fourthly, feminist research has an emancipatory goal. To paraphrase Sandra Harding (1987), in the best of feminist research the purposes of research and analysis are to provide useful information that will empower people so they can challenge and fight their manipulation, control and exploitation by the powerful; the objective is to transform the status quo. This last characteristic implies that to "study up", namely, to study the powerful, is consistent with the goals of feminist research.

There is enormous diversity in feminist research methods or techniques. Although experiments and survey research are used, qualitative approaches to the production of knowledge are used more often by feminist scholars. Feminist researchers find interviewing appealing because it offers access to people's ideas, thoughts and memories in their own words, while the interviewer can observe the non-verbal communication and emotions of the subject. Most feminist approaches to interview research are conversational and, thus, are suitable for researching the powerful in education.

Business leaders and educational reform

The federal government's publication of *A Nation at Risk* (National Commission on Excellence in Education 1983) marked the renewal of large-scale attempts to reform public education by business, government and educational leaders in the United States. A major impetus to business involvement in this effort has been the declining position of the US economy in international competition. Business critics charged that, because America's public schools failed to educate the workforce properly, the US position as an economic superpower was in jeopardy (Shea et al. 1990). Taking much of their rationale from the business critique of education, the Reagan and Bush administrations proposed many market-based educational reforms, including parental choice of schools, accountability, increased standards and greater professionalism of teachers.

During much of the 1980s the business community's response to the perceived crisis in education was aimed primarily at the local or state level, which is not surprising given the 50 states' responsibility for education.[2] Individual businesses became involved in partnerships with local schools or sponsored local task forces to investigate the status of public education in their communities. At the same time, national business organizations also began to direct their resources to the study of the relationship between education and the workforce (Business Roundtable 1988, Committee for Economic Development 1991). The New American Schools Development Corporation (NASDC) stands as an organizational manifestation of corporate leaders' perception that weak education was the source of many of their problems and excellent education was a key solution. Formed in 1991 in response to President Bush's urging, NASDC has raised $40 million in corporate donations and in 1992 it funded 11 "break-the-mould" projects. Today, NASDC's chief officer is David Kearns, the former CEO of Xerox and Deputy Secretary of Education, who has been in the forefront of the national corporate push for educational excellence through market-based reforms.

Educational reform in Charlotte

During the last decade, some of Charlotte's corporate leaders, like their counterparts around the nation, expressed dismay over the apparent scarcity of "qualified" young workers. To address this problem, in 1987 key Charlotte corporate executives began vigorous involvement in the local school reform process. Although school improvement was the formal motivation for business activism in educational reform, the informal motivation of the business elite was to end Charlotte's mandatory bussing utilized since 1971 to racially desegregate the county-wide district. The racially desegregated schools had become a liability for the local business elite, who found the public schools were not perceived favourably by national firms contemplating a relocation to the Charlotte area (see Mickelson & Ray 1994 for details of this movement to end desegregation).

Emblematic of the business elite's effort to reshape the reputation of Charlotte's schools was their instrumental role in the hiring of a new reform-minded pro-choice superintendent in 1991. During his first year, the superintendent convened a panel of nationally prominent educational experts. In late 1991 and early 1992 this "World Class Schools Panel" met in Charlotte to chart the directions for educational change in this district. Members of the panel included a former Secretary of Education, a former Deputy Secretary of Education, former heads of the National Institute of Education, presidents of the Spencer and Carnegie foundations and leaders of major national educational organizations.

Given the imprimatur of the World Class Schools Panel's prestigious but vague recommendations, a number of significant curricular, instructional, organizational and assessment reforms were instituted by the superintendent during his first year. Arguably the most controversial and far-reaching of these was the end of mandatory bussing for racial desegregation and its replacement with a parental choice plan built around a series of magnet schools. It is within this context of sweeping educational reform, unique in the American landscape because of the direct and indirect influence of so many powerful national actors, that I conducted the interviews that I will now discuss.

Four interviews

In the following pages, I will draw from the transcripts of interviews with four nationally prominent and powerful individuals whose interviews are particularly useful for illustrating the points I wish to make. In all cases I obtained signed consent forms from the interviewees. The excerpts are from interviews with H. Ross Perot, Denis P. Doyle, Chester A. Finn, Jr and Donald E. Stewart. During all the interviews I was keenly aware that the conversational nature of the verbal exchange meant I was both gathering data and providing knowledge to my interviewees. Moreover, I was guided by the premise that there is no such thing as the neutral construction of knowledge; certain knowledge is privileged and serves certain interests (Edelsky 1992). The interviews reveal the tensions inherent in a dialogue between a powerful person and an interviewer who is attempting to conduct scholarly research while remaining true to her feminist principles.

Perot

H. Ross Perot spoke publicly in Charlotte in October of 1991, a period during which the business elite and school board were making crucial decisions about the direction educational reform would take in this community. During his speech Perot had referred to the de-industrialization of the major cities of the USA and the flight of capital to the developing world, and linked these to the low levels of education among the workforce, a problem he believed is caused by the general poor quality of the schools. I sought an interview with him in the hopes of learning to what extent someone at his level in the corporate world was aware of the contradictions inherent in calls for a more educated workforce at the same time that the majority of current and projected jobs produced by the economy require minimal skills and education (Ray & Mickelson 1993).

I interviewed Perot during a 35 minute trip from the University of North Carolina Charlotte UNCC campus to the airport after his participation in a forum at the university (this was prior to his bid for the US Presidency). He sat in the front seat while I and my tape recorder were in the back. I had requested a formal interview through his office but his secretary declined, stating that he was too busy. Undaunted, I arranged with the conference staff to ride with him back to the airport and requested the interview en route. Perot graciously agreed to be taped. Recall that in his speech Perot referred to the weak competitive stance of the de-industrialized American economy. I challenged his claims that poor students and terrible schools were responsible for the state of the economy.

R.M.   My own work looks at school achievement and I have found that kids who come from poor and working-class backgrounds on a day-to-day basis see around them that education doesn't pay off, that in fact there are relatives and older siblings and members of the community who have good educations but they don't have jobs, so from the kids' point of view, education doesn't pay off and that is why they drop out of school.

H.R.P.   Anybody that has a college education and claims they can't get a job, I'd wonder about. If you're a minority and you have a college degree and you're breathing normally, then you've got corporate America standing in line for you because of the need to bring in more minorities in the mainstream . . .

137

R.M.   What if I told you that you are wrong on that? [I had recently read Franklin Wilson's report, "Racial equality in the labor market: Still an elusive goal", 1991 which indicated that the ratio of black to white male unemployment increases with every year of education.]

H.R.P.   [incredulous] What?

R.M.   . . . black males with a college degree have a greater chance of unemployment than the white males with similar degrees.

H.R.P.   [incredulous] What?

R.M.   In other words, among black males the probability of being unemployed relative to whites with comparable education is greater for college educated compared to less well educated.

H.R.P.   Now, again, for example, we have one new young person with us who is a Major in the Marine Corps who was on the White House guard and had a scholarship to Yale whose wife has a PhD and speaks eight languages. I'm looking for all the talented people I can find and this guy is a super achiever, "love to win, hate to lose" personality, very aggressive but in a nice way . . .

R.M.   Most of the people I am talking about are people who have a high school education, a couple of years of college . . . the problem from their point of view is that the good jobs for people with this kind of training are not in their communities. The jobs have moved from Detroit and Pittsburgh to Charlotte or Mexico. And so, they're working class without work, so to speak.

H.R.P.   Okay. You've got to go where the jobs are. Stop sucking your thumb. Go West; go East; go Southeast, right. That's just – life is hard.

Although Perot consistently turned my structural analysis of poor student performance into a matter of individual initiative (i.e. his counter-example of the black Marine or his call to follow the jobs), I was able to present to him, my captive in the automobile, an alternative perspective on why so many American students do not do well in school. I do not know if this information entered his stock of knowledge, but I presented him with an interpretation of poor student performance linked to the damaging consequences of capitalists' decisions to restructure the economy in certain ways.

Finn

June, 1993 I interviewed World Class Schools Panel member and frequent consultant to the Charlotte–Mecklenburg school district, Chester A. Finn, Jr (Checker to his friends), at his current job with Whittle Communications in Washington, DC, several blocks from the White House. Chris Whittle, the educational entrepreneur who hopes to open a chain of private for-profit schools, is a friend and business associate of former Secretary of Education, Lamar Alexander (Kozol 1992). During the interview, Finn, casual and relaxed in his demeanour, sat behind his desk and occasionally leaned back and placed his feet on it. Because of his extensive writings advocating school choice and other market-based reforms, I was particularly interested in this former Reagan educational official's perceptions of the social and political sources of educational reform in Charlotte. In the following exchange, my questions and probes were aimed at eliciting his understanding of the business elite's offer of $25,000 bonus to the new superintendent after his first year in office. Reinharz indicates that, when feminists engage in research on men, upper-class people and those with considerable power, they are likely to demand less from their subjects. It is crucial, however, that feminist researchers persevere and consciously probe. The following exchange illustrates the fruits of such efforts.

R.M. Given what you know about Charlotte, and the changes that [the superintendent] was able to effect the first year, why do you suppose the business people wanted to tip him?

C.E.F. I didn't even know about the event. How can I possibly know what they – what was in their minds?

R.M. I thought you could speculate.

C.E.F. You're beginning to remind me why I don't like sociology as a discipline. How on earth am I supposed to know *what* they are doing, is in their minds, when I didn't even know they did this until you just told me it?

R.M. Well, it is conceivable you did know, and the nature of the question has to do with how you see Charlotte and how you see the role of education and the business community. And why business leaders would be so delighted with [the superintendent's] accomplishments after one year.

C.E.F.   . . . it's so bizarre that you would ask me why – what was going on in *their* heads. [Pause] That there is an economic development rationale for education reform is manifest throughout the country and was crystal clear in Charlotte the night of the dinner party that kicked off the World Class Schools Panel on the top of that bank [First Union Bank, the eighth largest in the United States, has its corporate headquarters in Charlotte and its CEO is an active member of the business elite]. That there was a substantial business community interest in the fate of education in Charlotte, has been crystal clear from the time I first had any communication with Charlotte. But that's true of any community – any city in the country that's got a significant push for better education. The sources of that push are rarely the educators. They are ordinarily the consumers, and that is often represented by the business community – by employers – and that's clearly true in Charlotte. So it would be perfectly consistent with that interest if they wanted to reward [the superintendent], but I have no idea what they were thinking at the time.

R.M.   When you say it was crystal clear when you were at [the dinner party on] the top of First Union, what made it crystal clear?

C.E.F.   The people, the talk; the remarks, both formal and informal, the – it was crystal clear. We weren't meeting in a homeless shelter and talking to the homeless people about whether they thought Charlotte would be better served by improved education.

R.M.   Uh-huh.

C.E.F.   Who was present? It was the business leaders, school board members, a handful of other civic leader types, but it wasn't a meeting called by the president of UNCC [my university]; it wasn't a meeting called by the Urban League [an established national civil rights organization with branches in major cities]; it wasn't a dinner hosted by the AFL-CIO [one of the largest trade unions in the United States].

It was perfectly clear whose party this was. Despite his angry disclaimer that he had no understanding of it, his full answer revealed a very clear, systematic and sophisticated understanding, consistent with the other data I had gathered from respondents, of why the business elite were happy with the superintendent's initial accomplishments. His comments were especially useful for their clear delineation of the relationship between the specific impetus for school reform in this district, the specific interests of the business elite in its outcomes, and their key participation in the process.

Doyle

Another frequent consultant to the Charlotte–Mecklenburg schools and World Class Schools panelist was Denis P. Doyle. With NASDC head David Kearns, Doyle co-authored *Winning the Brain Race* (1988), which was required reading for the Bush Cabinet. Perhaps more than any other conservative tome, it links the competitiveness problems of the American economy to inferior public schools, and argues that the solutions lie in market-oriented reforms. Formerly associated with the American Enterprise Institute, Doyle currently works for another conservative research organization, the Hudson Institute. I interviewed Doyle in an office in the headquarters of the RJR foundation, on whose board of directors Doyle serves. The RJR foundation is the philanthropic arm of the RJR Nabisco corporation, a conglomerate whose many products include cookies, candy and cigarettes. The foundation's offices are in a tastefully refurbished old hotel across the street from the White House in Washington, DC. I was struck by an incongruous sight of lovely porcelain bowls filled with small packages of cigarettes and candy throughout the well-appointed corporate suite. One of the lines of my questions centred on the personal and professional networks of the powerful national people involved in school reform in Charlotte. I began with Doyle's own extensive involvement in Charlotte.

R.M. I would like to turn the conversation a little bit to more general issues and that concerns your broad – what I believe is a broad involvement in Charlotte's reform process. You're on the World Class Panel, you're on the RJR Foundation board which funded the Highland/Tryon project [Next Century Schools project], you are on the [NASDC] team that wrote Modern Red Schoolhouse . . .

D.D. [interrupts] No one else has picked up on this; you'll be the first . . .

R.M. [continuing] . . . what else are you doing?

D.D. That's essentially it – I've done some ongoing consulting in Charlotte. I did until the World Class Schools Panel. Now I'm off the consulting roster in Charlotte because that would be a conflict of interest. But those are essentially it and the three are designed to interlock, interconnect. I mean it's no accident that the little Modern Red Schoolhouse proposal is similar to the Charlotte 14 points [the document that emerged from the World Class Schools Panel]. A lot of the same people were involved and Next Century Schools, which RJR runs, was kinda the precursor organization for NASDC so – so far they continue to fit.

Another line of questioning I pursued concerned school choice and the privatization of schooling, particularly vouchers for private schools. This interchange cast into sharp relief the tension between scholarship and advocacy, thus forcing me to clarify "what side I was on". I had the opportunity to provide to an individual at the national epicentre of the powerful in education empirical data that supported the non-feasibility of private for-profit schools (schools that would require educational vouchers, a policy that I consider to be a disastrous threat to American public education and any semblance of equality of educational opportunity for the less privileged in US society). To the extent that my data would enhance his ability to argue more forcefully against private for-profit school vouchers in his many sites of power and influence, my actions advanced my political and social goals. However, to do so was clearly pushing the limits, or at least complicating, my position as a social scientist conducting an interview.

R.M.　A lot of people on the World Class Schools panel are also working for the Hudson Institute and Whittle Communications.

D.D.　One.

R.M.　Isn't Checker [Finn] and isn't Bennett [William E. Bennett, former Secretary of Education during the Reagan administration]?

D.D.　No, Bennett thinks Whittle is going to fall flat on his face . . . No, in fact, he and I have told Checker that we just don't think Whittle is going to make it – for a lot of reasons. As I said, one caveat is if Whittle gets vouchers for non-sectarian schools. If vouchers were generally available for private schools of all kinds, Whittle would stand a chance. I mean there's no way Whittle could compete with [the religious schools that don't make a profit]. There simply isn't 15 per cent profit to be made around the schools and anybody that can make 15 per cent profit would be out-competed by somebody who was willing to work without the profit. That's what religious orders do and they would simply clean Whittle's plough.

R.M.   Actually, I have a clipping from the *Los Angeles Times*. There's an interview with some people who run a very successful school in Los Angeles . . .

D.D.   A for-profit school?

R.M.   Yeah, and basically they come to the same conclusion. The question is could this be duplicated and they say no it can't because of all the things that you mention and also the fact that you cream off – I'm saying once the self-selected group of families with funds, so on and so forth.

D.D.   I'd like to see it.

R.M.   Yeah, I'll send it to you.

D.D.   I'll give you a card so you'll remember.

Arguably, the centrepiece of reform in Charlotte during the first two years of the new superintendent's tenure was the replacement of mandatory bussing for desegregation with parental choice among magnet schools in the public sector. US proponents of choice often cite Harlem's District Four as the quintessential example of how choice improves the quality of education for children, especially poor and minority youngsters. I challenged this notion in the following exchange.

R.M.   It seems to me that in District Four, choice came, if you look at a 16-year period of reform, after about 11 years and [mention of several other reforms], then choice and so it becomes very hard to argue that choice brought about the success [rise in students' scores]. Maybe the success has brought about choice? How do you tease out . . . the contribution to school reform success made by choice and . . .

D.D.   It's an empirical question how you find it. Well, to part without being utterly evasive, the choice argument is essentially a moral argument rather than an instrumental argument. This is really an argument about human dignity. It would be the same fundamental argument if you would advance about choice with right-to-life [abortion opponents]. It is really a hard and fundamental moral decision about the dignity of the person and his or her right to make a selection about his or her life. So, I would say the instrumental arguments are less important than the principal moral argument. But having said that, if a choice system exists, the question still remains does it make a difference instrumentally?

R.M.   Well, choice hasn't made a difference in Milwaukee [a limited group of low-income Milwaukee, Wisconsin, parents were awarded vouchers to be used in the private schools of their choice. Achievement results from the first two years show no academic advantages accrue to students who attend private schools].

D.D.   But that's such a little truncated bizarre, almost grotesque situation . . .

R.M.   I mean, it is such an important question since so much of the school reform debate today is centred around issues of choice and all other issues – curricular, instructional, etc., have, at least in the public discourse, taken a back seat and . . . if it's simply a moral question – people are not talking about it in terms of a moral. Chubb and Moe [authors of a widely read book prescribing choice for what ails American schools] don't talk about it in terms of a moral – they talk about it as the panacea, the linchpin which will bring out . . .

D.D.   [interrupts] Well, it is very difficult to find out in part because we don't have very many examples from which to draw and examine so it would be very hard to find out. So we don't have a lot to look at to tease out [the effects of choice] empirically.

It's a philosophical or moral issue in the first instance. Key in this exchange is the fact that, when pressed on the crucial issue of the empirical basis of proponents' claims that choice improves schools, one of its most ardent and articulate advocates relies on a moral argument and dismisses evidence against his position as bizarre.

Traditional approaches to interviewing require the researcher to be rather like a sponge soaking up what the interviewee says, influencing the course of the discussion only through the nature of the questions asked. On the other hand, feminist interview techniques may involve an exchange of information or interviewer self-disclosure, especially with subjects of less power and privilege. Interviewing powerful people requires the feminist researcher to be more circumspect or less self-disclosing than with subjects of similar or lower status because self-disclosure diminishes one's power and, arguably, one's ability to engage the subject seriously on the same critical plane. There are, however, times when self-disclosure or sharing sensitive data with a powerful person engender trust and result in greater access, openness and the development of a working relationship with the individual – all of which may support shared social or political goals. My experience interviewing Donald Stewart, president of the College Board, illustrates this point.

Stewart

The College Board is the national organization that sets educational policy in a number of key areas; an example is the Scholastic Aptitude Test (SAT), which is widely used for entrance into higher education. Donald Stewart, the only African American who actually participated in the deliberations of the World Class Panel, is its president. Formerly, he was the president of Spellman College, one of the most prestigious historically black colleges for women. I interviewed Donald Steward in his offices across from Lincoln Center (the home of Carnegie Hall) in the heart of New York City. Our scheduled interview was cut short by a crisis, but Dr Stewart allowed me to return several hours later in the afternoon. My questions concerned the tension between excellence and equity in school improvement strategies discussed by the World Class Panel.

R.M.   So how do you end up on a panel with Bennett, Finn and Doyle [all conservatives who lament the ways that attention to equity in education has crippled excellence]?

D.S.   Well, you see, they want that voice. I mean, I'm a minority person. I obviously care deeply about such matters. I happen to think that I also believe in high standards and quality but I think for a nation and a society or a school district that you best achieve excellence through equity by providing as superb an educational experience to all students, doing what you may need to do that is supplemental for poor students and minority students so that high standards are achieved. And I don't see the quality–equity trade-off. I think they are – I don't think you have to sacrifice one for the other. Obviously this reflects my values and it explains why I would separate myself from a Bill

Bennett, or a Checker Finn or a Denis Doyle on that issue, but I totally embrace the high standards aspiration . . .

Earlier in the interview, Stewart said that one reason he had agreed to let me interview him was because he "wanted to learn from [me] more about what's going on there". I made a conscious decision to share information with this key national actor who, like me, held equity as an important goal but mistakenly believed the reforms of Charlotte's superintendent were wholly consistent with this. Mindful of the superintendent's sensitivity to the views of powerful national actors, especially those with grant money such as Stewart, I hoped my information to Stewart would work as a countervailing force against the influence of more conservative consultants who uncritically support market-inspired reforms like school choice. I made the decision to tell Stewart about the reforms underway in Charlotte in a clinical fashion but to identify in clear terms the concerns held by many people concerning the adverse equity implications of a number of reforms, particularly the direct consequences for black children, parents and educators of the end to bussing and the institution of choice among a few magnet schools.

D.S.   Well, it's an interesting piece of social engineering. I'm not sure I have problems with the mainstreaming of kids for whom English is not their first language. But the other part [the way in which magnet schools were organized and implemented], however, is alarming – interesting is not the word. Some damage may be done in the process – may be done. The impact of magnet schools and the losing of minority teachers and kids . . . I mean it's a form of gentrification . . . It would appear as if the Finn, Bennett, Doyle notion of how you deal with excellence and equity is being played out in Charlotte–Mecklenburg with equity not being allowed to dilute or get in the way of increasing academic excellence as measured by performance on standardized tests or whatever . . .

A few days after I returned from New York, I received a note from Donald Stewart in which *he* thanked me for sharing with him the information I had discussed and requested that I keep him informed about the reform process in Charlotte. Of course, I have no way of actually determining if our conversation prompted him to act in ways to elicit greater attention to equity from the superintendent, but my information was heard and appreciated.

Ethical dilemmas

Reinharz (1992) notes that a common ethical dilemma feminist scholars face is trying to avoid further exploitation of the less privileged who are often the subjects of their research. My own work involved an interesting twist on this ethical concern. My interviewees were powerful people who were, in many cases, directly involved in formulating or implementing state and business policies that directly affect the lives of millions of people. In the dilemmas I will describe, my research potentially could contribute to or work against the exploitation of people, depending on what I did during the interview and what I did with the information I acquired. My response to each ethical dilemma was informed by the answer I gave to the question, "Whose side am I on?"

Candour

I was not completely candid when I interviewed these powerful people. I am far more genuine and candid when I am interviewing non-powerful people. I am comfortable in my interviewing personae because I believe it is the best way that I can gather the data I seek from these individuals. Guided by the scholarly as well as the political and social goals I hope my research will serve, I selectively choose the degree of candour I exercise with the powerful actors I interview. For example, Denis Doyle asked if I was on the faculty of the College of Education at UNCC. I answered, "I'm a sociologist." Doyle replied, "Oh, well, no wonder your questions are so good. I couldn't believe it." His candid response suggests the low regard in which he holds professors of education. And, because of the disrespect Doyle displayed towards professional educators, I did not reveal that, indeed, my PhD is in education although my appointment is in the department of sociology.

Confrontation

At times, the powerful have uttered abhorrent comments in the course of an interview or during an event I observed. When this occurred, the ethical dilemma I faced as a researcher was rather simple: to say nothing and thus tacitly condone the remarks because to speak risked ending the interview (or access to observe other events), or to challenge the comments with counter-evidence, arguments or sociological analysis. In a

1990 interview, a former education official in the Bush administration defended school choice as a reform that would help the poor. To claims that choice would hurt poor parents, who are less likely than the middle class to participate in choice or to make informed decisions about choice schools when they do, he argued:

> We don't, uh, act paternalistically toward the low-income parents in all of these other very basic domains of their lives as people and parents. On the notion that parents, uh, low-income and minority parents cannot be expected to make rational decisions for their kids, um, we let them have kids. We let them decide what to feed their kids. Uh, we let them decide whether the food stamps we give them to nourish their kids, something more basic than education, are gonna be spent for milk or vodka.

Where does one begin with such a statement? Point out the inherent paternalism of the actual words despite his disclaimer of exactly the opposite? Note that empirically the poor are controlled in where they may live and what they do with their food stamps – and one control is that they cannot buy alcohol with them? I said nothing, in part because his remarks left me speechless. As I looked back at this interview, one of the first I conducted with a powerful actor in national education, I concluded that it was a mistake not to challenge his conception of the poor and his analysis of choice in these terms. I have since adopted a much more consciously assertive stance when I encounter racist, elitist or reactionary rhetoric.

Community

A final ethical dilemma stems from my involvement as a scholar, parent and citizen–activist in this community. I serve on a committee designed to ensure that the switch from mandatory desegregation to magnet schools compromises neither educational quality nor equity for any child. But I am different from my colleagues on this committee because I am an academic: I have been studying school reform for six years and am immersed in the scholarly and popular literature on the topic. Yet I seek to work with the others on the same critical plane. I want to be a source of information without being pedantic. I want to communicate what I know with fellow committee members, parents and community activists who contact me without either alienating or overwhelming them. In one sense, this situation reverses my status vis-à-vis the powerful ("Ask the professor what she thinks", "We don't know as much as you, Dr Roz").

Conclusion: Feminism and action research

My experiences over the past few years as a feminist researching powerful people in education have presented me with a practical, conceptual and ethical minefield, which I continue to negotiate each day. I face dilemmas in attempting to combine the roles of researcher and advocate; in attempting to balance my scholarly and political goals. After six years of observing and interviewing these actors in the school reform movement, I am convinced that a feminist approach to research on the powerful in education not only is not an oxymoron, but is necessary.

I have concluded that my research on the powerful in education is most true to a self-consciously feminist epistemology and praxis when my data demystify powerful people and reveal their feet of clay, and when I put the knowledge I extract about the powerful into the hands of the less powerful so they can better struggle and resist efforts by the powerful to shape the direction of school reform in their narrow interests. My construction of a feminist research methodology not only fights against oppression and privilege through the results of my enquiry, but also attempts this struggle while I conduct the research itself.

Notes

1. Research reported in this chapter was supported, in part, by a grant to the author from the National Science Foundation (No. SES–8910865).
2. Unlike almost all other industrialized societies, the USA has no national education system. The federal government provides only about 6 per cent of school funding. The responsibility for public schooling falls to the 50 states and the 15,000 local school districts within them. Public schools are almost always funded by local property taxes supplemented by a per pupil formula addition from the state government. Consequently, there are great inequalities directly linked to funding (see Jonathan Kozol's superb critique, *Savage*

Inequalities, 1990). The federal government's role is, therefore, rather limited. It becomes directly involved when individual school districts fail to provide equality of educational opportunity on the basis of gender, race/ethnicity, language, physical handicap or learning disability. Federal statutes which mandate certain practices are enforced through carrots (federal funds, coveted special programmess) and by sticks (court orders, withdrawal of funds).

References

Business Roundtable Ad Hoc Committee on Education 1988. *Business in educational reform: A blueprint for action*. New York: Business Roundtable.

Committee for Economic Development 1991. *The unfinished agenda: A new vision for child development and education*. New York: CED.

Edelsky, C. 1992. A conversation with Carole Edelsky about politics and literacy. *Language Arts* **69**, 324–9.

Harding, S. 1987. *Feminism and methodology*. Bloomington, Ind.: Indiana University Press.

Harding, S. & J. O'Barr 1987. *Sex and scientific inquiry*. Chicago: University of Chicago Press.

Kearns, D. & D. P. Doyle 1988. *Winning the brain race*. San Francisco: Institute for Contemporary Studies.

Kozol, J. 1990. *Savage inequalities*. New York: Crown.

Kozol, J. 1992. Corporate raid on education: Whittle and the privateers. *The Nation* **255**, 272–5.

Mickelson, R. A. & C. A. Ray 1994. Fear of falling from grace: The middle-class, downward mobility, and school desegregation. In *Research in Sociology of Education and Socialization*. Manchester: JAI Press.

National Commission on Excellence in Education 1983. *A nation at risk*. Washington, DC: US Government Printing Office.

Ray, C. A. & R. A. Mickelson 1992. Restructuring students for restructured work: The economy, school reform, and noncollege-bound youth *Sociology of Education* **66**, 1–20.

Reinharz, S. 1992. *Feminist methods in social research*. New York: Oxford.

Shea, K., E. Kahane, P. Sola (eds) 1990. *The new servants of power. A critique of the 1980s school reform movement*. New York: Praeger.

Smith, D. 1984. The deep structure of gender antithesis: another view of capitalism and patriarchy. *Humanity and Society* **8**, 395–401.

Wilson, F. D. 1991. Racial equality in the labor market: Still an elusive goal. Discussion Paper No. 91–33, Center for Demography and Ecology. Madison, Wis.: University of Wisconsin.

CHAPTER TEN

Researching the locally powerful: a study of school governance

Rosemary Deem

Introduction

This chapter will explore questions about gaining access to and researching the locally powerful, as well as about what power educational researchers possess and the likelihood that policy research can seek to empower (or disempower) those being researched. The concerns examined here are derived from the experiences of an Economic and Social Research Council (ESRC) funded project directed by myself and Kevin Brehony, with assistance from Sue Hemmings and Suzanne New, between 1989 and 1993. This study analyzed the impact of recent educational reforms on the processes and power relations of lay participation in the administration of education, as evidenced in the governing bodies of local education authority (LEA) maintained schools in England. Governing bodies, in addition to containing headteachers (school principals) and teachers' representatives, are comprised mostly of lay people from three different but overlapping constituencies: the parents of school students, governors nominated by LEAs (many of whom have a political party affiliation), and co-opted members of local communities, including business people. The educational reforms specific to school governance were set out in a number of pieces of legislation including the 1986 no 2 Education Act and the 1988 Education Reform Act, encompassing increased parent and co-opted governor representation on governing bodies and the establishment of new governing body responsibilities for budgets, resources, the de facto hiring and firing of school staff, a range of other personnel issues and site maintenance.

The project described

The research team carried out a detailed case study of 10 primary and secondary school governing bodies in two English LEAs over a four-year period during which the reforms described above were being implemented. We wanted to carry out some research on governing bodies that would enable us to gain some detailed understanding of the processes and micro-politics of governing schools in England in the late 20th century. By the end of the 1980s, lay school governors had moved from a largely symbolic function to a role in the administration of schools that was extremely demanding and responsible. Furthermore, during this period the composition of governing bodies had shifted from a predominance of local politicians to a much more mixed group including parents and business people. In addition, LEA schools themselves had begun to acquire much more autonomy over their decision-making and many were beginning to engage in competitive marketing for pupils as their funding became more dependent on the numbers enrolled. Thus previous research on governing bodies had become to some extent outdated.

We began our field study in October 1988 with an exploratory pilot study based on observing the workings of 15 governing bodies in two contrasting local education authorities. The pilot fieldwork was intended to run until December 1989. Our cases included schools in different areas: urban, suburban and semi-rural. Their pupil intakes ranged from predominantly white and middle class to Asian and working class.

Late in 1989, as our pilot study neared its end, we received an ESRC grant to continue the research for a further period of three years, which meant that we would be able to continue to observe our governing bodies for their entire first four-year term of office operating under the provisions of all the 1980s educational reforms. At this point we decided to reduce the number of governing bodies we were studying from 15 to 10. We had already found that keeping up with the activities of 15 governing bodies was very time consuming and it threatened to become more so as all but one, following changes in 1989 to the regulations under which they operated, began to establish networks of subcommittees or working groups, some of which met on a more frequent basis than the governing bodies themselves.

Throughout the pilot and main study we used a range of mostly qualitative methods (some of which yielded both quantitative and qualitative data), thus also ensuring triangulation of data sources. We attended, as observers, all the formal meetings of our selected cases, and also, from 1990 onwards, a selection of subcommittee meetings, taking near-verbatim notes at all of these. We included what was said, details of who was speaking, the length of discussion items and a seating plan. We administered two questionnaires to all the members of the case-study governing bodies: in 1989 we enquired about why they had taken on the task and in 1992 we asked them to reflect on their experiences over the past four years. We carried out semi-structured interviews with 43 governors including headteachers, chairs of governing bodies and chairs of finance and other subcommittees, parent, LEA, business, co-opted and teacher governors. We also collected a range of documentation connected to each governing body, including agendas, minutes, headteacher reports and briefing papers. We observed the selection process for three headteacher appointments, attended governor training sessions and held informal discussions with LEA officials.

Definitions of the locally powerful

Defining power is notoriously difficult. Researchers are also unable to agree about whether power carries mainly negative or mainly positive properties or both. As Lukes (1986) notes, the search for a single unifying definition is probably mistaken. One way of exploring different theories of power, he suggests, is to distinguish the kinds of questions that researchers have asked about power – "Who can adversely affect the interests of whom?" (Lukes, 1986: 9), "Who can control whom?" (p. 10), "Who can get what?, where not all can get what they want or need" (p. 11), "Who can secure the achievement of collective goods?" (p. 12) and, finally, asking where power is located or "whom to hold responsible for the effects" of power (p. 13). In addition, we can enquire about "who gains by bringing about, or helping to bring about, the outcomes" of power (p. 14) and the sources of change in the distribution of power: "Power lies where a certain proposed difference to significant outcomes can be made or resisted" (p. 15). Lukes' questions about power are based on a notion of power as a scarce resource available to some but not all individuals or institutions, and his views could also be interpreted as perceiving power as mostly positive for those who are power holders but mostly negative for those over whom others wield power. Some poststructuralist writers, notably Foucault, take issue with Lukes' premises about power, insisting that power is not a property of people, that it is not inextricably linked to the relations of production and that power can be facilitating as well as repressive (Rabinov 1984). However, Lukes' questions seem to exclude only the first of these poststructuralist critiques, and there seem to be fewer problems with agreement between different theorists in relation to the second and third points.

Not all of the questions as posed by Lukes were of central relevance to the project we undertook. We were particularly interested in identifying those on a governing body who could adversely or positively affect the interests of heads, schools, teachers, pupils and other governors; which governors (including the headteacher) seemed able to control other governors and school personnel; which governors got their wishes and concerns dealt with and acted upon, and which governors were significantly involved in the definition and redefinition, as well as provision, of state education. The question about location of power was also especially relevant in relation to current debates in the UK about shifting power from the producers of education to the consumers (Deem 1990, Deem & Brehony 1993a), as a result of recent educational reforms. Finally we were concerned to discover whether there were sources of resistance to, as well as sources of support for, the reforms of governing bodies from amongst governors themselves. We operated with a wide definition of the sources of power and political interests, ranging from professional or other occupation, party politics and religion through social class to gender and ethnicity. The notion that power is important in governing bodies is a controversial idea, since some writers deny that political interests and power relations are at the heart of governance, seeing more neutral concepts like participation as forming the core of gubernatorial activities (Mahoney 1988, Sallis 1991).

The governors we studied were not in the main nationally or internationally known individual figures. However, many of them were powerful in three important senses. First, some exercised a good deal of local power within their communities, in one of several ways. They might be headteachers of schools and hence responsible for the education and wellbeing of many children, local councillors who helped shape local and municipal policies and services, business people who provided employment for many members of the local adult population and "urban gentry" (Brehony 1992, Deem 1993a), who were prominent in community affairs and voluntary organizations. Secondly, some governors had the power to provide and/or withhold information and, collectively, all possessed the power to influence the distribution of resources within schools and shape the philosophy of education operating in the school for which they were responsible. Finally, whereas we wanted to research governors, few of them actively wanted to be studied. As members of bodies that can legally restrict public access to their meetings, governors had the power to exclude us, either altogether, or from certain of their activities.

Within the context of the governing bodies themselves, a fourth set of power relations also made itself known to us. This included those who were prominent in the activities of the governing body by virtue of their frequent and sustained participation or their occupation of a key office. Headteachers, chairs of governing bodies, chairs of finance committees and representatives of the LEA were especially likely to fall within this subset. Also included in this category were those who exercised power over others because of their gender. These were usually men who, though not numerically dominant on every governing body, generally participated much more in meetings and were more likely to be members of key subcommittees like finance (Deem 1991). These men were usually also white. There was only one exception to this, at Birchdene primary school (all school names are pseudonyms), where there were frequent struggles and arguments between the white female head and a number of Asian governors and the head was driven to resign early because of the pressures she experienced. Social class was also a significant source of power; the majority of governors in our study were middle class and in professional, executive or managerial posts, which is consistent with the pattern found by national surveys (Jefferies & Streatfield 1989, Keys & Fernandes 1990). Even in schools with a predominantly working-class pupil intake, the social composition of their governing bodies rarely reflected this fully.

These various kinds of power relations affected our research in a variety of ways, both anticipated and unanticipated. We experienced no particular difficulties meeting and interviewing headteachers or chairs of governing bodies, although occasionally the other commitments of chairs made arranging to interview them rather time consuming.

At times we had to be careful that we were not over-identified with this group. All of the research team were familiar with and had worked in education, and until the end of 1991 I was myself chair of a secondary school governing body, though not one of those included in the study.

This was not the full extent of possible identification between members of the research team and the governors being researched. Seven of the chairpersons in the case-study organizations were governors who had been appointed by their LEA, and between 1988 and 1991 I was both an LEA-appointed governor and, for the first seven months of the pilot study, an elected councillor sitting on the education committee of an LEA. Another member of the team had previously served as an LEA governor and a further member was so appointed in the final stages of the research. Hence we found relatively few problems of access in relation to LEA-appointed governors, headteachers, chairs of governing bodies and teachers.

How we gained initial access to and acceptance by our case-study governing bodies is explained in the next section and in general this was negotiated without too many problems. We did, however, encounter resistance and access problems in relation to our assumed ideological opposition to Conservative government education reforms. Thus one Conservative governor who had missed the initial meeting of his governing body, where it was collectively agreed to grant the research team access to observe meetings, tried subsequently to prevent the research team having access on the grounds that ours was not a neutral study. The governor in question had seen an article by one of the research team that was very critical of the 1986 Education Act and the 1988 Education Reform Bill and believed we were about to conduct ideologically biased research. This is an interesting illustration (not the only one we encountered) of differing views about the epistemology, values and ethics of social science research being held by the research team as compared with some of those being researched. In this particular instance we were able to outwit the complainant, both because his governing body had already granted us access and because the local LEA officer to whom the complaint about us was sent happened to be a headteacher on secondment whom the research team knew well and who was very supportive of the research.

Getting to know business governors was more challenging than getting to know LEA-appointed governors, heads, teacher governors and chairpersons. Some business people, in common with the sole LEA governor already described, regarded the research team as an arm of the left-wing education lobby that the 1986 and 1988 Education Acts were intended to restrict, and others thought people in education were part of a different, inferior world compared with their own. The latter was usually described as the "real world", implying that ours was an ivory tower world for which they had little time or sympathy.

So far as powerful men in general were concerned, the only male researcher (the project co-director) probably encountered fewer problems with men than did the female members of the team. For instance, at one secondary school governing body meeting attended by me and my co-director, the male head in conversation with the latter referred to me as "your assistant", though for months he had been receiving correspondence and reports on the research indicating that I was a professor whereas the other co-director was a lecturer. However, there may be a more positive side to this apparent gender discrimination since it is also possible that men revealed more about their views on governing bodies to the women in the team than to the male co-director precisely because the women researchers were regarded as relatively unimportant and therefore entrusted with the kinds of confidences to which men's secretaries and wives might also be made party (Pringle 1989).

It was not only in situations where the researched seemed more powerful than the researchers that we encountered both positive and negative aspects of working with the locally powerful. Women governors, working-class governors and ethnic minority governors presented us with other kinds of difficulties, also to do with power. Although some of these governors had little or no power in Lukes' sense of the concept, they did have the power to resist our invasion of their lives. So, for instance, it might be expected that a largely female research team would have instant rapport with women governors; indeed, many writers on feminist research suggest this is likely to be so where female researchers meet with other women whose experiences might be assumed to be comparable (Roberts 1981, Bowles & Klein 1984). However, in a number of respects some of the women in the research team were very unlike some of the women governors in the study. The female researchers were highly educated and politically aware, had much committee experience and were confident and assertive. Although there may have been ideological differences between team members and those women in the study, including female heads, chairs of governors and women councillors, who most resembled us, in other respects we met on equal grounds. However, not all women governors could be described as highly educated, experienced in committees and assertive and confident. Some were amongst those we termed "silent" governors, who participated little in meetings and did not consent to being interviewed. Those who did sometimes apologized that we might find them uninteresting, something I also encountered when researching women's leisure (Deem 1986).

Access – who has the power?

Most contemporary empirical social research is likely to face problems of access. In some projects the major obstacles to access arise at the outset, but in any kind of extended, qualitative study there is always a problem of continuing to convince people of the legitimacy of the research activity. Long after securing access to our case-study governing bodies, we were faced with the problem of continual re-negotiation of access, as headteachers, chairs of governors, clerks and the membership of our governing bodies changed. It was not governing body meetings that raised access issues for us after the initial stages but access to subgroups and individuals, as well as documents relating to governing body activities.

The starting point of the research in the pilot stage was to gain access to sufficient governing bodies to make the study possible. We began by trying to find eight governing bodies in each of the two LEAs we had selected, but we did not use the same method of gaining access in both cases. In Northshire, we had existing contacts with a variety of LEA officers and schools and so it was possible to gain some "inside" information about which school governing bodies and heads might not be too overtly hostile to our presence at meetings. We were also able to find out how different governing bodies were perceived to operate, which was helpful since we did not want our cases to consist only of the supremely well organized and efficient. An approach was also made to the Chief Education Officer (CEO) in Northshire so that, if anyone should ever raise questions about our presence at governing body meetings, we could say it had been officially "cleared" at top level in the authority. This proved useful on one or two occasions. In Southshire LEA we initially had only one officer contact and never gained more than two or three because governing body work was not an area in which that LEA was very interventionist. We did not approach the CEO in Southshire, since it was felt to be unnecessary. We did have some contacts with individual schools in Southshire and with the LEA governor training officer, which enabled us to pick some likely contenders for the study. Other governing bodies were chosen from a list of Southshire schools in such a way that we had both primary and secondary sector representatives and a varied geographical/catchment area distribution. The night on which governing bodies held meetings was a consideration in both LEAs; with only two of us, and the need to fit the fieldwork round a mass of other commitments, we wanted to avoid having to attend several meetings at the same time.

In all we approached 17 schools at the pilot stage, adopting a similar strategy in each instance. The changes to governing bodies posed by the 1986 Act meant that all previous governing bodies had been dissolved in the summer of 1988, so that in September 1988, when we sought access, there was at best an acting chair until the first formal meeting. We sent a detailed explanatory letter to the headteacher and the acting chair, where one existed, and a copy for every governor. Accompanying this was a suggestion to heads and chairs that, our request be discussed at the first formal meeting, or before if possible, as some formal meetings were not scheduled until late in the autumn term. Where the formal meeting was to be held in September or October, we asked that unless otherwise notified beforehand, we be allowed to come to the meeting venue, remaining outside the door until a decision was reached on whether to permit access. Otherwise we would have missed the first vital formal meeting.

The question of gaining initial permission to observe governing bodies then was a crucial one for the study and very much bound up with issues of power. For some governing bodies the presence of an observer might have been felt to be threatening, perhaps because of the fear that the governors' lack of competence (however defined) might become public property and that the school would then suffer as a consequence. However, in all but two cases our strategy of gaining access was successful and we acquired 15 case-study governing bodies. Nevertheless, access had been negotiated only for a pilot study of at most three terms and was restricted to formal meetings only. When our ESRC funding commenced in February 1990, we did not encounter any significant problems in continuing our research with the 10 out of the 15 original cases that we decided to include in the main study, although we were at that stage able to take into account the reactions of the different governing bodies to our presence, so, while selecting the 10 on a range of criteria that we thought would be interesting theoretically, we also excluded one where we had encountered problems obtaining papers for meetings and where the head and chair of governors had not been very forthcoming.

What counts as access?

Having obtained initial access to governing bodies, in some cases we still needed further negotiations in order to secure access to documents and to subcommittees. As researchers interested in power we knew that we would also require access to individual governors and informal meetings. We were of course aware that, even so, some aspects of governing schools, including telephone calls and private conversations, were not going to be available to us in any circumstances. Later on in the study we were generally able to negotiate access to subcommittees without too much difficulty, though Knighton primary school remained reluctant to let us in on the grounds that the decision to establish subcommittees had been much contested by some governors and that our presence at subcommittees might cause the controversy to continue. There were also a number of grey areas in relation to access, including confidential items on the agendas of formal meetings, where the extent of our access varied. In some governing bodies we were asked to leave the room for these. In other governing bodies simply putting down our pens and folding our arms, thereby making it clear that we were not seeking to make notes about the confidential items, was held to be sufficient. Which researcher was present did not seem to affect exclusion from or inclusion in confidential discussions.

Another grey area was extra meetings of the governing body, arranged at short notice or outside the normal calendar. We sometimes did not hear about these until after they had taken place. On other occasions, as at Moatmeadow Secondary where a special meeting was arranged to discuss grant-maintained status, we knew that a meeting was to be held but could not persuade either the head or the chair to let us attend. In this instance it was argued that my presence in the research team, when I was at the time chair of governors at a GM school, could prejudice the outcome of the Moatmeadow meeting, even though we were quite happy to send a different researcher to that particular meeting.

It was in instances like this that the power of the researchers was pitted against the power of the governing body gatekeepers, and we did not always have the upper hand. Governing bodies had something useful to offer us. We had much less to offer in return – the prospect of future knowledge about governing schools, even in the form of a personalized presentation or a jargon-free report, was not a big incentive to those struggling to govern them then and there. We were always quite open about our intentions of observing how governors coped with the demands of the 1986 and 1988 Education Acts. In Gans' words we were trying to persuade people "that . . . research is useful and desirable" (Gans 1968: 309). In a political climate where research in education is seen as unnecessary or of no value, it was difficult to make too many other claims for the utility of what we were doing. Some governors were puzzled about why we wanted to attend so many of their meetings, but they generally accepted our argument that the research would be in some sense "useful", though to whom was left open. A minority of other governors believed that we were really left-wing activists in disguise as researchers, and that our intention was to destabilize and undermine the whole system of educational reforms of which governing bodies were but one facet. This notion of our power as researchers was certainly greatly exaggerated!

Researcher power

Our project thus raises some interesting issues about the balance of power between researchers and those being researched. These include the relationship that exists between researchers and researched, who has the power to do what and the nature of any bargains struck between the two partners. Another issue concerns the validity and power of the explanations and accounts of action put forward by researchers vis-à-vis those put forward by actors participating in the study. Furthermore, research on the policy process raises questions not only about power relationships per se but also about the political and economic context of research, especially if researchers take a different perspective on policy from some or all of those whom they are researching. The last was an issue for a number of those governors whom we researched, who believed in the need for radical education reform, thought that power should pass from the producers of education to the consumers and assumed that anyone who worked in education lived in an unreal world and had nothing of much value to say about anything. Potentially such governors might contest our accounts of the governing process, question the extent to which we were detached observers or cast doubts on the value of qualitative research. Indeed, some views of this kind emerged in some of the interviews we conducted. However, the holding of such views did not appear to have any very significant impact on the data we collected.

In part the issue about who holds power in the research process is dependent on the social location of those being researched as well as of those doing the research. This was a very complex affair in our governor research. Despite the relative homogeneity of governor recruitment, governing bodies may contain members of both dominant and subordinate groups, since schools differ in the social areas and groups from which they draw pupils as well as in relation to the kinds of communities within which those schools are located. Thus we encountered working-class as well as middle-class, female as well as male and Asian and African Caribbean as well as white, governors. Where research is conducted only on oppressed groups, the power differentials being dealt with may be more easily identified. But such research is in itself limited, since in order fully to research the oppressed it is necessary also to research the oppressors.

Recognizing that a problem about power relations exists in the research process is widely accepted. Views about strategies for dealing with this situation are more divergent. Thus, for example, a number of feminist writers have raised concerns about the possibility of a power imbalance between researchers and those they seek to research, seeing researchers holding the upper hand. Such analyses, especially in the early 1980s, were often accompanied by an argument that researchers needed to overcome this imbalance (Roberts 1981, Stanley & Wise 1983, Bowles & Klein 1984). More recently the debate has taken on new forms. Thus some postmodern feminist writers have suggested that it is not possible to use social theory at any significant level of abstraction in order to explain female oppression (or presumably any other form of oppression) nor is it possible to provide any representational relationship between reality and textual accounts of it (Lather 1991). Stanley & Wise (1993) further argue that there is nothing distinctively postmodern or poststructuralist about such a critique, which is not dissimilar to those they first presented, from a different theoretical perspective, in 1983 (Stanley & Wise 1983). The postmodern and cognate positions (including that of Stanley & Wise) would make it difficult to undertake the kind of research that has been described here.

What kind of research would be possible on the basis of such positions? Stanley & Wise (1993) proffer the view that theoretical accounts of research "should be continuous with the experience of the conclusions, interpretations and analyses of the researcher as the agent in constructing them" (p. 201), thereby rejecting both representational views of research that redescribe "post hoc a slice of social reality" (p. 201), and interpretational views that subordinate lay accounts of reality to "scientific" ones. It is not difficult to agree with Stanley and Wise that we should make apparent the role of the researcher in constructing the interpretations and analyses of research; this is clearly an important part of the research process widely recognized by qualitative researchers. Nor is there any difficulty in relation to our project in rejecting representational views of research. However comprehensive a descriptive account of qualitative research is, that description is always a selection from reality and therefore in some sense interpretational. Thus, even when we described what governors did or said, that description was analyzed from a particular point of view and viewed through a certain framework. However, rejecting both representational research and interpretational research does not appear to leave many alternatives. Indeed, interpretational research does not seem to preclude making the research and knowledge process open to the scrutiny of others. But do we not need to consider which others we are talking about? Audiences for research such as the project described here vary from teachers to members of political parties and research funding council evaluators; what is appropriately laid open to one audience would be inappropriate for another, especially in contexts where competition for research funds is intense and where some regard criticism of current government policies as inappropriate behaviour by researchers (which happened for example when one of the research team presented a paper critical of some aspects of governor activity at a governor pressure group meeting in the presence of a DES official).

There are, of course, several ways in which the researcher role can be made more "vulnerable" to the needs and interests of those being researched (Stanley & Wise 1993). Thus Bowles & Klein (1984) suggest that vulnerability can be ensured by not excluding the researched from the design of research, though of course this can be done by any researcher, with any philosophical position on research, using any method. Thus, we could have consulted governors about our question-naire or interview schedule design, or asked them to vet our publica-tions and accounts, especially those dealing with issues about racism and sexism. We did undertake some consultation with some governors in our piloting of questionnaires and interview questions, though to have consulted all those we were researching would have been too time consuming. However, to ask governors in our study to vet our draft pub-lications would have raised important questions about our political and academic autonomy and our right to be critical of the status quo. Since we did not name either governors or their schools in our published work we felt we had some freedom of manoeuvre in this respect. In addition, in relation to issues of racism and sexism as well as the efficacy of the new models of school governance, sending draft publications to gover-nors in the study might have curtailed our access to those governing bodies and prevented us saying anything about important aspects of power relations in governing bodies. That is not to say that we hid the details of our research findings from the governing bodies concerned. On the contrary, we drew their attention to the short articles on the study that we had published in the popular educational press, offered them talks and presentations, invited them to a conference on governors that we ran, and sent them regular lists of our more scholarly publications, together with the offer to provide them with copies of any of these that interested them (only one person took up this offer). However, to do more than this would have been immensely problematic. We were already fairly vulnerable as researchers in a contentious area of contem-porary educational policy; to have increased this vulnerability still fur-ther might well have resulted in us acquiring less knowledge about the process of governing schools rather than more.

Of course, as Stanley & Wise (1983, 1993) suggest, it is important for researchers to make use of their own experiences. We did this where it seemed appropriate: as white middle-class women and men, as femi-nists, as Labour Party members, as governors, as teachers and, in my case, as a local councillor. But we were not business men or women, we were not headteachers, we were not parents, we were not black or Asian or working class and, even where we shared some experiences with gov-ernors in the study, we were not governors of those schools. Indeed, we had to be careful not to over-identify with those governors whose experiences most closely matched our own, since this might have resulted in reducing our credibility, and therefore access, to other governors with whom we shared fewer experiences. This happened to an extent anyway. We found it difficult to arrange to interview certain governors, some governors missed a lot of meetings or said nothing in them, there were always people with whom casual conversations never took place and there were those who did not return our questionnaires. However, if, as Stanley & Wise (1993) suggest, the only kinds of research that are epistemologically and ontologically valid are those that result in us finding out only that which we already knew, it would hardly have required four years of very intensive fieldwork. There is also the more complex but related question of whether anyone, let alone us, "knew" what would happen as lay governors took over more and more of the responsibility from LEAs for setting the administrative and policy parameters of schools. Of course we had hunches and ideas about this, but, as in all genuinely inquisitive research, some of those hunches (for example that many governors would resign once they realized the extent of their obligations) proved wrong, while others (for instance the view that governors would cope with their responsibilities by concentrating fully on only some of them) proved more fruitful.

Empowerment and qualitative research

Ideas about the empowerment of those researched have often been closely linked to analyses of the unequal power relation between researcher and researched (Roberts 1981, Bowles & Klein 1984, Troyna 1993). Thus, it is suggested by these writers, from the standpoint of relatively powerless groups including women and ethnic minorities, that the point of research is to bring about change and that this can be achieved, in part at least, by ensuring that research empowers those whom it studies. By providing people with critiques of existing practices and policies, they can develop better ones or at least challenge the status quo. Leaving aside concerns about whether considerations of difference amongst categories, such as women or ethnic minorities, mean that simple assumptions about powerlessness do not apply across the board, there is also on occasion an apparent slippage between thinking that the outcomes of research can critique the status quo and imagining that the critique will have any effect upon that status quo. Here many research-ers are also relatively powerless.

There is also another problem about the discussion of empowerment: it is rare to hear anything about disempowerment, yet for every person involved in the research process that the researcher may wish to empower, there are also likely to be some whom they wish to disempower. The latter is particularly likely when research involves socially, politically or economically powerful groups. The ground rules for both empowerment and the wish to disempower are unlikely to be the same, and yet the issue of whether the researcher has the capability to bring about change is invoked in both instances.

The notion of a relationship between political intent and research goals has been criticised strongly by Hammersley (1992a, 1992b), who suggests that the integrity and validity of social research as an end in itself is impugned by attaching political purpose and values to it. How-ever, Hammersley's views on this are not widely shared. Ramazanoglu (1992) says of Hammersley's critique of feminist methods: "What femi-nist thought and practice have done is both to empower women and to problematise yet again what we mean by knowledge, reason, objectivity and validity . . . Hammersley . . . approaches sociological research with-out a theory of power" (Ramazanoglu 1992: 209). Ramazanoglu's com-ments are important ones, especially her arguments about the importance of recognizing the place of power in research. But can social research empower people, as opposed to merely adding to the stock of knowledge in a given society?

To a large extent this depends on the purpose of the research. The notion of empowerment is often defined at a low level of abstraction, to include only those researched (Lather 1991, Stanley and Wise 1993). This kind of empowerment was never part of our intentions. We wished to arrive at some assessment of an aspect of current educational policy we were both curious and about which we also had some misgivings. We did not see individual governors as a group to whom the research might offer some powers to transform schools, partly because we were scepti-cal about this possibility anyway but also because, given the timespan of the research, such an aim appeared unrealistic. By the time our findings appeared many of the governors whom we researched would have moved on. However, we did want our research to inform national and perhaps international debates about the role of lay people in the admin-istration of publicly funded schools (Deem 1994).

Other researchers may have more immediate political and social purposes than these. Thus Troyna (1993) argues that his research on multicultural and anti-racist education policy "figured prominently in the framing of anti-racist struggles, especially in the local arena" (p. 12) and helped to set up a campaign for change directed at a local education authority. It would be hard to make similar claims for our research, although we do see it as having some wider significance than simply the collection of knowledge about 10 governing bodies and how they operated over a four-year period. We have tried to feed the findings of the study into the wider educational policy debate and on occasions this may have resulted in the empowerment of particular social categories, rather than individuals. One example was the 1991 Department of Education and Science consultation about whether teachers should be debarred from standing for election as parent governors (Deem & Brehony 1991). The second example, which has not so far resulted in any empowerment of anyone, has been interventions in discussions about what form future governance of education should take (Deem 1993b, Deem & Brehony 1993b, Brehony & Deem 1993).

The issues of disempowerment also arose in our study. Amongst our case-study governing bodies it was on occasion difficult to resist intervening (for instance, when at several governing bodies teacher governors were excluded from taking part in discussions about the pay of the headteacher and in the debate about selective and comprehensive schooling at Moatmeadow and Cotswold), but if we had done so we could not have claimed to be attempting any kind of coherent and detached assessment or analysis of what was happening. Of course our presence at meetings had some effect on governors; it would be naïve to believe otherwise. But we did not "take sides" in disputes and we did not feel it was desirable, or indeed possible, actually in the meetings to empower or otherwise assist those who felt silenced or powerless. Equally, the presence of a researcher was not sufficient to disempower those who thought that schools were a waste of public money and out of touch with the real world and needed to become more like businesses.

Two governing bodies where our decision not to intervene was particularly hard for us to sustain were Birchdene, a primary school, and Cotswold, a mixed comprehensive. At Birchdene, which had a high percentage of ethnic minority pupils but an almost entirely white teaching staff, a number of ethnic minority governors were locked in struggle with a white headteacher over such issues as mother tongue teaching and pupil achievement. The meetings were, in our view, often chaotic, with shouting, difficulty in sticking to an agenda and many disagreements. However, we recognize that some of the participants may have seen the meetings as their only opportunity to challenge what they defined as white racism; interference from us would have been seen as another example of this. But in any case the concerns and debates were not constructed by either us or the governors in such a way that we could easily identify an oppressed group and oppressors. Although there may have been genuine anxieties about the achievements of ethnic minority pupils at Birchdene, there was also a strong possibility (in our view) that the attitude of some governors on this issue was also a way of making the female white headteacher feel uncomfortable. This in turn seemed based on sexism as well as issues to do with racism. There was little we could do to ease the disputes at Birchdene, which reached such proportions that no clerk would agree to take the minutes, so that the proceedings had to be taped, and which finally brought about the early retirement of the head. We were not a party to all the issues at stake and would have been denied access altogether if we had attempted to intervene. Surprisingly, we were never excluded from formal meetings at Birchdene (and were, in due course, also allowed to observe the appointment of a new head) nor did our presence appear to have any ameliorating effect on the behaviour of some governors there.

At Cotswold, with a mainly white working-class pupil intake, the scenario was different but equally intractable. The head, chair of governors and a number of other governors were strong supporters of comprehensive education for all children, whatever their attainment level, though this did not mean that they attached no importance to academic achievement. However, two further governors, for a while joined by a third, were opposed to comprehensive education and spent their time at the governing body meetings pointing out the failings of the school and of comprehensives generally. Outside the meetings they used their position to promote the cause of selective education and to bring to the attention of the public at large (as they saw it) the poor standards of education and exam results found in comprehensives. At this school, too, it was not possible to empower the group with whom we identified most – the supporters of comprehensives – any more than it was possible to disempower the proponents of selective schooling. A clear taking-up of sides by us would have meant either that we would have been denied access to the meetings or that some governors would have refused to assist us in the research. It would also have constituted undue interference in the processes of governing at that school, a position that we found ethically as well as politically unacceptable.

Conclusion

The chapter has concentrated on three main issues – the relative power of researcher and researched in gaining and maintaining access to research locations, the balance of power between researchers and researched in the research process and outcomes, and the issue of whether research on contemporary educational policy can empower or disempower those being researched rather than simply contributing to future debates about policy. It has been argued here that, in research on locally powerful people, the balance of power rarely lies with the researcher. This is not to suggest that all our governors were locally powerful; variations in gender, social class background and ethnicity helped to ensure this was not always so. But, even with governors who were relatively powerless in their role as school governors, it was not always evident that they were in a similar position vis-à-vis the research team. We could not simply read off from the social status and group membership of governors their likely views about education, the more so if they seldom spoke during meetings and did not agree to be interviewed by us. In investigating a politically contentious set of education reforms in a critical way, we implicitly, if not explicitly, set ourselves against current prevailing ideologies advocating greater exposure of the education system to the market. Furthermore, because our research was not "official" research for the Department for Education, we could not claim any legitimacy in the eyes of those who supported government policy on school reform. We did, however, claim some legitimacy in relation to those who worked within education or had a notion of school governance as benevolent service to the community rather than as a way of consumers of education claiming their individual rights (Brehony 1992, Deem forthcoming).

Any endeavour to intervene in the affairs of the governing bodies we were studying would have either resulted in us being denied future access or impugned the credibility of the research team in the eyes of some or all of those governors being researched. Both of these would have affected what we saw as the validity of our study, that it offered a description, albeit a selected and interpreted description, of the processes of governing schools during a period of considerable change and reform, which in turn allowed some analysis of the wider policy context in which those reforms and changes were set. Our analysis may offer to both the currently locally powerful and the currently disempowered some tools for change and/or resistance, but the research described here did not and could not offer direct empowerment of such individuals where they were governors of the schools being studied. Our project, as indeed is the case with all social science research, had its deficiencies as well as its strengths, but the nature of what we were studying, the political and social context in which it was set and the dominant views about educational researchers, all ensured that the power to change either policy or individuals was never significantly within our grasp.

Acknowledgements

Thanks to Kevin Brehony and Mary Maynard for their comments on the first draft of this chapter.

References

Bowles, G. & R. D. Klein (eds) 1984. *Theories of women's studies*. London: Routledge.

Brehony, K. J. 1992. "Active citizens": The case of school governors. *International Studies in the Sociology of Education* 2 (2), 199–217.

Brehony, K. J. & R. Deem 1993. Democratising school governance. Paper to Fabian Society Education group, London, July.

Deem, R. 1986. *All work and no play: The sociology of women and leisure*. Milton Keynes: Open University Press.

Deem, R. 1990. The reform of school governing bodies: The power of the consumer over the producer? In *The 1988 Education Reform Act: Its origins and implications*, M. Flude & M. Hammer (eds). London: Falmer Press.

Deem, R. 1991. Governing by gender? School governing bodies after the Education Reform Act. In *Gender, power and sexuality*, P. Abbott & C. Wallace (eds). London: Macmillan.

Deem, R. 1993a. Education reform and school governing bodies in England: Old dogs, new tricks or new dogs, new tricks? In *Managing the effective school*, M. Preedy (ed.), London: Paul Chapman.

Deem, R. 1993b. Governing schools in the 1990s – autonomy or collaboration? In *School co-operation: New forms of governance*, S. Ranson & J. Tomlinson (eds). London: Longman.

Deem, R. 1994. Free marketeers or good citizens? Education policy and lay participation in the administration of schools. *British Journal of Educational Studies* **42** (1).

Deem, R. forthcoming School governing bodies – public concerns or private interests? In *Accountability and control in educational settings*, D. Scott (ed.). London: Cassell.

Deem, R. & K. J. Brehony 1991. A labour of love. *Times Educational Supplement*, 21 June, 23.

Deem, R. & K. J. Brehony 1993a. Consumers and education professionals in the organisation and administration of schools: partnership or conflict? *Educational Studies* **19** (3), 339–55.

Deem, R. & K. J. Brehony 1993b. Governing bodies and local education authorities: who shall inherit the earth? *Local Government Studies* **19** (1), 56–76.

Gans, H. J. 1968. The participant observer as a human being: Observations on the personal aspects of fieldwork. In *Institutions and the person*, H. S. Becker, B. Geer, D. Riesman & R. S. Weiss (eds). Chicago: Aldine.

Hammersley, M. 1992a. *What's wrong with ethnography?* London: Routledge.

Hammersley, M. 1992b. On feminist methodology. *Sociology* **26** (2), 187–206.

Jefferies, G. & D. Streatfield 1989. *The reconstitution of school governing bodies*. Slough: NFER.

Keys, W. & C. Fernandes 1990. *A survey of school governing bodies*. Slough: NFER.

Lather, P. 1991. *Getting smart*. New York: Routledge.

Lukes, S. (ed) 1986. *Power*, Oxford: Blackwell.

Mahoney, T. 1988. *Governing schools: Powers, issues and practice*. London: Macmillan.

Pringle, R. 1989. *Secretaries talk*. London: Verso.

Rabinov, P. 1984. *The Foucault reader*. London: Penguin.

Ramazanoglu, C. 1992. Male reason versus female employment. *Sociology* **26** (2), 207–12

Roberts, H. (ed.) 1981. *Doing feminist research*. London: Routledge.

Sallis, J. 1991. *School governors: your questions answered*. London: Hodder & Stoughton.

Stanley, L & S. Wise 1983. *Breaking out*. London: Routledge & Kegan Paul.

Stanley, L. & S. Wise 1993. *Breaking out again: feminist ontology and epistemology*. London: Routledge.

Troyna, B. 1993. Critical social research and education policy. Paper presented at "New Directions in Educational Policy Sociology" conference, Southampton, March.

PART IV

Historical perspectives

CHAPTER ELEVEN

Research perspectives on the World Bank

Phillip W. Jones

Introduction

If we are concerned with the exercise of power in education, a central consideration must be the influence of ideas that shape views of educational theory, policy and practice. These ideas and views are often local in origin, and tightly bound up with local tradition and convention and the exercise of power on a domestic level. But in the world as we currently know and understand it, local factors cannot be viewed in isolation from the outworking of agendas that are global (or at least regional) in scope. In analyzing influential ideas about education, we need to understand something of the background to them, their origins and their promoters, whether their background is domestic or international.

Around the world, processes of educational policy formation reveal not just the combined influence of local and international forces. There is often a very real tension between them, perhaps as they compete for dominance. This is commonplace in many developing countries, struggling to consolidate the achievement of political independence through the building up of freedom in a variety of dimensions – cultural, intellectual, technological and economic – usually in the name of national development. Often what we see is a battle between ideas. At the very least, ideas reveal something of the exercise of power, if only its justification or rationalization. More usually, if we can learn something about the origins of influential ideas and the motivations of their purveyors, a new dimension in our understanding of education might open up.

INTRODUCTION

When a particular educational imperative appears on the scene, one that is either irresistible in nature or inescapable because of the power of its promoters, we might well enquire as to both its origins and its pathway. Such an imperative might be appearing, in fact, in many parts of the world at once, and it is worth pondering if this might be more than an accident of history. Indeed, why is it that in many dispersed and disparate parts of the world we see homogeneity in educational decision-making? Differences of local tradition, convention and politics would normally suggest a far greater diversity in educational developments than we are currently witnessing world-wide.

A starting point, however limited its potential to explain all, can be those actors on the global educational scene who admit an institutional role in exerting global influence on education. Prominent here must be the range of international and regional organizations that include in their mandates the development of education and the promotion of educational change. Their mandates, of course, might be far broader than education alone, but might find in educational change both a means and a sign of effective promotion of those mandates.

The work of international organizations in education is part of the process whereby the pattern of educational change around the world is being increasingly influenced by global, not local, agendas. In accordance with these agendas, governments can be seen to be behaving in remarkably similar ways when addressing educational policy. They pose similar questions about education, and emergent policy responses bear striking resemblance from place to place. Climates of opinion about education that originate locally might well maintain their customary diversity, but those operating as international phenomena, by contrast, seem decidedly more homogeneous in nature. The standardization of education – and mass schooling in particular – is a global trend of considerable force in our time, and is of enormous cultural and political significance as the world approaches the achievement of universal schooling.

Whether structural or cultural explanations are sought for the emergence of global agendas in education, the influence of international organizations bears on each. The organizations of relevance are numerous and varied, their mandates touching on economic, cultural, technological, intellectual and development co-operation. Those within the framework of the United Nations often have their work summed up under the themes of peace, human rights and development, three interrelated aims promoted through a bewildering array of international arrangements and programmes. I have described their educational work and significance elsewhere (Jones 1993), and have examined two agencies of direct relevance in detail, Unesco (Jones 1988) and the World Bank (Jones 1992). In Unesco, we find an agency whose poverty of financial resources forces it to rely for influence on the intellectual clout of its arguments. In the World Bank, we find a complex agency whose influence stems in a variety of ways from its financial might, the conditions attached to its loans, the impact of its projects and its attempts to exert direct influence on the educational policy process of governments the world over.

Access for research purposes

Many publications about the World Bank begin with introductions lamenting the difficulties faced by researchers in gaining the kinds of access to the Bank deemed necessary to address specified concerns. Such laments indicate just how secretive the Bank can be, even by Washington standards. The question of access to large organizations is both important and complex, but the persistent and imaginative researcher can be well rewarded by a careful approach to the challenges of access.

In my case, I approached by letter the director of the Bank's education department, and outlined what I hoped to do and what I intended to do with my findings. The noncommittal response I received was nevertheless warm, and I was welcome to go to Washington, meet senior education officials in the Bank and, presumably, get looked over. The necessary approvals were forthcoming: the timeframe for my in-house research was agreed upon, arrangements made for a pass in order to obtain physical access to Bank buildings, and arrangements made to make my work comfortable and efficient. An office was provided with good furniture, telephone and, importantly, access to photocopying, the library, archives, project files and Bank staff. Much of this was unprecedented. Furthermore, I was left to my own devices to shape my research in my own way. No attempt was made by the Bank or any official to colour my research or mould its findings. The Bank made no request to vet or veto the draft of my book. In fact, the senior official responsible for determining the fate of my request for access was emphatic on the desirability of a "warts and all" account of Bank work in education.

My own experience indicates that considerable discretion rests with individual department heads within the World Bank for granting or denying access to researchers. Once access is granted, however, it should be noted that the Bank itself has produced a document outlining its rules for outside researchers. In my case, it was never referred to me. I came across it in the course of my research, but nevertheless felt bound to abide by its provisions.

One constraint I faced was of a major kind. Bank standing rules insist that all Bank documentation is "for official use only" and there are blanket bans on its unauthorized reproduction or release. The Bank sees this as essential in its often sticky relationships with its borrowers, i.e. governments, and with the international financial community. Access on my part to Bank documentation posed no problem to the Bank; the issue was what use I would make of that documentation. The approach I proposed was acceptable to the Bank – that I would resist extended citation from Bank documents, that I would identify individual documents and their authors in a vague way, and that my final book draft would be available to the Bank for checking for errors of fact and areas where the Bank might wish to point out any disagreement with my analysis or conclusions. In several important senses, I entered into a relationship with the Bank that was partly codified in written agreements but more left to mutual understandings, governed by my willingness to abide by my word, my sense of fairness and a researcher's code of ethical practice. Many occasions have arisen, particularly when writing or speaking about the Bank, when I have had to invoke those understandings and stem the desire to go beyond them. There has been an academic price for this, of course, in that I am not always in a position to provide the detailed referencing, documentation, citations or other evidence conventionally required in scholarly work. As far as Bank documents are concerned, I needed to forge a trade-off between the option of unrestrained access to the documentation I felt I needed to see (if only for "background") and scholarly conventions of documenting my argument and conclusions.

The issue of access to such international organizations as the World Bank is a major one for researchers. We all have our own style of working, our own approach to methodology and our own agendas and questions. For me, the overarching point to be made about access is this: as a researcher, why is access needed and what benefits is it intended to provide? International organizations are most likely to be respectful of researchers who come to them already well informed, who are constructive in their pitch and who do not seek to embark on vague fishing expeditions. They favour specific, focused investigation. A researcher seeking access needs to be able to come down to detail about what particular kinds of access are needed, and why. Access is a dimension of the broader issue of research purpose, design and methodology, and is inseparable from it. Until a researcher can give precise answers to fundamental questions about the need for access, then requests for access are probably premature and best left to a later stage.

Researching institutional diversity – which World Bank?

The World Bank is not the only large, complex organization of interest to educational researchers. All of us at some stage will be interested in what goes on inside educational bureaucracies. Should issues of access be resolved, and on acceptable terms, the question remains: which part or parts of the organization are relevant to my research agenda and how can I know?

In the case of the World Bank, I quickly discovered that this complex agency was several organizations bundled up into one. Some parts exist comfortably with others; some appear to function in marked opposition to others. Even within a Bank department, staff can be pitched against one another, as they vie for policy supremacy, project approvals, visibility, career opportunities, ideological ascendancy, or whatever. Large organizations, especially of an intergovernmental, intersectoral and multipurpose kind, are far from monochrome or homogeneous, and the wise researcher needs to take account of this and explore the implications.

There are many options open in this area of access and research focus. One closed door might be more than adequately made up for by another. At any rate, good research inevitably requires the cross-checking of information and other data, coming at the same issue from as many angles as possible, checking and comparing continuously and as a matter of course. No single, objective reality is there to be discovered, and the real story is one of how competing and contrasting perspectives interact and intersect. In the World Bank, on major as well as minor issues, Bank staff rarely agree, even if the Bank itself has published an official, straightforward line.

I have mentioned that the World Bank is a multifaceted organization, pursuing its objectives through a range of means. Those researching the Bank need, as a result, to be aware of and sensitive to this range. A piece of data or evidence about one function might easily be misapplied to another. Tension exists, for example, between the banking functions of the Bank and functions more to do with development assistance. Some staffers, for example, see themselves as bankers and loan officers, reflecting the culture of the financial world, while others carry cultural baggage that is more commonly seen in bilateral aid or international welfare agencies. Where each sits in the Bank determines the view of things adopted, and this is of profound significance to the researcher conducting interviews and assessing internal Bank documentation. One needs to get into the mind-set of the interviewee or writer, understanding the underlying motivation and perspective in each instance. For example, it is fascinating to get hold of a Bank policy paper, and then unearth the many drafts written along the way, examining the comments made by officials in their various capacities, with their own agendas, preoccupations and institutional turf to protect. The successive drafts, frequently enough, are more revealing than the final version!

Another example has to do with the Bank's in-house research work. A department in the Bank might initiate a piece of educational research, setting out to demonstrate the validity of a particular argument, policy option or project design. The underlying purpose might not be straightforward, however. It might be to persuade a government to alter a loan application in a way more acceptable to the Bank. Or it might be to undermine the policy influence of another section of the Bank by calling into question some prevailing policy orthodoxy. Or there might be an ideological or intellectual dispute under way (e.g. between proponents of cost–benefit analysis and manpower planning). Or there might be personal rivalries between Bank staffers, or a desire to discredit policy positions adopted in earlier times by one's predecessors. In every instance in which the Bank has embarked on educational research, there can be found in-house dynamics such as these. Bank research has always had a story behind it. This is another example of what I mean by institutional diversity, whereby things are not so straightforward or just what they seem to be. Just as educational power around the world is exercised through a battle for ideas, so too do such battles for ideas rage within the World Bank.

My own interest in the Bank concerned the historical development of its policies on education, how these were put into project loan form and how the Bank reshaped its policies as it looked back on completed projects. In a nutshell, my research was about how the Bank's power and influence have been purveyed in the realm of ideas. The Bank itself would agree with the proposition that its most important single function is to influence government policies around the world. The following are the more prominent of the means it adopts to achieve this: furnishing very large foreign exchange loans and credits for specific, identified purposes; attaching to loans and credits side-conditions (covenants) that act as leverage on borrower governments, principally to adopt policies laid down by the Bank; direct advice through conventional patterns of technical assistance; and direct involvement in the world of ideas through research, published policy positions on issues of direct concern to governments, and influencing the work of other development assistance and financial organizations. The point I am making is that the Bank works in numerous and complex ways and on a very large scale. Those researching the Bank can easily find themselves missing the wood for the trees, or looking at the wrong trees.

Documentation

I have already touched on issues of gaining general access to in-house documentation and the handling of confidential papers. Of further concern are issues of interpretation and assessing the significance or reliability of printed materials.

International organizations such as the World Bank produce vast quantities of printed material. Most researchers will find that the problem of having too much documentation is more likely to arise than the problem of having too little. It is in the scheme of things to end up with a mass of items, each piece requiring judgements concerning its import for the research task at hand. At the same time, most documents are of some interest, as they display something of in-house thinking, possibly of prevailing climates of opinion, or personal views held by staffers, or embryonic policies yet to find their fullest expression.

In each instance, I find it constructive to determine why a document was produced. Its fundamental purpose will reveal much about it. Was it a definitive statement of institutional policy, carefully drafted and meticulously worded? Was it more speculative, exploring some policy options? Was it produced as an information piece, and for whom and for what reason? Was it framed for public consumption? And so on. Officials of such agencies as the World Bank rightly display indignation when documents are seized on by outside commentators as official statements of policy when they are manifestly not. I cannot overstate, from my own experience, the importance of getting under the surface of documentation, probing and analyzing the story behind its production.

Documents designed for public information need to be handled with particular care. In general terms, they tend to reduce complex policy and/or technical matters to a simple and unsubtle level. I can recall many instances of policy and programme failures celebrated in official publications, at a time when in-house papers were damning. By no means all public documents are cover-ups, but they do tend to put a good gloss on things, and a wise researcher will seek out (through other documents or interviews) the full story.

In the World Bank we have an organization that succeeds in achieving a high level of discipline among its staff. Even on the most contentious issues, once the Bank has formed a policy its staffers are expected, and seem to manage, to toe the official line. Various points emerge from this. One is that on policy matters of tortuous complexity about economic and development policy (about which governments and experts agonize) the World Bank can often appear to be decisive, issuing policy statements and other documentation that boldly appear to solve complex matters. What official Bank documentation fails to reflect, of course, are the profoundly interesting pathways taken inside the Bank to achieve such policy certainty. The vehemence and vigour of debate and disputation in the Bank are considerable, to an extent and depth quite invisible in policy documents.

The secrecy surrounding much of the Bank's operations and decision-making is by no means the end of the matter. The World Bank, as a specialized agency of the United Nations, is an accountable organization. In its case, it is governed by a board of governors representing its member governments. Between annual meetings of the board of governors, there are the weekly meetings of the executive directors. The EDs are nominees of member governments (usually senior officials of finance ministries), approve all loans and projects and receive reports on their progress. I go into this detail because the executive directors have established their own evaluation unit – the Operations Evaluation Department (OED) – which is detached from the Bank bureaucracy and which reports directly to the board. OED project reports are the formal evaluations of Bank projects, and are more or less in the public domain, i.e. to the extent that the EDs and their governments are prepared to release them. OED assessments not only address individual loans and projects; they also look to broader themes, such as the quality of Bank work in a particular sector (there was an influential OED report on education in 1978), or the Bank's relationship over time with a particular country. Impact studies appear from time to time. These reports, in particular, tend to find their way to bilateral aid agencies and other UN agencies, and can frequently be obtained through them. In fact, there is a good deal of document exchange among international organizations, opening up a range of avenues for researchers.

With the World Bank, project failures are the norm, given the nature of the business. No project lives up to the expectations announced at its inception. The Bank, however, usually has in its borrowing governments (which implement Bank projects) a convenient scapegoat for failures of implementation, most frequently citing problems of poor management or lack of commitment. Experienced readers of Bank documents find in-house "codewords" or argot that might point to lapses at the Bank level but that might be glossed over by the general reader. For example, if a document indicates an official belief that "policy approach A" has been demonstrated to be particularly effective, evidence must exist somewhere as to why "policy approaches B and C" are regarded as less effective, even if one would never expect to come across a potentially public document outlining the deficiencies of B and C. Much needs to be inferred.

Interviews

A good researcher will be willing to come at his or her object of research from as many angles as possible, placing no absolute reliance on any one form or piece of evidence. Cross-checking is a must, and here the relationship between printed and oral evidence assumes importance. A dry, one-dimensional document can come to life in conversation with its author, especially if that conversation opens up means of interpretation not apparent to the reader.

It is not at all difficult to gain personal access to international civil servants. Their work embodies the expectation that they are ready to explain institutional policy and programmes. The real issue is a matter of gaining maximum benefit from each interview, and getting beneath the surface of the official line.

With such disciplined organizations as the World Bank, the interviewing researcher will quickly discover the official line – all staffers will know what it is and how to talk about and around it. In particular, general questions will elicit general answers, but not always! Although I would always advocate the use of highly specific, well-informed questions, much can also be gained from the occasional question of a highly general kind. In the context of a highly structured and organized interview, a controlled performance by an official can become a little unsettled by a surprisingly general question, eliciting highly interesting "background" or "off-the-record" information.

Interviews take many different forms. They might be carefully structured or be very loose. They might be recorded on tape. The interviewer might write furiously during the interview, or immediately afterwards. Many factors will determine the forms adopted, but I consider it absolutely essential – and a matter of research ethics – to come to explicit understandings with those interviewed. Any person interviewed in an official capacity is fully entitled to know what use will be made of their remarks, how their statements are being preserved and how they might appear subsequently. A background briefing must remain as such; a taped conversation whose transcript was promised to the interviewee for editing must be handled as agreed; a promise to preserve anonymity must be scrupulously honoured; an undertaking to furnish the resulting paragraph in the interviewer's thesis, book or paper should not be forgotten with the passage of time.

Interviews are all about the relationship between two persons. The interviewee is not an impersonal cog in some large bureaucracy, but is a person who deserves to be treated with all human dignity. The interviewer who constantly complains that they are getting nothing more than dry, bureaucratic responses from subject after subject might well be shaping that result by their own approach. A genuine interest in people is a splendid tool in exploring one's interest in an organization and its work.

I am convinced, perhaps contrary to a good deal of prevailing organizational theory, that the characteristics of organizations – even large and complex ones – derive in large measure from the characteristics and qualities of the people within them. For my part, I try to learn about the people I interview as people, not merely as functionaries. This becomes pertinent when considering the interviewing of persons with whom one might have significant differences of viewpoint or opinion, or persons who are members of organizations about whose work one has major reservations. It is rarely impossible to suspend judgement until all the facts are in! Because I consider interviews to be essentially a matter of relationship, there is considerable room for how precisely that relationship is defined, especially in terms of how explicit a researcher needs to be in terms of the perspective adopted for the research. Often, very difficult and complex terrain is traversed in interviews, and straightforward answers to questions of values are often elusive. Again, we all have a great deal to learn from each other as people, not least from those with whom we do or might disagree. In particular, I frequently need to remind myself not to pre-judge persons interviewed, especially in value or ideological terms. I need to be patient, not to rush to judgement, to be open to them and to respect not only their opinions but also their professional and career commitments. Again and again, I am impressed by persons of very great integrity who struggle daily with weighty matters in complex organizational and political settings, persons I would never have identified as such had I closed my mind to them before even meeting them.

Conclusion

Each of my remarks needs to be understood from the perspective I have adopted in examining the World Bank. My angle was to get inside the Bank and explore policy formation and review within it. Others seeking to examine the Bank and to assess its work might well adopt a different viewpoint, not least researching in detail the story of Bank involvement in education within developing countries themselves. More than 100 countries have borrowed foreign currencies for well over 400 projects, each project being large, costly, protracted and ambitious. Many projects merit a book in themselves, and each country's educational relationship with the Bank is well worth researching in detail.

Researching such a powerful organization as the World Bank involves the primary challenge of distinguishing its blunt instruments of power from those that are more subtle and shadowy. Those of the blunter kind – the sheer magnitude of its financing, its direct influence on the international financial community and its attempts to influence government policies through loan covenants – may not in fact constitute the primary means whereby its power is exercised at all. Those researching the Bank should make themselves aware of the far more subtle ways in which the Bank shapes the thinking of key decision-makers around the world. That story is the real one.

References

Jones, P. W. 1988. *International policies for third world education: Unesco, literacy and development*. London and New York: Routledge.

Jones, P. W. 1992. *World Bank financing of education: Lending, learning and development*. London and New York: Routledge.

Jones, P. W. 1993. United Nations agencies. In *Encyclopedia of educational research*. New York: Macmillan.

185

CHAPTER TWELVE

Interviewing the
education policy elite

Sharon Gewirtz and Jenny Ozga

Introduction

This chapter is concerned to explore a number of issues in interviewing a particular, historically specific, education policy elite. The chapter describes issues that arose during work on a project, "Elites in Education Policy-making", funded by the Open University, which investigated the role and nature of elites in education policy-making generally, with particular attention to their contribution to the 1944 Education Act and the postwar reconstitution of education provision. In the remainder of the chapter we concentrate on discussion of methodological and ethical issues. However, before doing so we feel that it might be helpful to say something about the project and our intentions in using interviews as a source of data.

The nature of the project

The elites project is historical. That is, its subject matter is historically located in that it is concerned to explore the world of post-1944 education policy-making in England, with particular reference to the influence of officials and officers on the construction of the postwar system and on the shaping of provision in the period up to the late 1960s and early 1970s. The project is also historical in an analytical sense, in that it is part of an attempt to explain and understand education policy-making within its historical context, which, we submit, has a strong impact upon its current and future development. This is not to suggest that historical events *determine* current outcomes, but to place current developments – which may appear radical or revolutionary – within a longer-term framework, where they may be seen as part of a larger, less immediate, narrative. Our concern to give proper attention to history and its lessons stemmed from an accidental convergence of background – we were both trained historians – and from some frustration with what we perceived as a generally unproductive relationship between history and sociology prevalent at the time of the origin of the project in the early 1980s. Rather than enthusiastically embracing C. Wright Mills' dictum that all worthwhile sociology was history, it seemed to us that attempts to bring the disciplines together brought out their worst characteristics – obsessive empiricism on the one hand and cavalier disregard for the messiness of historical evidence on the other. We felt that a closer relationship between history and sociology could produce more powerful explanations of education policy. It should be emphasized that we were committed to a close and interdependent relationship between the two disciplines, and that we did not see the emphasis on historical enquiry as a substitute for theory. We need to discuss our view of the connections between theoretical frameworks and historical enquiry a little further here, if we are adequately to contextualize the methodological issues that then arise.

History, theory and education policy

Historical investigation is not at all free of theory; it does not exist in some theory-free zone in which the "facts" of the matter are revealed by historical investigation. Historical scholarship is pervaded with assumptions; indeed it is necessary to study these assumptions in order to uncover how they have helped to shape current understandings of education policy. In particular, it is necessary to uncover assumptions about educational theory as natural progression, as this results in a narrative heavily biased towards pluralist interpretations. In that narrative, the achievement of representative democracy leads to the creation of state institutions that serve that democracy. The major interests – parents, teachers, local education authorities (LEAs) and central government –

work together in broad agreement to negotiate education policy. We would wish to contrast this type of account with more critical histories that search for explanation of the growth of provision and connect that growth to the transition to industrial capitalism in 19th-century Britain and to the consequent high level of social unrest and organized political activity.

We would also wish to draw attention to the extent to which uncritical assumptions about progress and growth have permeated explanations of recent and current education policy. They contributed to a somewhat anodyne and superficial account of education policy in the postwar years, and sustained the emphasis on explanation at the level of system organization rather than purpose. The concentration of policy scholars on the visible rituals of exchange and bargaining between the three "partners" in policy-making distracted them from attending to the more fundamental and deeply sedimented patterns beneath the surface. Assumptions about educational progress and state provision also left policy scholars unprepared for the narrative shift of the 1980s.

It is our concern to explore more fundamental patterns of education policy, particularly those that result in the stratification of provision so characteristic of English education (Johnson 1989) that has led us to seek for ways of understanding policy that are historically grounded.

Having spent some time in defence of historical method, we now propose to set out our conditions for the proper understanding of education policy. Once again, we will try to limit ourselves to those aspects of our argument that have a bearing on the methodological issues to come. Readers interested in a more extended version of this discussion are referred to Dale and Ozga (1991), as the text below follows that discussion very closely. Some of what we will say has been indicated above, particularly in relation to our attempt to challenge conventional, pluralistic accounts of policy-making with their privileging of partnership. We believe that the recent changes in education policy-making expose the inadequacies of pluralist analysis and show that explanations that focus on partnership are neither sufficiently robust nor flexible to cope with change. Essentially, as we indicated earlier, they had taken as the problematic the more visible features of the policy-making process and sought to explain these, rather than looking for the deeper conditions on which these features depended.

It is not sufficient to respond to this criticism by saying that the explanations had been overtaken by events. We reject this defence on the grounds of absence of historical perspective, and because such explanations will always be vulnerable because they are ad hoc explanations, whereas what a comprehensive theory of education policy-making seeks to establish are sustainable *a priori*, or basic propositions, that link education policy to the institutions and discourses of wider society. We therefore need an approach like the one set out in summary form below, which puts forward a number of features that are necessarily characteristic of *any* education policy. This approach reflects the assumption that it is possible and desirable to provide explanations of education policy at a level of abstraction sufficient to enable generalizations and comparisons to be made, yet not so remote from the detail of any given policy that it has nothing of immediate relevance to offer. Briefly, we take it as axiomatic that any education policy must have a *source* (or sources), a *scope* and a *pattern*. That is, any education policy has to originate somewhere, it has to contain, however implicitly, some notion of what it is desirable and possible for education systems to achieve, and it has to carry within it an awareness of the workings of the system and the potential for change.

So, rather than talking about partnership or pluralism or policy communities, we start from the position that education policy can be made by only three major groups within the social formation: the state apparatus itself (including the professionals in the state service), the economy, and the various institutions of civil society. There is no implication that any one of these groups is always necessarily dominant in all three dimensions of source, scope and pattern. However, we do assume that the working of the dimensions can always be explained by a particular combination of these groups, and that particular combination can itself be explained by the economic, political and social conditions and conjunctures of the wider social formation.

We cannot, in this already over-long preamble, discuss the means whereby we might explore and develop the three key dimensions – source, scope and pattern – of education policy. Here we wish only to emphasize that the sequence of source, scope and pattern given above should not be equated with the conventional usage of formulation, execution and implementation of policy. Additionally, not all sources of problems lie outside the education system. If we attempt to connect this theoretical model to our earlier argument, then we could also point to the effects of the "pattern" of provision, and its capacity to act back positively and negatively on the definition of policy. Not only do existing, historically rooted patterns of education policy and practice set effective limits to the solutions available to education problems, in so doing they refine the definitions and the shape of the forms taken by educational problems. As well as setting limits, they can reveal opportunities.

We now hope that enough of the underlying and organizing framework of the larger project – that is, understanding education policy – is sufficiently visible for the scope of the elites project to be more clearly understood. We felt that it was necessary to provide this context, because the elites project is part of a bigger picture. Some of that picture has been developed with a focus on teacher–state relations, and the alternative strategies of direct and indirect rule attempted in the regulation of those relations (Lawn & Ozga 1986, Ozga 1986, 1987). The development of the discussion of indirect rule led to a closer examination of partnership, which is a variant of indirect rule. The historical analysis of state management of the education system in that bigger picture drew attention to two things foreshadowed in the earlier discussion – the endurance of differentiation as an organizing and informing principle of education policy and the significance of permanent state personnel. These, then, were the topics at the heart of the elites project.

The contribution being made to the "bigger picture" is structured by these concerns. We cannot claim that the elites project illuminates *all* the dimensions that we regard as necessary for a comprehensive understanding of education policy; it is better thought of as a spotlight on specific aspects, which may cast some light on others. The aspects of the picture that we highlight relate to exploration of aspects of source, scope and pattern through the interrogation of assumptions held by a key group of postwar policy-makers. We seek to elucidate their views about the scope of education, and to examine that impact on the pattern of provision. Source is interrogated through exploration of the nature of the group, particularly through the attempted characterization of the group as an elite fraction of the state apparatus, with attention to associated issues of class location.

The project methodology

It is relatively simple to set out what our intentions were and what we did: essentially we made use of documentary source material relating to individuals, to LEAs and to particular policy cases, and we also recorded lengthy unstructured interviews with 15 former directors of education or senior Department of Education and Science (DES) officials.

Here again our intentions and motives were more complex than is readily explicable. As far as "straightforward" historical scholarship was concerned, we were doing nothing untoward but following accepted practice in using the recognized secondary sources to guide us towards primary sources. We also used our knowledge of where to look for documentary evidence. There is a great deal of it, not over-used, in archives in the Public Records Office, the Alexander collection at Leeds, Lady Simon's collection in Manchester, and other public and private collections of educational papers. (See, for example, Gosden 1981.) We made use of such sources both in order to find out more about the period and its events, and to compare and cross-check our informants' accounts.

Here we come to the less straightforward element. This followed from our decision to interview as many surviving officers and officials of the postwar period as we could, and to interview them using a slightly diluted version of the life-history method. The reasons for this are embedded in the earlier discussion, but were also simple – we wanted to know more about these people. A more explicit defence of our method would underline our criticism of the tendency of pluralist accounts to privilege political (governmental) activity and to neglect the state bureaucracy. It was also obviously linked to our concern with continuity. Moreover we were critical of pluralists for their casual identification of actors and their roles, without taking account of the beliefs, motives and explanations of those actors. Again, we hope that the connection to our informing framework is clear, in that we were interested in cultural, political and economic cohesiveness that went beyond the shallow category of "interest group" and connected to ideas of class or class fraction.

We did not set out with the intention of achieving a comprehensive coverage. Rather we were drawing on Bertaux's notion of "representativeness" (Bertaux 1981) in that we felt that we would achieve a fuller understanding of postwar administrators through extended study of some of them – study that extended beyond their formal functions and engaged with their constructions of themselves and their "assumptive worlds" (Young & Mills 1978; cited in Raab 1987), that is, their subjective understanding of the environment in which they functioned, which also reflects interconnections of belief and perception.

There are, then, a number of methodological issues raised by the project, and the following are among the more substantial:

- the nature of the evidence and its interpretation: how did we relate relatively loose and ill-defined categories to more theorized ideas about class fraction?
- the relationship between such fractions and individual agency and with the larger structure of the state apparatus.
- the extent to which organizing theoretical frameworks and categories influenced the interpretation of interview data.

We will return to these below.

Identification of informants

We identified informants through routine activity – for example, establishing the terms of office of directors of education in most postwar LEAs, combing of the educational press, mapping administrative careers, identifying "stables" of administrators clustering round particular directors. Publications, correspondence with the department, Society of Education Officers' archives – these gave us information on who was active and influential. We also tended to follow up individuals who were involved in areas of controversy – for example in particularly protracted negotiations over development plans.

All our interviewees talked about one another, and introduced us to former colleagues and friends, or told us about individuals whom they identified as significant in some way. We had more such references than we could easily follow up. The interconnectedness of the people we studied was at one and the same time an aid to the research process and a finding of the study. We are aware of the possibility that it might have created an impression of "community" that may not be strictly accurate.

Access and gatekeeping

Many researchers have identified the problem of access and the significance of gatekeepers (Burgess 1983, 1985, Ball 1981). There are very many possible difficulties here, including misrepresentation of the research intention, loss of researcher control, mediation of the research process, compromise and researcher dependence. Access for us was relatively unproblematic – indeed it was surprisingly easy, which led us to reflect more self-consciously and self-critically on what we were doing. Access was considerably eased by the fact that one of us had worked closely with a former Deputy Permanent Secretary, who was invaluable in directing us to his colleagues and friends, and who gained their cooperation by describing us as "perfectly harmless". Interestingly, almost the same phrase is reported by McPherson and Raab in their major study of postwar education policy-making in Scotland. They report: "'They are quite harmless' was the way Dickson told us he would describe us to Rodger. We were not sure whether to be pleased or disconcerted" (McPherson & Raab 1988: 61). Other contacts included former local education authority directors of education, and some recent or current members of the directorate who put us in touch with their mentors.

We believe that there were other "access-easing" factors too. These included a widespread feeling of disillusionment and waste among our informants, as they witnessed considerable change in the style of policy-making, and particularly the growth of political influence (and they were united in their disparagement of politicians). In addition, our informants were in retirement and had been accustomed to considerable activity and to recognition. They were not necessarily reconciled to inactivity, and welcomed the opportunity to revisit their active pasts and to comment on the shortcomings of their successors. More mundane reasons might relate to their interest in former colleagues, and a certain pleasure in disparaging them. They were a little curious, but not much, about our motives and intentions. Many of them felt that they were helping to document a remarkable period of public service as it drew to a close.

Access was also aided by the fact that we were both (relatively) young women, and not "important". Of course our informants were, for the most part, extremely confident people, but we did not threaten their self-confidence. We were informed, interested and to a certain degree cast by our informants in the role of audience – a role that has its problems in life-history work, as well as its advantages, as Plummer (1983) has indicated. On reflection, we did not feel that the material was compromised by this, as there were so many other checks on what was said – notably other informants and the knowledge of our interviewees that we would be seeing them too, and documentary sources. There was an impact on us, however: we were vulnerable to being patronized, and were; and we needed to be alert to a tendency to discount material from informants who had been particularly self-important. It is worth considering this point further, as it is significant. We had agreed that access to the powerful (or once-powerful) would be relatively difficult and that interviewing them might also prove challenging. We were wrong on both counts.

Indeed, we feel there may be a case for arguing that within the education research community there is a tendency to overestimate the difficulties associated with researching the powerful and a concomitant tendency to underestimate the problems associated with researching those without power. This is illustrated by the experiences of one of us (SG) who, after completing the fieldwork for the elites project, became involved in a study that involved interviewing working-class mothers about their choice of school for their children. During the elites project, academic colleagues had frequently asked how SG "coped" with interviewing retired directors of education, the assumption being that, for a young female researcher, interviewing high-status older males would be problematic. The enquiring colleagues would express surprise at her confidence about and comfort with the process of elite interviewing. On the other hand, similar questions were not asked about her work with working-class women; for interviewing the non-powerful was assumed to be relatively unproblematic. Our own experience suggests that such presumptions are misplaced. Our elite respondents had an understanding of what academic research involves, they were used to being interviewed and tape-recorded, and, as we have already noted, we were perceived as being non-threatening. As a result, they were very forthcoming. Clearly there are problems associated with a familiarity of the researched with the research process and we needed to be aware of the tendency of our elite respondents to give rehearsed, sometimes platitudinous, replies and of the skilful way in which they were able to dodge awkward issues. However, there were obvious advantages associated with their confidence: they were comfortable with the interview as a social event, which in turn made us, as researchers, feel at ease, which resulted in us obtaining a significant volume of, on the whole, rich oral data. The same cannot be said of many of the working-class female respondents from the parental choice project, who often appeared distinctly uncomfortable with, even threatened by, the research process (however non-threatening the researcher tried to be); who frequently seemed to doubt that they could have anything of interest to say to a middle-class interviewer from "the university"; and whose replies were sometimes inhibited by a concern that they were "getting the answers wrong". The impact of such responses on the interviewer was to make her uncomfortable with the interview situation, which often led to tense, stilted conversations with short, sometimes monosyllabic, replies in place of the long flowing narratives of the elite interviewees.

Doing the interviewing

We did the early interviews together, but as the project progressed one of us did more of them. Most interviews were recorded in informants' homes, and they controlled the event. As a result the setting varied considerably, from a formal and relatively austere exchange in an obviously seldom-used front room, to generous and relaxed lunches where additional family members might be present. We did not have an interview schedule, but we sometimes had particular things that we wanted to explore, and if this was the case then we would send background prompt material in advance, and we would rehearse with one another what we needed to know. The pace and range of the interview depended on the responses of the informant. In this we were attempting to follow good practice in life-history interviewing. We aimed for the "unstructured interview as conversation" as elucidated by Burgess (1982), with perhaps an even stronger emphasis on allowing the interviewee to "speak for himself". (There was only one woman, a point we return to below.)

Among the important early lessons that we learned was the absolute necessity of thorough preparation. Our desire to allow our informants control over their own narratives meant that we had to be prepared for changes of direction. The age of our informants and their busy working lives meant that they sometimes needed help with a name or a place, while their experience made them alert to gaps in our knowledge. These points reinforce the excellent advice in Plummer's chapter, "The doing of life histories". This discussion highlights the basic problems with such work, and deals with them under the following headings:

- *the social science questions*: these are, broadly, to do with the justification for the research;
- *the technical questions*: these relate to sampling, adequate interview-

ing, assessing validity;
- *ethical and political questions*: these relate to the political justification for doing the work and to ethical dilemmas;
- *personal questions*: the dual impact of the research on the researcher's personal life and of the personal life on the research.

(After Plummer 1983: 84)

The first point has been covered – if not dealt with. The technical questions, too, have received some attention. Interview technique is perhaps the area where the nature of our enquiry made for some difference from conventional life-history interviewing. There the convention is for the interviewer to be as passive as possible. That was not quite our mode. As we've indicated, we were sometimes called upon to provide information. We were also "tested", to establish that we did have some knowledge of events and personalities. Much life-history work has been done with marginalized or underrepresented individuals or groups, and the political justification that has been used to meet the ethical dilemma presented by intrusion into personal and private lives has been the necessity of researching a situation and thus making it visible. Our interviewees, obviously, were placed very differently from Thomas and Znaniecki's (1958) "Polish peasant". This had an effect on the interviewing and on the relationship between researcher and researched, which is why we referred earlier to "diluted" life-history method.

The other issues that resonate with us from Plummer's list relate to ethical dilemmas concerning the relationship between us and our interviewees. First, there is the gender issue. Feminist researchers (for example, Finch 1984) have diagnosed the extent to which researchers control and direct their "subjects", and moved from expression of their sense of the inappropriateness of the forms and methods of research in exchanges between women to a more general critique of the assumptions about appropriate power relations that are encapsulated in much social science research – in data collection and analysis. Our gender did have an impact on the research and on the relationship with our informants, but in a way that provided a rather ironic commentary on the feminist critique (with which we were familiar and which we endorsed). In effect we felt that we were viewed as women in very stereotypical ways, which included being seen as receptive and supportive, and that we were obliged to collude, to a degree, with that version of ourselves because it was productive for the project.

We were given a great deal of help by our interviewees, and they told us a great deal about themselves. As McPherson and Raab put it, "if help and trust took us into the policy community, were we also 'taken in' in other ways? Was it gullibility that rendered us harmless?" (McPherson & Raab 1988: 62). We like to think not and that our interest in the "complete" life, rather than in the policy process, gave us material that was unavailable to McPherson and Raab. (Indeed, the lack of a convincing picture of Scottish political and educational culture is one of the most trenchant criticisms of *Governing Education*. See, for example, Grace 1989.) However, we must admit to some consciousness that, in our self-presentation and in our presentation of the project to our interviewees, we probably played up the aspect that recorded the apotheosis of partnership and down-played our search for a "policy elite".

Analyzing the data

Our first intention in interviewing anyone was to find out what kind of person they were, and we tried to do this by working through the life, asking, for example, about the influence of family background on career choice. To summarize, we had interview data that told us about the people we had talked to – it told us about their backgrounds, their education, their experiences of life. It gave us insights into what they took for granted in their worlds, what had been difficult, what experiences they viewed as formative. We had different kinds of questions once the person reached an established career point and could be asked about specific incidents or policy areas. This represents our intentions. In fact, accounts could go in many directions simultaneously. That makes them enormously rich and extraordinarily difficult to manage.

The process of analysis of life-history data is not well documented, perhaps because it is so difficult to describe in terms that go beyond the exhortation to read and re-read the material, take notes, develop organizing categories, read and read again. As indicated earlier, we were incorporating other source material into our analysis, and this played a part in the development of organizing categories. Life-history data are notoriously difficult to manage. Transcripts are very lengthy, and we found that, even with relatively succinct accounts of "lives", we had difficulty absorbing the material so that we could readily make connections across interviews. We did not wish to break the flow of the stories, and kept files that reflected sensitizing concepts such as educational background, entry into educational administration, networks and mentoring, development planning, views on other significant policy-makers – and kept the appropriate extracts in those categories as well as within the whole account. We would like to emphasize at this point that we are talking about a process of analysis that is not yet complete, and that has been interrupted by changes in our circumstances. We are therefore talking about emergent categories and current (if intermittent) activity, and about a continuing and developing process.

Prominent within the narratives were variations on the "nature of administration" theme. We became aware that the different "stables" represented different views of the nature of educational administration, which themselves reflected personal characteristics and strategies. We became immersed in the exploration of these different cultures of administration and of the networks they maintained (perhaps too immersed, as we have far too much information about too many directors). The pursuit of networks as a theme was confirmed in its significance by this line of enquiry, however, as we learned a great deal about the "following of form" and the social cohesiveness of the group. As well as pursuing the theme of administration and its meanings, we became drawn into further exploration of the nature of the central–local relationship. This followed from our pursuit of the indirect rule into partnership idea, but it also emerged spontaneously from our informants, often in contradictory ways. We have written elsewhere (Gewirtz & Ozga 1990) about the ways in which we would wish to use our material in our critical analysis of partnership and in support of our attempts to place partnership as an ideological construct that obscures underlying patterns and assumptions about appropriate provision. The methodological problems of interest here relate to the potential tension between the organizing concepts and the subjective experience of our informants. Did our organization distort these accounts?

For the most part, at this level of analysis, we think not. Once again, we refer to the historical grounding of the project and our reading of other significant evidence. In particular, we were able to supplement first-hand oral accounts of events with behind-the-scenes documentary evidence, which included correspondence between LEA officers and civil servants based at the Ministry of Education and memos prepared by Ministry officials for the private consumption of other Ministry officials. (These are held at the Public Record Office and released to the public under the 30-year rule.) Because they were highly confidential, the papers are extremely revealing and we were faced with having to explain apparently quite significant discrepancies between what appeared in them and the versions of events recounted to us in the interviews.

It is worth noting here that the experience of doing historical research with access to a whole variety of sources provides a useful reminder to those of us involved in contemporary studies that there is a great deal we do not yet know about current policy-making processes. Contemporary policy analysts are rarely able to refer to private documents of the kind available to historians and, as far as documentary evidence goes, have to rely almost exclusively on material produced specifically for public consumption. There is the added problem in contemporary research that elite informants often have a stake in being somewhat "economical with the truth" – on the whole, more so than is the case with retired respondents, because of the closeness of events in contemporary research and the fact that the informants may still be in office or at least still be politically ambitious. Such shortcomings in oral evidence in conjunction with limited access to key private documents make it very difficult when doing contemporary policy research to discover what actually went on behind the policy-making scenes. This was pointed up very strongly in subsequent research on City Technology Colleges (CTCs) where two authors of a briefing paper that was allegedly the source of the CTC policy within the DES were interviewed. The informants – Robert Dunn and Stuart Sexton – gave significantly contradictory accounts of what that paper contained and hence conflicting impressions of the intentions underlying the CTC policy as initially conceived. The researchers in that project had to try and make sense of those contradictory versions of the origins of the CTC policy within the DES without having seen the briefing paper in question (Gewirtz et al. 1992). (At the same time, it may be worth noting some of the advantages that the contemporary researcher has that the historian does not. The former is likely to have access to more key informants, because they are still living, and those informants may provide very detailed accounts of the emergence of particular policies because the events are close at hand.)

Part of our explanation for the apparent contradictions between oral and documentary sources in the elites project came from reading the oral accounts in a number of ways – in the same way as historians read conflicting documentary accounts, with an ear tuned for the selective and favourable self-presentation, for *post hoc* rationalization, and for the settling of old scores. In particular, we felt that we were being offered a version of "partnership" that was enhanced by distance and comparison with current developments – a comparison that was often explicitly made. Another possible distorting factor, which our one woman informant alerted us to, was the macho-ness of the male presentation of self. She pointed out that the male directors whom we interviewed were likely to exaggerate their roles in local policy-making, particularly in relation to their control over the education committee:

> I often got the impression that chief education officers felt they told their committees what to do. But I wasn't convinced that it was necessarily like that but it was part of them putting forward the male view of their position, that in fact they might well have been more obviously challenged than they said but they weren't going to admit it when they were talking outside the authority.
> (Gwenneth Rickus, Chief Education Officer for Brent, 1971–84)

We were reluctant, however, to raise the "rose-tinted spectacles" syndrome or the macho-ness of male-self presentation simply to explain away the rosy version of "partnership" conveyed to us in interviews. In trying to make sense of the apparent discrepancies between our oral and documentary evidence, we came to understand partnership not just as an ideological construct that functioned to obfuscate the high degree of central control and in particular the imposition of tripartism by the centre. The evidence suggests very strongly that partnership was also very much a concrete phenomenon, but one that differed markedly from the open democratic version conveyed in the pluralist literature. This was essentially a closed partnership of officials from largely similar class and educational backgrounds who tended to have a shared view about the direction of education policy, including the belief that selection ought to be an integral part of the English education system (although there were exceptions to this tendency). The documentary evidence on the whole would seem to support the impression conveyed to us in the interviews of cosy amicability in the relationship between officials, but from which local politicians tended to be excluded.

We were thus able to support our critique of partnership, and to extend and strengthen our understanding of postwar policy-making through a developed appreciation of the role of permanent officials. Our researches uncovered their commitment to particular organizational forms and patterns of provision. The diluted life histories, in particular, gave us access to the community between them and to the coherence of their assumptive worlds. They also allowed us to understand the strength of the bureaucracy and the mechanisms by which it maintained control through the definition of patterns of provision.

Theorizing from the elites project thus takes the form of a contribution to understanding the nature of the education state apparatus and the powerful, if often contradictory, position of elite members of that apparatus. The theoretical underpinning for a focus on elites within the state apparatus owes much to the work of Poulantzas, in particular the aspect of his work that stresses the state's role in securing political class domination and social cohesion (Poulantzas 1975). The "irresistible rise of the state administration" and the emphasis on the state bureaucracy as a leading actor offered us a justification for further exploration of that bureaucracy and for discussion of its class location and class character. Going further, we wished to explore the state's role in ensuring social cohesion through unifying the power bloc, producing knowledge, and using knowledge to reproduce power relations. Poulantzas' suggestions that research, technology, management and in particular bureaucratic organization are always closely woven with the dominant ideology (Jessop 1990) were of interest to us, unfashionable though these ideas are. If we take Poulantzas' ideas further (i.e. beyond recognition of the significance of state power), we particularly wish to stress the importance for our thinking of his emphasis on the reproduction of class contradictions within the state apparatus, and the incoherence and chaos of state policies that follow from that contested and contradictory character.

That briefly indicates some of the theoretical background on which we draw, and it is related (theoretically and methodologically) to our background as historians and our connection to the growing and powerful body of work that moves historical sociology forward (see, for example, Skocpol 1979).

Methodologically, we draw on the work of life historians, oral historians and feminist historians, whose work combines to offer ways of using the elusive, fragmentary and illuminative insights of such historical (and contemporary) scholarship to interrogate the tension between structure and agency. We do not make assumptions about the character of state bureaucracies, or indeed about the character of the specific bureaucracy concerned with education policy in postwar England, but we do assume that it is important and that it may be understood through particular forms of exploration. Hence, the combination of structural analysis, historical investigations and illuminative, subjective exploration.

References

Ball, S. J. 1981. *Beachside Comprehensive*. Cambridge: Cambridge University Press.

Bertaux, D (ed.) 1981. *Biography and society: The life history approach in the social sciences*. Beverley Hills, Calif.: Sage.

Burgess, R. G. (ed.) 1982. *Field research: A sourcebook and field manual*. London: Allen & Unwin.

Burgess, R. G. (ed.) 1985. *Strategies of educational research: Qualitative methods*. Lewes, Sussex: Falmer.

Burgess, R. G. 1983. *Experiencing comprehensive education: A study of Bishop McGregor School*. London: Methuen.

Dale, R. & J. Ozga 1991. *Understanding education policy: Principles and perspectives* E333 Unit 1. Walton Hall: Open University.

Finch, J. 1984. "It's great to have someone to talk to": The ethics and politics of interviewing women. In *Social researching: Policies, problems and practice*, C. Bell & H. Roberts (eds). London: Routledge & Kegan Paul.

Gewirtz, S. & J. Ozga 1990. Partnership, pluralism and education policy: A reassessment. *Journal of Education Policy* **5** (1).

Gewirtz, S., G. Whitty & T. Edwards 1992. City Technology Colleges: Schooling for the Thatcher generation? *British Journal of Education Studies* **40** (3).

Gosden, P. 1981. Twentieth century archives of education as sources for the study of education policy and administration. *Archives* **15**, 66.

Grace, G. 1989. Education policy studies: Developments in Britain in the 1970s and 1980s. *New Zealand Journal of Educational Studies* **24** (1).

Jessop, B. 1990. *State theory*. Pennsylvania: Pennsylvania State University Press.

Johnson, R. 1989. Thatcherism and English education. *History of Education* **18** (2).

Lawn, M. & J. Ozga 1986. Unequal partners: Teachers under indirect rule. *British Journal of the Sociology of Education* **7** (2).

McPherson, A. & C. Raab 1988. *Governing education: A sociology of policy since 1945*. Edinburgh: Edinburgh University Press.

Ozga, J. 1986. A social danger: The contested history of teacher–state relations. In *The state, private life and political change*, H. Corr & L. Jameson (eds). London: Macmillan.

Ozga, J. 1987. Studying education through the lives of the policy-makers: An attempt to close the macro–micro gap. In *Changing policies, changing teachers: New directions in schooling*, S. Walker & L. Barton (eds). Lewes, Sussex: Falmer.

Poulantzas, N. 1975. *Classes in contemporary capitalism*. London: New Left Books.

Plummer, K. 1983. *Documents of life*. London: Allen & Unwin.

REFERENCES

Raab, C. 1987. Oral history as an instrument of research into Scottish educational policy-making. In *Research methods for elite studies*, G. Moyser & M. Wagstaffe (eds). London: Allen & Unwin.

Skocpol, T. 1979. *States and social revolutions*. Cambridge: Cambridge University Press.

Thomas, W. I. & F. Znaniecki 1958. *The Polish peasant in Europe and America*. New York: Dover Publications.

Young, K. & E. Mills 1978. Understanding the "assumptive worlds" of governmental actors. A report to the SSRC panel on central–local government relations.

CHAPTER THIRTEEN

Writing school history as a former participant: problems in writing the history of an elite school

Susan F. Semel

This chapter examines the problems involved in writing the history of a school that one was intimately involved in, as a student, teacher and parent. It is concerned with the difficulties in writing history as a participant, a participant-observer, and, finally, a former participant. It looks at the processes I engaged in during the research and writing of my book on the history of *The Dalton School* (Semel 1992), and suggests that I relied on anthropological and sociological methods of field research, as well as traditional methods of historical investigation to examine a school where elites send their children. Given these field methods, it examines the problems endemic to such research and how I dealt with them. Lastly, it suggests that this type of research is to some degree a psychoanalytic journey, in which I had constantly to make sense of my own subjective experiences as they related to the larger historical record. Despite the problems encountered, I conclude that writing history as a participant and former participant is a valid form of research.

The research setting

The Dalton School is a coeducational, independent day school located on the fashionable Upper East Side of Manhattan. At present, the Middle and High School, grades 4–12 are housed in a 10-story brick building at 108 East 89th Street. The Lower School, grades K–3 is housed in two cleverly connected townhouses at 53 and 61 East 91st Street.

The neighbourhood in which the school is located contains some of the most costly real estate in the USA. Apartment prices generally range from half of a million dollars to over several million dollars. It is a neighbourhood of extreme wealth, loosely bounded on the north by 96th Street, on the south by 59th Street, and encompassing Third to Fifth Avenues. Politicians refer to it as the "Silk Stocking" district of New York; its residents tend to vote Republican.

It is readily apparent to those who approach the school from Park Avenue, an avenue of trees with islands of cultivated greenery in the middle, that the neighbourhood is one of elegance and affluence. Regal apartment houses of neoclassical or Beaux Arts design, constructed in the 1920s and 1930s, line both sides of the avenue. A sense of wealth and wellbeing is further underscored by the early morning scene of white-gloved, uniformed doormen hailing taxis or opening doors of limousines for smartly attired, mostly white residents on their way to Wall Street law or investment banking firms, or, somewhat later, their clubs or shopping excursions downtown.

Whereas the majority of students at the 89th Street building travel to school by themselves, those at 91st Street must be transported by car or escorted, by either parents, nannies, housekeepers or au pairs. This in part accounts for the fact that most of the students in the First Program are fairly affluent and white, and live within the confines of the neighbourhood. The other factor that determines racial composition at 91st Street is the tuition fee. Parents of Dalton students pay an average of $12,000 per year to send their children to school. They are also solicited for voluntary contributions of several hundred dollars in addition to the tuition, school benefits and the endowment fund. Thus, sending a child to Dalton (or any comparable independent school in the area) is an expensive proposition; in fact, the current headmaster, Gardner Dunnan, has frequently noted that parents who have incomes totalling $100,000 are just "making it" – and probably not, in the current economy. Scholarship monies are available and currently 18 per cent of the student body receives scholarship aid; however, a disproportionate amount, 21 per cent is concentrated in the High School. This would account for the more socially and economically mixed student body in the Upper School.

Because of the costliness of sending children to Dalton, the school must struggle to maintain a diverse student body. Under its founder, Helen Parkhurst, and her successor, Charlotte Durham, the school was a haven for the children of professionals in the arts, intellectuals, successful German Jews and WASPs interested in progressive education. There was always a commitment to minority representation and to financial aid. This configuration shifted somewhat under Donald Barr, as the student body almost tripled in size and the physical plant expanded to 91st and 94th Streets. Increasingly, the children of German Jews and WASPs were eclipsed by a large cohort of children of affluent, successful, often high-profile, predominantly East European Jews. This trend has continued under Gardner Dunnan, although recently there has been a serious effort to attract more minority students to Dalton. Nevertheless, the student body that visitors encounter today reflects a significant number of children of affluent, successful, talented and visible individuals in real estate, investment banking, law, medicine and the fashion industry. Children of intellectuals and children of parents in the arts are also represented; today the difference being that these children are often the offspring of more affluent, more established and less media shy individuals than in past decades. It is this trend from a low-profile, frequently offbeat parent body, to a successful, high-profile one, that has created both negative and positive images of the school.

Returning to the First Program, little of the high profile image of the school is present as visitors pause at 53 East 91st Street. Rather, visitors to the school are struck by an aura of order and tradition, suggested by the location as well as by the architectural facade of the building. Few parents applying to the First Program at Dalton today are actually aware of or interested in Dalton's progressive roots. Significantly, at one open house, prospective parents posed many questions but "None of them were about the school's philosophy or operation. All were related directly or indirectly to the admissions process. 'What do you have to do to get in?' one father asked"(Kanner 1987). Perhaps this incident is an important indication not only of the lack of knowledge of the progressive tradition Dalton represents, but also of the current concerns of parents when admission to the school is the bottom line – a group buying a credential rather than a particular educational philosophy. In any event, the setting of the school at 91st Street would scarcely indicate Dalton's roots in an important historical movement in education, which has dominated educational thinking for so much of this century: progressive education.[1]

The history of Helen Parkhurst's administration, the school's founder, and the subsequent administrations of Charlotte Durham (1942–60), Jack Kittell (1962–4), Donald Barr (1964–75), and Gardner Dunnan (1975–

present) illustrate an important theme in the history of Dalton, namely, that the head of the school makes the school what it is; that "life in a school – the quality of its culture – [is] in large part a function of its principal" (Sarason 1971: 207). Roland Barth (1980) states that, 'only recently have educational policy makers come to realize, for instance, that the school principal has an extraordinary influence over the quality of education and the quality of life under the roof of the schoolhouse'. In the years since Barth's statement the importance of leadership has become acknowledged throughout the education reform literature (Lightfoot 1984, Grant 1988, Sadovnik et al. 1993).

Once a non-competitive, progressive school, today The Dalton School is a highly competitive, elite college preparatory school. Although vestiges of progressive practice remain, it is certainly no longer a progressive school in the tradition of its founder. My research sought to understand how and why the school changed over the past 73 years. It examined the role of leadership, the effects of cultural and social change, shifts in the demographic composition of the neighbourhood and the student body, among other factors, and argued that leadership by the school head is an important component of school change.

Methodological issues

My association with The Dalton School has spanned over a quarter of a century, as a student, teacher, parent and researcher. I attended Dalton as a student during Charlotte Durham's administration. I returned to teach social studies during Donald Barr's administration and continued as a teacher through Gardner Dunnan's administration until 1988, when I joined the faculty at Adelphi University as an Assistant Professor of Education.

I have also been a Dalton parent. My son, John, attended Dalton from kindergarten to grade 8, during Gardner Dunnan's administration.

In the course of my years at Dalton, I have personally known three of its heads and two of its interim heads. Many of the faculty members I write of have either taught me or been my colleagues. Many children I have taught have been offspring of former schoolmates. Many of the events I have described I have witnessed first-hand. Thus, I have approached my subject with my own special history, my own personal landscape. Given this subjective landscape, I have worked diligently at bracketing out my personal experiences and have attempted to analyze the history of the school as an historian of education. Nevertheless, writing the history of a school in which one has been so intimately involved poses significant methodological concerns.

My research began in 1978, when as a Klingenstein Fellow at Teachers College, Columbia University, I began to research the history of The Dalton School for my doctoral dissertation. My dissertation, completed in 1984, under the mentorship of Lawrence A. Cremin, examined the history of the school through the Barr administration. As I was still a member of the Dalton faculty, Professor Cremin and I agreed that the dissertation would not include the Dunnan years, for obvious pragmatic considerations. When I left Dalton in 1988, I decided to turn the dissertation into a book by completing the history through the Dunnan administration. I discovered that I could not simply begin to write the history of the Dunnan years without first sufficiently distancing myself from the events in which I was so intimately involved.

The process of bracketing out my own experiences discussed above proved to be significantly more challenging for the period closest to my writing. As an historian it was essential to have sufficient time lapse between the events and their analysis. Thus, although I began to think about returning to this history in 1988, I did not begin the research for this book until 1990, when I felt I had gained the requisite objectivity necessary to write solid history. When I left the school, I still felt so much a part of it that it was difficult to analyze its most recent history from anything other than my own subjective landscape. As my departure, although voluntary, was painful and less than satisfactory, for reasons I will discuss below, I needed to work through my own negative feelings about the current leadership before I could write its history objectively.

Although my research does not constitute participant observational field research in the strict sense as practised by anthropologists and sociologists, as I did not conduct research as a participant, I am cognizant that many of the problems of participant observation as a participant are applicable to my research (Whyte 1981, Lareau 1989, Bogdan & Bicklin 1992, Glesne & Peshkin 1992). Whereas participant observers are involved in the organization that they are studying as they are conducting their research, I was a part of the organization that I looked at historically. None the less, the problem of "going native", a central issue in field research, presented an interesting dilemma, since to some extent I have always been native. Thus, I constantly had to examine my own perceptions of the history of the school as a participant in that history and compare it with other evidence, such as archival documents and interviews (I conducted over 100 interviews). Sometimes my perceptions as a member coincided with other sources; sometimes they varied. As an historian I had to treat my own perceptions as just another piece of evidence, and then I had to make sense of any contradictions. This required a type of psychoanalytic journey, one that most historians do not need to take so explicitly in their work. Suffice it to say that at times this was difficult; so much so that, when I began to research the Dunnan years, I realized that I needed some time before I could separate my feelings as a participant from my role as an historian. Through constant self-examination, reflection, criticism and ongoing discussions with colleagues both inside and outside of Dalton, I am confident that I have confronted the problems associated with this type of research. My awareness of the possibility of researcher bias kept me honest and I have tried to be as objective as anyone doing history. Since complete objectivity is a myth of positivism, I believe that I have kept within the boundaries of writing good history.

School histories written by participants or former participants are not unusual. More often than not, however, they are celebrations of the school, with little historical rigour or criticism of the school's practices. They are often written to celebrate particular pedagogic practices or ideologies and therefore rarely look critically at questions of organization and leadership. One about The Dalton School, edited by the Dalton archivist to celebrate the school's sixty-fifth anniversary is such a book (Feldman 1984). It is therefore important to note that my own history was not such an enterprise. Rather it was a scholarly attempt to explain the transformation of an experimental progressive school into a competitive, college preparatory school. Certainly, my own experiences teaching at the school, as well as my own dismay at the path the school has taken, shaped my interpretations. None the less, I diligently bracketed out my own story as I interpreted the historical data. That is not to say I was completely objective, as this is never possible. But, as Glesne and Peshkin point out:

My subjectivity is the basis for the story I am able to tell. It is the strength on which I build. It makes me who I am as a person and as a researcher, equipping me with the perspectives and insights

> that shape all that I do as a researcher, from the selection of a
> topic clear through to the emphasis I make in my writing. Seen as
> virtuous, subjectivity is something to capitalize on rather than to
> exorcise.
> (Glesne & Peshkin 1992: 104).

Lareau (1989: 214–15), in discussing her fieldwork methods, states that, contrary to popular myth, field researchers rarely go off alone to make sense of their data. Rather, interpreting data is a social process, which involves an ongoing dialogue with others. For my own research, overcoming what Lareau labels the "lone ranger" problem was essential. As a participant in the history of the school I was studying, I had to step outside my insider self. This was an essential first step in writing history; it was important for me to view my own perceptions as shaped by the same institutional forces that shaped its history. My own taken-for-granted notions and assumptions about the school needed to be challenged or I could not begin to write its history. My dissertation adviser, the historian of education Lawrence A. Cremin, also an insider as a member of the school's board of trustees and a parent of two of my Dalton students, helped me to do so, as I shall discuss below.

During the second stage of my research, once I left Dalton and started to turn the dissertation into a book, this process intensified. For the first time in over 25 years I was not intimately involved in the life of the school. From 1988 to 1990, I attempted to step back and gain the distance required to complete the school's history. Also, my professional collaboration with two Adelphi sociologists of education on two other projects provided me with another lens for seeing my own subjective view of Dalton. In discussing my research on Dalton with them, they constantly forced me to examine my own history and how it affected my writing history. Their own more radical critique of Dalton as an elitist, rather than progressive school helped me to make sense of the contradictions of the school's transformation. Thus, through constant dialogue with people outside of Dalton, I was able to overcome the "lone ranger" problem. If I had gone off by myself to write the history, without such reflective interaction, I am certain I would have written a different book.

During this second stage, I had to overcome another potential source of personal bias. When I left Dalton in 1988, after 23 years as a teacher, I left in silence. There was no institutional good-bye; no party, no celebration, no official recognition. My department took me to lunch, along with someone else who was leaving. There was no mention of my leaving in the student newspaper, the *Daltonian*. I was instructed by my chair not to make a public announcement to my students. To the best of my knowledge, Gardner Dunnan did not want it perceived that he forced me out, as I was one of the last faculty members of the "Old Dalton" still at the school. Because I knew that I would need his permission to gain access to the archives to complete my research, I acquiesced. I did say good-bye to my long-time students and had the opportunity for some closure with many. None the less, I left that June bitter about my treatment after a long and dedicated career. During the summer, I received letters of thanks and good wishes in my new career as a college professor from my chairperson, the director of the High School, and the headmaster. Somehow, this did not ease the pain. The following year, when I returned to Dalton to supervise student teachers, some of my former colleagues were still not aware that I had left. From 1988 to 1990, I had to work through my own anger toward the headmaster in order to be objective enough to write the history of his administration. I believe that I have been so successful at this that some readers with knowledge of his administration have suggested that I have been too kind.

From the time I left Dalton as a teacher to the time I returned to speak to alumni as the author of a book on its history, I have maintained an uneasy relationship with the headmaster. I have, as well, struggled with my own relationship to the school. Although I no longer consider myself part of the Dalton community, except as an alumna and former teacher, I still sometimes use the word "we" when I talk about the school. I am convinced that because I left the school in a cordial manner the headmaster continued to give me access to the archives, which allowed me to complete writing its history. After the book's publication, he has used the book for his own ends, including fundraising among alumni, and has been cordial and, at times, helpful. None the less, as I didn't write the book he would have written, especially pertaining to his administration, it makes for an uneasy relationship. I will expand upon some of the problems related to the reaction to a school history by students, parents, teachers and administrators in the final section.

The sociologist Jack Douglas (1976), analyzes the problems associated with investigative field research. In his discussion of research based upon direct experience as a member, he outlines the major criticisms of in-depth involvement and concludes that, despite problems of possible researcher bias, the experienced researcher, through careful and constant self-reflection, can overcome these dilemmas and in doing so gain important insights impossible in other, less involved circumstances. In the same vein, writing history as a participant (and former participant), although posing serious challenges, provided a perspective that a non-participant might never have achieved.

My affiliation with the school provided important access that other researchers might not have had. Because I was a graduate of the school, as well as having taught at the school, I was afforded me entry to interviews with numerous key informants. Students, graduates, teachers and former teachers, parents and trustees, for the most part, seemed eager to talk with one of their own. Moreover, we shared a language and history and therefore were able to avoid the usual awkwardness of the interview. I sometimes had to be careful not to become caught up in nostalgia or to lose my perspective as a researcher.

My position as a participant and historian posed some ethical dilemmas. The most important problem concerned the use of information given to me as a participant, when I was teaching at Dalton, rather than as a researcher writing about the school. Since I participated in the school for over 25 years, I was witness to events that most historians would never have witnessed first-hand. More importantly, the question of whether to include information offered to me in my role as a participant, not as a researcher, presented the most serious ethical dilemma. Although I have based my analysis on information given to me in both roles, the book does not reproduce private conversations in which I was involved as a participant. Further, I have attempted to corroborate important historical data with at least two sources.

A word must be said about the historical sources used in my research. In addition to documentary sources, I have relied on interviews and conversations with administrators, faculty, students, alumni, parents and board members. In all instances the individuals were informed of my research project. Some individuals specifically agreed to talk to me on condition that they were granted anonymity. In the case of formal interviews, where the individual agreed to be identified, I have included this information in the footnotes. In no case have I quoted anyone who did not make a statement with full knowledge of the research. Therefore, I never quoted, even anonymously, anyone who said something to me in my other roles as teacher or parent. Finally, in no instance did I quote anyone who spoke to me as a participant, but not as a researcher, with the exception of statements made in public settings. In these cases, I have for the most part not referred to individuals by name, with the exception of the major figures in the school's history – its heads.

The Dalton archives provided significant data for the study, albeit patchy. There were few archival records for the early years, and spotty records for the Barr years. Only the Dunnan years proved a treasure trove of archival material, and this is reflected in the increased use of documentary sources for the Dunnan chapter.

My research on the history of The Dalton School has used both traditional historical methods as well as methods used more traditionally in anthropological and sociological field research. As an historian, I relied on interviews, documents and other archival material. However, as a participant for a large portion of the school's history, I witnessed at first hand events that other historians would have "witnessed" only through documents and interviews. Although my participation required that I step back from my involvement sufficiently to write solid history, I believe this has been possible. It has required a difficult psychoanalytic process, in which I have constantly attempted to make sense of my own experiences in relation to the other historical evidence. I had to examine fully my own taken-for-granted assumptions about my own experiences, and, at times, this has been painful. In some ways, writing the school's history has been, in part, like writing my autobiography. If I could not transcend autobiography then I would have failed as an historian. The major challenge, therefore, was to use my subjective perspective gleaned from experience and to incorporate it as part of my historical lens. Although difficult, I believe it was possible, and the final product is informed by the rich interplay between my own experiences and those of others. Thus, although there are problems with writing history as a former participant, what is important is that I have consciously removed myself in the writing of the school's history from my actions as a former participant. The result, I believe, is a study that is informed by both the subjective understanding of an insider and the historical insight of an outsider. Although this was not easy, Douglas's conclusions about in-depth direct experience support its validity as a form of social and historical investigation. This is not to say that sociological or historical research is ever truly objective; there is always a tension between "scientific" objectivity and human subjectivity. What is important is that as a former participant I had always to be aware of how my own "insider" subjectivity affected my own construction of an historical analysis.

In the course of this research, given the nature of the school and its clientele, I came into contact, both as a teacher and then as a researcher, with many of New York's academic, economic and cultural elite. The next section discusses some of these experiences and how I managed to do research among the powerful.

Doing research on elites

As I stated above, my book, *The Dalton School: The transformation of a progressive school* (1992) began as a doctoral dissertation. My dissertation adviser was Lawrence A. Cremin, one of the most important historians of American education and, at the time, President of Teachers College, Columbia University. Cremin was also an insider. As a member of Dalton's board of trustees, a parent of two of my former Dalton students (both of whom I taught), and the person responsible for finding two of the school's heads (Donald Barr and Gardner Dunnan), he also saw the history of Dalton as both an historian and a participant.

Cremin was always gracious and welcoming; we would meet during his office hours, Mondays, late in the afternoon. At the time, he occupied the President's office, a rather intimidating room, replete with echoes of the past greatness of Teachers College. Needless to say, I was very much aware of the power relations involved in this relationship, although he always acted as my mentor, not as the President of the college. Moreover, Cremin never let his role as a former Dalton board member interfere with his role as my mentor, although the former capacity allowed him to provide a perspective that he, as an historian, might not have been able to give. In this respect, in the initial stages of my research both Cremin and I balanced the dual roles of insider and outsider – he as a former board member and I as a teacher. We clearly represented different constituencies in the school; nevertheless, as historians we were able to discuss the school's history with a unique balance of historical analysis and insider perspectives. None the less, there were times when Cremin and I had serious disagreements about issues. In these instances, he always let the final interpretation be my own. Most historians studying a school's history do not have the benefit of one insider view; in this case, I had the benefit of two.

Another member of my original dissertation committee was historian Diane Ravitch, who was working on her book *The Troubled Crusade* (1983), which included a chapter on the rise and fall of progressive education. At the time, Ravitch was married to a former chairperson of the Dalton board of trustees, Richard Ravitch, an important member of the New York City elite (former chairperson of the Metropolitan Transit Authority, former candidate for Mayor of New York City, and currently Chief Labor Negotiator for the major league baseball owners, Players Relations Committee). Both of Ravitch's children attended The Dalton School and one was my former student. Additionally, one of Ravitch's children baby-sat for my children, as did Cremin's children. In the end, Ravitch decided to withdraw from the committee, stating that she had been too personally involved in the history of the school to have the distance to evaluate my work objectively. As I had little contact with her, except as an outside reader, this decision did not greatly affect my work.

It is interesting to note that, whereas Ravitch had some difficulty distancing herself from her ties to the school, Cremin did not see his relationship to the school as preventing him from supervising the research. In fact, since we both had to balance our insider–outsider tensions, we were able reflexively to keep each other honest. As I argue in this chapter, although being an insider poses methodological problems, these can nevertheless be addressed, as long as one is conscious of them from the outset.

In addition to doing research among academic elites, I also worked among many wealthy and powerful New York City families that had over the past 75 years sent their children to Dalton. These families tended to fall into two groups. Those from the early years to the mid-1960s, the "old-Daltonians", consisted primarily of German Jews, such as Alfred Stern, and William Rosenwald (of Sears Roebuck and Company), some prominent WASPs, such as Mrs Marshall Field, Whitman Knapp (head of the Knapp Commission, which investigated police corruption under the Lindsay administration) and Eleanor Roosevelt, and members of the New York artistic and intellectual community, including William Shirer, Telford Taylor, Orville Schell and William Shawn (the long-time editor of the *New Yorker* magazine). The second group, from the 1960s on, the "new-Daltonians", consisted primarily of East-European Jews, many of whom are considered to be among New York's *nouveaux riches*, investment bankers and Wall Street brokers such as Bruce Wasserstein, and well-known entertainers and media personalities such as Woody Allen, Diana Ross, Robert Redford, Dustin Hoffman, Tom Brokaw and Leslie Stahl. Because of my ties to the school, which spanned over 25 years as a student and teacher, and because of my class position as an upper-middle-class, Park Avenue born New Yorker, I was afforded easy access to some members of both groups.

As an insider, I was privy to confidences that I do not believe an outsider would have had access to. However, with knowledge comes responsibility. I was careful to use information given to me only as it pertained to the goals of my research, only as it might shed light on events or documents I was studying. For example, I was entrusted with board of trustee minutes from the current headmaster's office. However, on close examination of the documents, I discovered personal correspondence as well, particularly confidential memos, that should not have left the office. Only after I had examined the discs did I realize that they were not for the public record. As they had no direct bearing on my study, I did not use them. Nevertheless, their contents certainly helped me to interpret public documents and historical events, and to form conclusions about leadership style.

One of the major problems I encountered was the perception by parents, teachers and students whom I interviewed formally, or encountered informally in the neighbourhood or at the school, that my research could be used as a forum for their discontent. In doing the research, it became immediately apparent that I had special access to numerous groups of people that an ordinary researcher would not have, owing to the various constituents' perceptions of me as a solidly ensconced member of the Dalton community. As I proceeded with my interviews, it became apparent that my agenda was perceived by my subjects quite differently than I had intended. In particular, I was viewed by them less as an objective researcher engaged in writing a serious school history and more as a champion of their various causes. For example, numerous faculty, who made me swear to respect their anonymity (there is no tenure at Dalton), gladly unburdened themselves to me, recounting numerous rumours and embarrassing episodes regarding the administration in the hope that I would act as their conduit and "tell all". In fact there were times during interviews when I felt as if I was a conduit for dissension and revolution. The same phenomenon occurred in my interviews with disgruntled parents, alumni and students. Each group had it own agenda; each group saw me as, if not the messiah, at the very least an agent of change, come to deliver the school from the leadership of corrupt incompetents who had derailed progressive education and who catered to "big bucks" instead.

I never stated that their grievances would be addressed in my research, but I did not dissuade them from their perceptions as their unburdening might provide important data. However, that is exactly how I treated it – as data to be interpreted through an historian's lens, not as facts to be used for political ends. Although an historian with no insider connection might have been able to elicit such responses, I believe that, given my insider status, such data were more easily available to me.

My insider status also made me privy to details about the private lives of students and their families. As a teacher at the school, I had inside information about family problems, sexual liaisons of parents, teachers and students, drug problems, financial problems and manipulations, etc. As the former head of the Dalton Thrift Shop, my mother thought she knew everything about everyone. Many people, including my mother, wanted me to write a best-selling novel rather than an academic history. One former parent and *New York* writer told me that I could publish it in the *New York Magazine* in instalments. In writing an academic history, I had to make sure that only information relevant to the history was included and thus these personal stories were almost always irrelevant. Certainly, if I had used them and named participants, I would have been likely to be sued, as is the practice of the powerful. A former student of mine, Jordan Orlando, has recently published a steamy novel about the school, from which he will make significantly more money than I will for my book.

One of my most memorable interviews with a member of the elite took place at the end of my research for the book in 1991. Winthrop Crane's aunt, Mrs W. Murray Crane, gave Dalton's founder the money to start the school. Although Mrs Crane was a New York "salon lady" and a founder of the Museum of Modern Art, the family originated in Dalton, Massachusetts. The Cranes are old money WASPs, who founded the Crane Paper Company in 1801 in Dalton, where today Crane Paper Company is the dominant industry in what is a company town. Crane factories can be seen from the highway that runs through the town; stores carry the name Crane on their signs, such as Crane Pharmacy. I needed to interview Mr Crane to corroborate data concerning the early years of the school in Dalton, Massachusetts, before it moved to New York City in 1919. I called Mr Crane at home and arranged to go to Dalton to see him. As soon as he heard that I had graduated from the school, as well as taught there, he agreed to see me. In fact, it was these personal ties to The Dalton School, rather than my academic status as a professor, that proved important to him.

Mr Crane lives in one of three identical Crane family houses (Georgian mansions) in a cul de sac road, set directly off the main thoroughfare through town. There are no markings or address numbers other than a discreet marker on the ground near the entranceway bearing his initials. Because it was so small, I missed it and had to go into the Crane Pharmacy to ask for directions. There I was greeted by a number of his employees who wanted to know why I was privileged to go to the Crane house, when none of them had ever been invited. After telling them why I was going to see Mr Crane, they seemed satisfied with my explanation and gave me directions.

Once there, I spent the afternoon with Mr Crane, who, in his eighties and despite some short-term memory lapses, had a definitive memory of the early years of the school in Mrs Crane's house. During our conversation, in his reminiscences of his own life, we discovered that my son had attended the same boarding school as had he and all of his sons. This information seemed to make me legitimate in his eyes and made the rest of the interview quite easy. Although I am in no way in the same class position, the fact that we had in common a connection to this elite boarding school, the Hotchkiss School in Lakeville, Connecticut, changed the dynamic of the interview to a much more personal one. In fact, he encouraged me to interview his half-sister, Louise Crane, the child Helen Parkhurst was originally employed to teach by her mother, Mrs W. Murray Crane.

Louise Crane lives in a stately New York City Fifth Avenue apartment overlooking the Central Park Zoo. It is one of those grand, old New York apartments that only the truly wealthy can maintain (as J. P. Morgan once remarked, "if you have to ask how much, you can't afford it"). I made contact with her secretary, Mr Chester Page, who informed me that I could not interview Miss Crane as she was suffering from Alzheimer's Disease, but that he would be glad to talk to me as her representative. Although he could not tell me anything about Miss Crane's direct experiences with Miss Parkhurst, he was able to provide important missing information about the family's relationship with her after the school was moved to New York. She also provided me with original, inscribed first editions of Helen Parkhurst's *Education on the Dalton Plan*, in English, Japanese and Italian, which Miss Parkhurst gave to the Cranes. Although I would have loved to interview Louise Crane, the opportunity to see her apartment gave me a small glimpse of the upper-class roots of the benefactress of the school.

Conclusion

In the final analysis, although my insider status helped me to gain access to many powerful informants, it remained the case that many wanted me to produce the book they would have wanted written. This was especially true of teachers, parents, students and administrators, both past and present. This was readily seen in the reaction to the book. The current headmaster, Gardner Dunnan, liked the book initially, as it legitimated the school as an important New York City school. He also believed that it provided a necessary historical perspective to faculty and parents and ordered 500 copies for faculty and board members. However, he disliked my portrayal of him, in his words, as a "mindless bureaucrat". None the less, I have been asked to speak about the book and the school's history at alumni events at the school. On the basis of conversations with alumni at these events as well as letters from those who have read the book, I feel that I have successfully addressed the methodological issues raised here. Although many have told me what I should have included, most have agreed that the book is on target. One former student wrote to me to thank me for helping her to understand what as a student she couldn't with respect to the rapid transformation of the school during her 12 years. A former teacher wrote a long letter, which included a number of items that she thought should have been included (which were anecdotal and would probably have led to lawsuits from the rich and powerful) and offered a gentle criticism, which I took as a high compliment. She stated that the book was too scholarly and academic and would do better if it had included more personal recollections of the school and its teachers and students. Her criticism told me that I had written precisely the book that I had intended: a serious scholarly history rather than a memory book. In order to write this history, however, I had to interview many powerful individuals about their memories and then to use the lens of an historian to make sense of it all. Despite the methodological problems and the constraints of writing about powerful people and an important school, I believe what emerged is a balanced portrait of the transformation of a progressive school.

Note

1. For full discussion of the history of progressive education see Cremin (1961).

References

Barth, R. 1980. *Run school run*. Cambridge, Mass.: Harvard University Press.

Bogdan, R. & S. Bicklin. 1992. *Qualitative research in education*. Boston: Allyn & Bacon.

Cremin, L. A. 1961. *The transformation of the school*. New York: Alfred A. Knopf and Random House.

Douglas, J. 1976. *Investigative field research*. Newbury Park, Calif.: Sage Publications.

Feldman, M. 1984. *The Dalton School book of memories*. New York: The Dalton School.

Glesne, C. & A. Peshkin. 1992. *Becoming qualitative researchers*. New York: Longman.

Grant, G. 1988. *The world we created at Hamilton High*. Cambridge, Mass.: Harvard University Press.

Kanner, B. 1987. The admissions go-round: private school fever. *New York Magazine*, 23 November, 40–7.

Lareau. A. 1989. *Home advantage*. London: Falmer Press.

Lightfoot, S. L. 1984. *The good high school*. New York: Basic Books.

Ravitch, D. 1983. *The troubled crusade*. New York: Basic Books.

Sarason, S. 1971. *The culture of the school and the problem of change*. Boston: Allyn & Bacon.

Sadovnik, A., P. Cookson, Jr and S. Semel. 1993. *Exploring education: An introduction to the foundations of education*. Boston: Allyn & Bacon.

Semel, S. 1992. *The Dalton School: The transformation of a progressive school*. New York: Peter Lang Publishing.

Whyte, W. F. 1981. *Street corner society*, 3rd edn. Chicago: University of Chicago Press.

Conclusion

CHAPTER FOURTEEN

Reflections on researching the powerful

Geoffrey Walford

Introduction

This book has presented a series of reflexive accounts of the methodology used in some major studies of the powerful in education. This final chapter will attempt to draw some insights from the various chapters and offer advice to those contemplating their own research projects in similar areas.

Access

Many of the chapters discuss the problems of access to the powerful for research. There are several conclusions that can be drawn. The first is that problems of access are likely to be intensified where research involves a policy initiative that is controversial and fiercely contested. A number of the contributions (e.g. Whitty & Edwards) make it clear that those promoting or implementing the initiative may resist any scrutiny by anyone not "on their side", while those opposed to it may refuse to co-operate because they feel that the initiative is best ignored.

Another very obvious finding is that already having some links with those with power in education significantly eases access. Ozga, for example, had previously worked with a former Deputy Permanent Secretary within the civil service, and already knew some local education authority chief education officers and former chief education officers.

Kogan has himself been Private Secretary to one of the ministers of education involved in his first collaborative study. Fitz & Halpin were able to make use of a former member of the research community who had moved to the Department of Education and Science. Already knowing people means that the researcher will at least be given a hearing and these contacts may also be prepared to introduce the researcher to other powerful individuals. Cassell (1988: 95) argues that the researcher of the powerful needs many of the characteristics of the social climber: "everyone who might possibly know someone, must be contacted and asked if they will give introductions, vouch for one, and otherwise help one's enterprise". But access in these circumstances may be on the basis of having "not caused any trouble" in the past. If the researcher eventually produces critical accounts, access may be far more difficult in the future. Conversely, a researcher who has been shown to be trustworthy and fair in earlier studies will find access for future studies easier.

Usually, the more sponsorship that can be claimed, the better. This may be in terms of "institutional" or "personal" sponsorship (Winkler 1987). Having your research sponsored by a respectable funding agency is clearly one way of authenticating the study and encouraging access. A connection to a respected university may be sufficient to show that the research is serious; support for the research project by a prestigious research funding agency will show that the project has high status as well. However, personal sponsorship is often the surest way of obtaining access. As McHugh shows, sponsorship through people already known to the researcher or through people already interviewed can sometimes be unusually effective. But the researcher has to be careful about both forms of sponsorship, for there may well be antagonisms and differences of viewpoint between the sponsor and the person to be approached of which the researcher is unaware. Sponsorship by the wrong people may make the prospective interviewee less likely to agree. This may be a particular problem where access needs to be achieved at various levels, or where both the centrally and the locally powerful are to be investigated. Extreme care may need to be taken over the order in which people are approached, and the researcher usually must not become over-identified with any one group.

It would seem that access is more likely to be granted if the researchers appear to be, as Gewirtz & Ozga were described, "perfectly harmless". In our sexist society, where it is men who hold most of the powerful positions, female researchers may be at an advantage in being perceived as being "harmless", especially if they are relatively young and not in senior positions within their own organizations. As many other researchers have noted (e.g. Easterday et al. 1977, Klatch 1988), being female is a great advantage in presenting a non-threatening image. Women may be granted access where men are denied it. Yet, as McPherson & Raab (1988: 61) make clear, academic men can also be seen as being unlikely to do any damage to those in power.

In general, persistence pays. The interviewer has to be flexible and to recognize that any arranged interview may be cancelled. As Fitz & Halpin observe, "The powerful can make you wait". Not only can they curtail the whole project, even if they are co-operative they can shape your research timetable. Writing about their study of the US Congress, Sinclair & Brady (1987: 63) explain that "arriving for an interview only to have it postponed is probably the norm rather than the exception". Such delays may be annoying to the interviewer, but one positive aspect of continued delays and rescheduling is that the interviewee may feel greater obligation to the researcher once an interview is finally achieved. The interviewer must, of course, always be polite and considerate to those who act as secretaries to the powerful. Such staff can greatly help or hinder access.

Several of the chapters also show that it is likely to be much easier to obtain access to those who have retired from positions of power than to those still active within them. One obvious reason is that, once retired, these once powerful people have far more time to give to the researcher than before. But it is also the case that many of them have been accustomed to being very active and influential people, and giving interviews to researchers is one way of partially compensating for their inactivity. Being chosen for an academic interview reinforces their self-image of at least having been influential in the past, even if no longer. However, retired interviewees, as well as those still in office, will have their own reasons for co-operating with the research. For those retired, it may be that they want to "set the record straight". They may wish to explain their own activities and indulge in self-aggrandizement. They may wish to disparage present incumbents of their former positions. Interpretation needs to be done with care.

This links with an interesting question raised by Gewirtz & Ozga about the relative difficulties of interviewing the powerful and the powerless. They had expected that gaining access to the powerful would be difficult and that interviewing them would be challenging. Yet they found, as have several of the other contributors to this volume, that both access and the process of interviewing were relatively straightforward. Those in power are used to their ideas being taken notice of. They are well able to deal with interviewers, to answer and avoid particular questions to suit their own ends, and to present their own role in events in a favourable light. They are aware of what academic research involves, and are familiar with being interviewed and having their words tape-recorded. In sum, their power in the educational world is echoed in the interview situation, and interviewers pose little threat to their own positions. In contrast, as Gewirtz & Ozga note, those with little power are unused to anyone taking their views and ideas seriously. They are likely to be intimidated by the interview situation and unaware of the purposes of research interviewing. Encouraging the powerless to become involved in interviews and to be forthcoming within them may be, in practice, more difficult than researching the powerful.

Indeed, one very important general finding from several of the chapters (e.g. Jones) is that it is very possible to obtain access to powerful people without any previous contacts. Indeed, it is becoming recognized that the difficulties of gaining access to members of elites and to powerful people may have been overemphasized. The belief that access to the powerful is difficult has a myth-like character to it, and it may provide researchers with a convenient excuse for not trying.

The interview

A common feature of all the chapters in this book is the demand for thorough preparation before interviews – to "do your homework", as Hunter (1993) describes it. This may appear to be an obvious point – all interviewers should be sure about what they wish to ask. But it would appear to be especially important that preparation is very full with the powerful, for the powerful are prepared to question the interviewer and to demand explanations as to why particular questions are being asked. They assume that the interviewer has already read what is published on the issues and is well aware of the general political and economic background. Generally, they will not be prepared to supply information that the interviewer could have obtained easily from published sources. They may also be knowledgeable about social science research methods and question how the interviews are to be used. They may ask questions about the researcher's motives and objectives. In short, the interviewer has to show competence.

This preparation might be divided into remote preparation and proximate preparation, as McHugh does. Both have to be given great care. The researcher must become knowledgeable about not only the "facts" of the events to be investigated, but also the procedures, symbols and terminology used by the powerful. The researcher has to be aware of potential problem areas and to have thought through how these are to be dealt with.

The proximate preparation is also central. It has become a cliché to write about "the tape recorder that did not work", yet most researchers appear to have experienced this problem during their research. The researcher may feel that it looks foolish to check that the tape recorder is working, but it certainly looks more foolish to end the interview and then discover a fault.

One common problem with interviewing powerful people is that they are used to their ideas being asked for; they are used to talking with others about their plans. The powerful may "just talk". As Ostrander (1993) argues, this is not simply self-centredness, but an accurate reflection of their position of power. The chapters here present a range of different styles of interviewing. Although the style adopted must be shaped by the theoretical objectives of the study, there is a clear danger that researchers may be intimidated by the powerful, and thus be too deferential or obsequious towards them. In a project that is concerned with life history, or similar detailed studies of individual people, it is appropriate just to let the powerful talk and to let them structure the interaction. Where a project has more focused aims, however, it may be necessary for the interviewer to challenge the assumptions of power and take an active part in the structuring of the interview. Mickelson, for example, reminds us that there is a danger of being so concerned with rapport that important questions are avoided and bland answers are insufficiently challenged. Her answer is to challenge interviewees face-on if their answers are evasive. She argues that, in practice, the powerful are often blunt and to the point, and they appreciate a clear indication of the researcher's intentions and objectives. Mutual respect is to be aimed at.

Thorough preparation is also important in order to ensure that the interviewee is not able to present a "public relations" account of the events that are discussed. It is necessary for the interviewer to show that a general discussion is not what is required, and that the interviewer already has considerable experience and knowledge about the issues. Several of the contributors to this book have used dual interviewers in their research on the powerful. Fitz & Halpin and Gewirtz & Ozga have conducted some of their interviews in pairs. This is, in part perhaps, a recognition that interviewing the powerful demands a great deal of concentration and work if the results are not to be platitudinous and self-congratulatory.

In most cases the actual interview with the powerful will probably be semi-structured rather than structured. It is usually not possible or desirable to pose a set series of questions to those with power, because it is the depth of understanding that they can give through their individual knowledge that is of greatest importance. Those who have influenced events directly have a detailed knowledge of events and a sophisticated understanding that is worthy of careful examination. The interviewer thus has to be prepared to be flexible in the interview, to structure questions specifically to the situation, to follow leads and to ask new questions as appropriate.

Good preparation for interviews will also show itself in the conduct of the actual interviews. With some powerful people there may be a good chance that an interview will be interrupted or discontinued before the allotted time. Both Fitz & Halpin and McHugh show that researchers sometimes have to be prepared to do the best they can in rushed circumstances. The interviewer may have to take the possibility of abrupt curtailment into consideration and ensure that some of the most important questions are asked early in the interview.

When interviewing the powerful it should be remembered that the interviews will often serve various functions. The first is obviously as a source of data on the specific research topic. Published and documentary sources may reveal much of interest, but it is often only by talking with the participants themselves that significant gains in understanding can be made. But this is far from the only function that interviews with the powerful can perform. As Moyser (1988) indicates, interviews with elite members differ from many interviews with those who are less powerful in that these interviewees can act as experts about events, processes, institutions and other powerful individuals. They will usually be exceptionally well informed about the issues in question, and may well have a good understanding of social science research. They can sometimes be used as sounding boards for tentative theories and as aids to guide the path of the research programme.

A further, and most important, function of interviews with those with power is that of charming the gatekeeper. If the researcher is able to build rapport in an interview and provide a convincing reason for the research, it is highly likely that subsequent access to other powerful individuals will be eased. Conversely, if an interview raises suspicions about the researcher's motives and aims, further access to a wide range of other powerful people can be inhibited. In this volume, McHugh, for example, explains how he was passed from one powerful person to another on the basis of personal recommendation. He was able to gain access to those centrally involved in influencing the 1988 Education Act by working from those on the periphery. After gradually building trust with them, they were prepared to help him obtain further interviews with those nearer the centre of power. The gatekeeping function will not always work in this way. Sometimes the researcher is forced to start near the top of an official hierarchy, and access to those lower down the ranks will be given only if these with the most power agree. In many cases, the interviewer will have to be careful that those with power do not exercise some of it to inhibit further interviews with others.

Analysis and the written account

Conducting the interviews is only a first stage of any research. The interviews then need to be interpreted and analyzed in the context of information gained from other sources and in the light of the researcher's theoretical concerns. Both Ball and Cookson alert us to the difficulties of interpreting interviews with the powerful. Political interviews are themselves highly political, and Ball illustrates the "game-like" nature of some of these interviews. He argues that, in interviews with powerful policy-makers, researchers need to recognize and explore more fully the interview as an extension of the "play of power" rather than as separate from it. In turn, Cookson highlights the idea of "power discourses" that profoundly shape public perceptions and the formulation of educational policy. He argues that, without sophisticated methodologies for investigating these power discourses, our understanding of the process of policy formation will be underdeveloped, naive and sometimes inaccurate.

In a similar way, documentary evidence cannot simply be understood at face value. The story behind the production of each document needs to be probed and analyzed, and the contents need to be triangulated against data from other documents and other forms of evidence. It is also always necessary to remember that there is never one objective reality to be discovered, but a range of competing perspectives that interact and intersect with each other.

The care with which researchers should analyze their data is one of the factors that distinguishes academic research from journalism. As Kogan points out, there are times when the two appear to be very similar, but the academic researcher will probably make greater use of triangulation of different accounts and data sources. More fundamentally, the academic researcher will test data against theory, and the whole enterprise will be theoretically informed. Thus, Gewirtz & Ozga, for example, structured their methodology in such a way that they can explicitly challenge pluralist theoretical frameworks.

Academic research about the powerful is different from most other educational research in that it is often not possible to offer confidentiality. As these people are in powerful positions, they are known to the public. To write about them necessitates their identification. But whereas the journalist focuses on the individuals involved and looks for short-term news and scandal, the academic is usually interested in longer-term analysis and a deeper theoretical understanding of events. Academic researchers are not interested in exposés and, apart from some forms of historical research, individuals are rarely the primary focus.

The necessity for identifying of individuals can bring particular problems of censorship and self-censorship. Both Whitty & Edwards and Walford note this potential when reporting on the powerful, and another of the contributors felt compelled to edit out the name of a very prominent politician from the chapter. In this case, although the author had copious notes on a particular meeting, which included some potentially scandalous statements, it was found that the tape record of that discussion was missing. The author felt that it was personally too risky to identify the politician with the statements without the tape evidence. The powerful have the means to challenge statements about them, which those without power rarely have.

Self-censorship may also occur because of various ethical and practical considerations. Whitty & Edwards, for example, raise the question of the extent to which official government papers should be used when they have not been obtained through "official channels". They decided that they should use them in part, while Kogan, for example, makes it clear that any information given "in confidence" should remain so. Jones felt obliged to follow the World Bank's rules for outside researchers even though the relevant document had not been drawn to his attention. Britain suffers from the particular problem of the Official Secrets Act, which often acts as a significant clamp on information. Fitz & Halpin and many others have found that senior civil servants sometimes use compliance with this Act as a reason for not answering certain questions. Additionally, where civil servants do give information it is usually on the basis that it is not attributable.

More practical problems that can lead to self-censorship include the necessity to retain good relations for further research. The researcher who has disclosed hidden information in one piece of research is unlikely to be given access to that research site again. With most educational research this is not a particular problem, but, for researchers who wish to look at the powerful, exclusion from, say, the Department for Education would have a major impact. Further, publishing reports that are heavily critical or that reveal secrets might not only affect the researcher directly involved. Other future researchers may be excluded to ensure that any similar disclosures do not occur again.

It would be wrong to overstate the problems of potential self-censorship, however. They exist but, like many of the other potential problems of researching the powerful, they can be minimized. The fact that the contributors to this book have been able to obtain access to the powerful, to obtain information about them and to publish their analyses, is an indication that others can do it as well. Indeed, part of the purpose of this book is to encourage others to "research up" as well as to "research down" and to tackle the problems of researching the powerful in education. It is a challenging task, but one that is most worth while.

References

Cassell, J. 1988. The relationship of observer to observed when studying up. *Studies in Qualitative Methodology* **1**, 89–108.

Easterday, L., D. Papademas, L. Schorr, C. Valentine 1977. The making of a female researcher: Role problems in fieldwork. *Urban Life* **6** (3), 333–48.

Hunter, A. 1993. Local knowledge and local power. Notes on the ethnography of local community elites. *Journal of Contemporary Ethnography* **22** (1), 36–58.

Klatch, R. E. 1988. The methodological problems of studying a politically resistant community. *Studies in Qualitative Methodology* **1**, 73–88.

McPherson, A. & C. D. Raab 1988. *Governing education. A sociology of policy since 1945.* Edinburgh: Edinburgh University Press.

Moyser, G. 1988. Non-standardized interviewing in elite research. *Studies in qualitative methodology* **1**, 109–36.

Ostrander, S. A. 1993. "Surely you're not in this just to be helpful?" Access, rapport, and interviews in three studies of elites. *Journal of Contemporary Ethnography* **22** (1), 7–27.

Sinclair, B. & D. Brady 1987 Studying members of the United States Congress. In *Research methods for elite studies*, G. Moyser & M. Wagstaffe (eds). London: Allen & Unwin.

Winkler, J. (1987) The fly on the wall in the inner sanctum: Observing company directors at work. In *Research methods for elite studies*, G. Moyser & M. Wagstaffe (eds.) London: Allen & Unwin.

Author index

233

Subject index